MW01290467

AWS Scripted

AWS Scripted

How to Automate the Deployment of Secure and Resilient Websites with Amazon Web Services VPC, ELB, EC2, RDS, IAM, SES and SNS

A QuickStepApps Guide

By Christian Cerri

(Second Edition 2014)

Table of Contents

Chapter 11 - MySQL Database 211

Chapter 12 - Java Servers 221

Introduction

How many Applications have you deployed only to be told by your boss to 'document' the process? Have you spent hours on pretty useless documents which read, "Now click Next, then, at the top click Open, then click Yes...". Forced to include screenshots? I empathise with you.

Which is why, when I realised the potential of the AWS Command Line Interface (CLI), I was incredibly excited because I realised I could deploy an entire application, servers and all, with Bash Scripts, and the process would be self-documenting. Instructions for a human are one thing, but can be misinterpreted. A solid script is a different world altogether.

Many months later, after much trial and error, I was able to deploy a rather complex web application to AWS from a single bash command. The process involved a whole range of disciplines, such as brushing up on my bashing, integrating the PHP, proper SQL scripts and much more. I was consumed by the need to script it all - leaving a few bits out just would not do. And this imperative took me in many new and interesting directions.

First and foremost, it is the AWS CLI that makes this all possible. I still get a thrill when I type a few lines into a command line and servers magically appear in the real world. The problem with AWS (as with so many things) is the documentation. It is such a vast topic that you can get lost in the details and it can be hard to understand high-level processes. Nowhere does Amazon provide a section 'Example Scripts for Common Tasks' - well maybe they do but in the general vastness of the docs I haven't found it.

Here's an example of what I'm talking about and a taster of the scripts to come later. Yes, I discuss topics and explain core principles, but more importantly, *every single topic is fully scripted* - nothing is left out. And it works! You can download the package containing all scripts from this book at the website I run at **http://www.quickstepapps.com**. They are ready to run (with a few configurations you can find in **Chapter 2 - Running master.sh for Development**). Give it a test! Anyway, back to our example:

[aws/snippets/snippet_vpc.sh]

```bash
#!/bin/bash

# example script to make a new vpc
vpcname=MYVPC
deployzone=eu-west-1

# make a new vpc with a master 10.0.0.0/16 subnet
vpc_id=$(aws ec2 create-vpc --cidr-block 10.0.0.0/16 --output text
--query 'Vpc.VpcId')
echo vpc_id=$vpc_id

# enable dns support or modsecurity wont let apache start...
aws ec2 modify-vpc-attribute --vpc-id $vpc_id --enable-dns-support
aws ec2 modify-vpc-attribute --vpc-id $vpc_id --enable-dns-
hostnames

# tag the vpc
aws ec2 create-tags --resources $vpc_id --tags
Key=vpcname,Value=$vpcname

# wait for the vpc
echo -n "waiting for vpc..."
while state=$(aws ec2 describe-vpcs --filters Name=tag-
key,Values=vpcname --filters Name=tag-value,Values=$vpcname
--output text --query 'Vpcs[*].State'); test "$state" = "pending";
do
 echo -n . ; sleep 3;
done; echo " $state"

# create an internet gateway (to allow access out to the internet)
igw=$(aws ec2 create-internet-gateway --output text --query
'InternetGateway.InternetGatewayId')
echo igw=$igw

# attach the igw to the vpc
echo attaching igw
aws ec2 attach-internet-gateway --internet-gateway-id $igw --vpc-id
$vpc_id

# create our main subnet
# we use 10.0.0.0/24 as our main subnet
subnet_id=$(aws ec2 create-subnet --vpc-id $vpc_id --cidr-block
10.0.0.0/24 --availability-zone $deployzone --output text --query
'Subnet.SubnetId')
echo subnet_id=$subnet_id

# get the route table id for the vpc
rtb_id=$(aws ec2 describe-route-tables --filters Name=vpc-
id,Values=$vpc_id --output text --query
'RouteTables[*].RouteTableId')
echo rtb_id=$rtb_id
```

```
# associate this subnet with our route table
aws ec2 associate-route-table --subnet-id $subnet_id --route-table-
id $rtb_id

# create a route out from our route table to the igw
echo creating route from igw
aws ec2 create-route --route-table-id $rtb_id --gateway-id $igw
--destination-cidr-block 0.0.0.0/0

# done
echo vpc setup done
```

You would have thought Amazon would make it easy to launch a new VPC (Virtual Private Cloud). The Internet is rife with 'Help! I can't connect to my EC2 instance!' posts. And that is because (as the above example shows) it is not trivial to launch a new VPC into which you can launch EC2 instances which you can then SSH to from the Internet. We're talking Subnets, Internet Gateways, Route Tables and harder still, how to make them all talk to each other! And whilst each individual AWS CLI command is well documented, there's nothing on how to connect them up. So, such and such a command needs a VPC ID, this command needs a Route Table ID - so where do I get these from? Another thing to take away from the above script is the power of scripting. Compare a set of instructions for the same VPC creation procedure applicable to the AWS Console (**Chapter 2 - Deploying from AWS**) - and as I say there - "Now do you understand the power of scripting?"

However, this book not only concentrates on fully automated AWS Deployment. It also focusses heavily on security, and the reason is this: security is a component of all the layers of an application (load balancers → web servers → Apache → PHP → MySQL). And security cannot be implemented independently at each layer. Rather what is needed is a comprehensive overall approach. Some examples of the integrated approach: ModSecurity (an Apache plugin) won't let Apache start unless the underlying network DNS structures are in place, and these have to be configured in the AWS CLI VPC creation scripts; inter-server communications won't work without the corresponding AWS Security Group configurations; the usernames and passwords for MySQL database access are put into the Apache httpd.conf file for greater security; and so on. The

Cloud Application you are building by definition is utterly interconnected and any approach which ignores this fact will fail.

Therefore, I provide fully working examples of a Public Website and an Admin Website which are deployed automatically with scripts. You will see that the Cloud Architecture explicitly requires certain things in the PHP and MySQL code (such as SSL integration). So they are included and fully working. Web servers are launched with a comprehensive set of security and other features such as: PHP Suhosin, ModSecurity, ModRpaf, Chrooting, Curl Compatibility, Monit, Mmonit, Rsyslog Centralised Logging, LogAnalyzer, PHPMyAdmin, SSL (valid and self-signed) and more. Again, everything is scripted - and that includes the creation, installation and configuration of these additional services. You may ask: how do you install and configure something like Apache or ModSecurity from a script? Well, you build a server; then you build a script to run on that server; you also build the configuration files you will need; upload everything, run it and hey presto! I hope you will be pleasantly surprised by the ingenuity of some of the scripted solutions you will find in this book.

Last, I devote considerable effort to the business of Development: the Development Cycle; Security outside of the Cloud; Migrating Data to your servers; and Secure Remote Access to your servers. Sorry to repeat myself, but, *again*, everything is fully scripted and working. And you will find all sorts of other tasty morsels which I have gleaned from the crypt-er-net and trial and error over the years.

The book is fully supported at **http://www.quickstepapps.com**, where I publish further articles and respond to Support Issues. The code from the book is also available as a single, working package. You could probably set up the provided example Application within about an hour. Give it a go - the proof, as they say, is in the pudding. Good luck with your scripting!

Chapter 1 - Architecture

Overview

This book shows you how to launch a resilient Web Application using Amazon Web Services. We will cover Elastic Load Balancers (ELB), EC2 instances running Linux/Apache/PHP (LAP) and a MySQL back-end with AWS RDS. In addition, we will tackle several areas which most applications will need, such as email (SES), networking (VPC) and Administration Tasks. However, almost all of the scripts and recipes are good jumping blocks for any number of other purposes.

The architecture of the proposed application is as follows:

1. an Internet-facing ELB, which distributes incoming traffic to any number of web servers
2. a layer of N web servers (hereafter referred to as Webphp Servers) running Apache and PHP
3. a single Admin Server which handles Centralised Logging and Administrative Access
4. a single RDS MySQL database all other servers connect to for persistent storage
5. other AWS configurations such as the underlying VPC, IAM accounts, SES setup and SNS Notifications

The aim of the book is to provide the ability to run ONE bash command to deploy the entire application. This command (from the aws directory) is:

```
./master/master.sh
```

As Security is the number one priority for all Web Applications, there is a strong emphasis on methods which raise an application to the required level to survive unscathed in the hostile landscape of the Web. This ranges from SSL to Apache configuration and plugins to PHP coding practices. We also cover the methodology of development: how to migrate from a development environment to a production one; how to deploy application updates; and how to access your servers securely.

AWS CLI

AWS provides stunningly effective tools for automating deployment and management of any and all AWS resources. It is the aim of this book to show how to implement fully automated deployment and access management strategies.

The importance of a fully scripted environment cannot be over-emphasised. Setting up these kinds of services requires hundreds if not thousands of instructions and configurations. Hence, documenting such a process is indeed a nightmare. By packaging everything into scripts you are, as it were, auto-documenting the process. And as a bonus, you can execute highly complex tasks with nothing more than a bash command.

AWS ELB

Elastic Load Balancers are an extremely effective way to increase the security and availability of your Web Application.

First, they are reasonably cheap when compared to an EC2 instance.

Second, they can act as a SSL decoder, which relieves your servers of the burden of SSL decryption.

Third, they allow web load to be shared between several servers, increasing resilience and availability.

Lastly, as ELBs are Internet-Facing, they protect your LAP servers which are by necessity not directly available from the Internet.

LAP Servers

Linux and Apache/PHP are by far the most common web server platforms in use today. They are free. They don't waste resources on graphical desktops and the like. They are highly reliable and, if configured properly, highly secure.

Discussion will range from setting up a secure base Linux image; installing software with maximum emphasis on Security; securing administrative access; and PHP code and techniques to integrate with the architecture selected. We will also cover ModSecurity, PHP Suhosin, ModRpaf and Chrooting Apache.

Admin Server

Any Web Application will require Administrative functionality, whether this is direct access to the Database (via PHPMyAdmin), running scheduled tasks, sending email, collating logs or managing your server farm. By setting up a dedicated Admin Server, we can minimise insecure code on the Internet LAP servers and maximise security for Administrative Access.

AWS RDS

The AWS RDS service is a highly reliable database server system. With the addition of Multi-AZ (Multi Availability Zone), this system provides near zero downtime. Setting up your own MySQL Server is not out of the question, but a huge amount of management and configuration is handled for you by RDS. At a small premium to EC2 instances, it is well worth using RDS.

Supported Platforms

All the examples in this book are tested on Macs and on the Amazon Linux platform. The main reason for this is that bash in Mac Terminal is fundamentally the same as bash on our linux boxes, so testing and running have no compatibility problems. This means you can run the supplied scripts from a Mac Terminal window or from an AWS Linux box. It is highly likely that the scripts will work on any Linux distribution, but this has not been tested.

The problem with Windows is that the underlying OS shell is not the same. Paths are specified differently (/ or \?), so migrating an Apache/PHP/MySQL website from a Windows Development Environment to a Linux Development Environment can be problematic. You may need to write substantial extra code to cope with the discrepancies. Given the costs of development, which run into tens of thousands of dollars per developer month, the price of a Mac Mini server and a few iMacs is a bearable cost. Or, if you are perforce tied to Windows, you can use the techniques set out in **Chapter 2 - Deploying from AWS** to obtain a compatible Linux OS and shell at negligible cost.

As a 20 year veteran of Windows NT, Windows XP, Visual Studio, IIS and MSSQL, I was understandably annoyed at having to shell out for a Mac when I started iOS development. And for a few months I needed to do the odd Internet search for the shortcut for this or that command, for how to configure such and such a setting. But overall it was pretty painless and now I am incredibly happy with my Macs. They require almost no maintenance and they don't annoy me with excessive popups - yes My Desktop is clean! In truth, a few weeks ago I was forced to use a Windows laptop at a convention and I must admit I felt a little queasy at how slow, unresponsive and intrusive it was.

Also, for our Secure Laptop, Macs are very much easier to secure than any other kind of box. I suppose you could use Windows, but why would you? Do yourself a favour - the MacBook Air 13" is gorgeous, technically superb and about US$1000.

Chapter 2 - Bash Deployment Framework

Where to Start

The downloadable zip package may seem bewildering at first. Don't Panic!

First, set up your in-house development environment (see **Installing on your Development Environment** later in this Chapter).

Then, get a feel for what you will be doing by deploying to a test AWS environment (see **Running master.sh for Development** later in this Chapter). You can then test the deployed website and take a look around the AWS Console to see how everything looks. Of particular interest will be EC2, VPC, RDS, SES and SNS. You can also SSH into your newly created boxes and take a look around (see **Chapter 14 - Remote Access**).

Once you are comfortable with master.sh and accoutrements, try doing a development deployment cycle. So change the development website a bit (such as adding some text to the home page) and then do a deploy run (see **Chapter 13 - Uploading a New Public Website**).

This will define your basic workflow: make changes to your development website, database or Java Servers, then upload them, then test them from AWS.

Directory Structure

This book comes with a downloadable package which contains all the scripts and development data to launch a simple, but secure website via AWS. All the scripts and data live in a folder 'aws'. The structure for the aws folder is as follows:

- *ami*

  scripts separated into services
    - *admin*

      create the Admin Server
    - *elb*

      create the ELB and SSL details
    - *email*

      configure SES and SNS
    - *rds*

      create the database with RDS
    - *shared*

      create the Linux Shared Image
    - *vpc*

      create the VPC
    - *webphp*

      create the LAP Webphp Server
- *credentials*

  passwords, .pem keys, other keys and remote access scripts
  are stored here
    - *oldpasswords*

      any existing passwords will be stored here if you
      recreate the passwords file
- *data*

  storage for deployable assets
    - *admin*

      deployable admin website
    - *database*

      database scripts
    - *java*

      jar files for deployment
    - *website*

      deployable public web site
- *development*

  proxy for your development environment
    - *database*

      development database scripts
    - *java*

      development java projects

- *website*

   development admin and public websites, and php includes
- *master*

   contains global variables, the master deployment script and the master delete script
- *minify*

   javascript/css compression folder
- *upload*

   scripts to deploy assets from the data folder
   - *admin*

      scripts to deploy the admin website
   - *database*

      scripts to deploy the database
   - *java*

      scripts to deploy java servers
   - *website*

      scripts to deploy the public website

To run all scripts, you must cd to the aws directory and run from there, so that any included scripts can be found. This is enforced by some commands found in most scripts which check you are in a folder called aws:

[aws/snippets/snippet_checkdir.sh]

```
# check dir
where=$(pwd)
where="${where: -3}"
if test "$where" = "aws"; then
 echo "running from correct directory"
else
 echo "must be run from aws directory with ./***/***/***.sh"
 exit
fi
```

How to Develop

Perhaps the most important aspect of any development is the methodology, but rarely is this given any emphasis. It's all about learning programming languages, taming operating systems or tailoring hardware. The point is that if your development methodology is wrong, you could waste significant effort and time, and, frankly, it's not that hard to do it right.

Long experience has taught me THE MOST IMPORTANT THING: the Proof of Life Test. Or, before you start writing reams and reams of code, write the minimum required to actually see something working. So if it's an iOS or Android App, start from a 'Hello World' shell app and actually get it running on a device. If it's a Java Server, get the main components running so you see something happening, and then plug in functionality modules. If it's a Website, get a minimum 2 page site up and running and actually see it working on the final deployment platform.

If you do this, you can then engage in what is known as *iterative development*. Which means, you iterate by changing something that you know works and then immediately testing. If you encounter a problem, you know the problem is with the last changes you made, and you don't have to go around debugging your entire app. Of course, the bug might be in code from a previous iteration, but at least you know the bug was *triggered* by your latest changes.

Early in my career I was ordered to get a Siemens TC35 GSM module 'sorted' via the now elusive COM port. Naive, I basically wrote the whole app in C without actually ever testing it. Then for the life of me I couldn't get the communication to the COM port working! Utterly frustrated, I tried some 'ping' tests with JavaCOM and found that everything worked fine. So I had to ditch my C code and move everything to Java. That's when I learnt about the Proof of Life or Ping Test. And now, I refuse to write even one line of code that I can't test 'in situ'.

It is very bad practice to start building your website proper until you have your Development Cycle sorted out. Don't start building your shopping baskets, contact forms and the rest until you have the basics like passwords, database queries and SSL fully working. Otherwise, you might find that you have made consistent mistakes in your pages which are annoying to fix. Or there may be a deeper, structural problem which can't be fixed, requiring a major rewrite. As you gain proficiency, you can deploy to your AWS Development Environment more rarely, but at the start, do it often and especially to test new functionality. Once you know it works, go ahead and roll it out across your pages. After all, if you've done it right, it only takes a couple of bash commands and about 2 minutes to update your website to AWS... Hardly a chore!

Funnily enough, it's never really that simple. Sometimes you have more than one decent starting point and need to choose which one will be your proof of lifer: should I start with the PHP User and Authentication module or the HTML/CSS web template I just purchased? My advice is to start with the most functionally complicated package, because normally it is easier to integrate simple stuff into hard stuff. So, you can probably port the HTML template into a PHP package quite easily (by sorting headers and footers most likely), but it would be much harder to edit an HTML template to include all the PHP code needed for users and authentication. Sometimes you just can't get access to the eventual final hardware, so you'll need to improvise. But the core principles are always the same: iterate and test.

Installing on your Development Environment

You can install the provided database and PHP website on your in-house development environment. The steps are as follows:

1. set up Apache so that 'It works!'
2. set up MySQL and have access with something like MySQL Query Browser with the root account so that you can run scripts, create databases and users
3. run the aws/development/database/dbs.sql script on MySQL
4. run the aws/development/database/dbusers.sql script on MySQL
5. delete all files for your Apache installation htdocs folder
6. copy the contents of aws/development/website/htdocs to your Apache installation htdocs folder

7. copy the folder aws/development/website/phpincludes to your apache2 folder (so it is at the same directory level as your htdocs folder)
8. start a development Google Recaptcha Account and copy the public and private keys into the relevant php config file phpinclude/globalvariables.php (see **Chapter 10 - Google Recaptcha** for more details)
9. point your browser to your Apache installation address and you will see the demo website
10. the Admin Website will be available at /admin - password admin

One Script To Rule Them All

How great would it be to run one bash command and your entire Application is deployed? Here is a script which does just that:

[aws/master/master.sh]

```bash
#!/bin/bash

# one script to rule them all...

echo $'\n\n********************\n SETUP AWS
APPLICATION\n********************\n'

# check dir
where=$(pwd)
where="${where: -3}"
if test "$where" = "aws"; then
 echo "running from correct directory"
else
 echo "must be run from aws directory with ./master/master.sh"
 exit
fi

# include global variables
. ./master/vars.sh

# make passwords
./credentials/makepasswords.sh

# order below is crucial

echo $'\n\n********************\n MAKING
VPC\n********************\n\n'
. ./ami/vpc/make.sh
echo $'\n\n********************\n MADE
```

```
VPC\n*********************\n\n'

echo $'\n\n*********************\n MAKING RDS
DB\n*********************\n\n'
. ./ami/rds/make.sh
echo $'\n\n*********************\n MADE RDS
DB\n*********************\n\n'

echo $'\n\n*********************\n MAKING SHARED
IMAGE\n*********************\n\n'
. ./ami/shared/make.sh
echo $'\n\n*********************\n MADE SHARED
IMAGE\n*********************\n\n'

echo $'\n\n*********************\n MAKING RDS DB
2\n*********************\n\n'
. ./ami/rds/make2.sh
echo $'\n\n*********************\n MADE RDS DB
2\n*********************\n\n'

echo $'\n\n*********************\n MAKING
ADMIN\n*********************\n\n'
. ./ami/admin/make.sh
echo $'\n\n*********************\n MADE
ADMIN\n*********************\n\n'

echo $'\n\n*********************\n MAKING
ELB\n*********************\n\n'
. ./ami/elb/make.sh $elbselfsigned
echo $'\n\n*********************\n MADE
ELB\n*********************\n\n'

for (( i=1; i<=$numwebs; i++ )) do
 echo $'\n\n*********************\n MAKING
WEB\n*********************\n\n'
 . ./ami/webphp/make.sh $i
 echo $'\n\n*********************\n MADE
WEB\n*********************\n\n'
done

echo $'\n\n*********************\n MAKING
SES1\n*********************\n\n'
. ./ami/email/make.sh
echo $'\n\n*********************\n MADE
SES1\n*********************\n\n'

echo $'\n\n*********************\n MAKING
DATA\n*********************\n\n'
. ./data/makedata.sh
echo $'\n\n*********************\n MADE
DATA\n*********************\n\n'

echo $'\n\n*********************\n UPLOADING
DATABASE\n*********************\n\n'
. ./upload/database/upload.sh
echo $'\n\n*********************\n UPLOADED
DATABASE\n*********************\n\n'

echo $'\n\n*********************\n UPLOADING
ADMIN\n*********************\n\n'
```

```
. ./upload/admin/upload.sh
echo $'\n\n********************\n UPLOADED
ADMIN\n********************\n\n'

echo $'\n\n********************\n UPLOADING WEB
SERVERS\n********************\n\n'
. ./upload/website/uploadall.sh
echo $'\n\n********************\n UPLOADED WEB
SERVERS\n********************\n\n'

echo $'\n\n********************\n UPLOADING
JAVA\n********************\n\n'
. ./upload/java/upload.sh
echo $'\n\n********************\n UPLOADED
JAVA\n********************\n\n'

echo $'\n\n********************\n MAKING
SES2\n********************\n\n'
. ./ami/email/make2.sh
echo $'\n\n********************\n MADE
SES2\n********************\n\n'

elbdns=$(aws elb describe-load-balancers --load-balancer-names
$elbname --output text --query
'LoadBalancerDescriptions[*].DNSName')
echo website=http://$elbdns
echo website=https://$elbdns
echo "domain registry: point a cname record www for your domain to
$elbdns"
echo "at your DNS Registrar, add a TXT record to yourdomain.com
containing: include:amazonses.com"

echo master script finished
```

The script calls all our other scripts and provides some output to make debugging easier. A good way to call this script is via tee which allows you to see output on the console and creates a log file for forensic purposes and is as follows:

```
./master/master.sh 2>&1 | tee deploy.log
```

Note that all subscripts are independent and can be run standalone. So, if after a few weeks you want to add a third webserver (for example) you could run:

```
./ami/webphp/make.sh 3
```

Running master.sh for Development

As with all development, you will be using an AWS Development

Environment and an AWS Production Environment. It is vital that you test the entire deployment process and any deployed assets, such as web sites, regularly on a test AWS account before deploying to the Production Environment. The main reason for this is that when you start using the Secure Laptop, it is not really a debugging platform - you will want to keep all activity on it to a minimum.

Security is a concern, even in the Development Environment. After all, you don't want unauthorised access to your data under any circumstances. The deployed application will contain all the security of the Production Environment. The only real security difference is that you will not deploy from a Secure Laptop. However, as you will deploy, test and tear down within a few hours, there is only a tiny chance of an intrusion. Look at it this way: if you have done your security correctly, the site will be highly unhackable anyway, and the only vulnerability will be, for instance, a key-logger on the machine you use for Development Deployment. So a hacker would have to be listening in, then download files, such as .pem keys, from your computer, then hack your AWS Development Installation, and all this in the 8 to 10 hours you will probably need to deploy, test and tear down your application. Realistically, this is highly unlikely. If you have done your security badly, it doesn't really matter as you will no doubt be hacked after your Production Launch. If you want to keep your AWS Development Environment on permanently, consider limiting public access via the ELB to just your IP.

A major difference between the AWS Development and AWS Production Environments is SSL. DO NOT use your real world certificate on your AWS Development Environment. The SSL key needs to be utterly secure or your PHP security will fall apart (SSL is THE major security component of PHP Session Authentication, see **Chapter 10 - Session Security**). Use a self-signed certificate for AWS Development (the code to automate this is provided in the **ELB Script**). Yes, you'll get some SSL warnings but these can be turned off. If you really need valid SSL (because for instance you are Curling to your site from somewhere else and VERIFY PEER is on), use your real world certificate but get a new SSL key before launching for Production. It is highly recommended that you set up your SSL Provider account from the Secure Laptop, even in this situation.

Prerequisites for master.sh:

1. create an AWS Account for Development
2. if your are rerunning the master script, ensure all AWS resources are deleted (from the AWS Console you will need to visit VPC, EC2, RDS, IAM, SES and SNS) and delete things in the right order (start with any EC2 instances and RDS, the VPC is last). A script is provided (see **Deleting All Assets** later in this chapter).
3. install AWS CLI with your Development Account (see **Installing AWS CLI** later in this chapter)
4. configure AWS CLI (see **Installing AWS CLI** later in this chapter)
5. edit aws/master/vars.sh (see **Global Variables** later in this chapter)
6. use a self-signed SSL cert, set elbselfsigned to 1 in aws/master/vars.sh
7. if necessary, edit the SSL scripts in aws/ami/elb/ssl to reflect your organisation
8. for the demo site provided, we are using Google Recaptcha, so you will need to create keys for a Google Recaptcha Account and then edit credentials/recaptcha.sh and copy in your private and public keys (see **Chapter 10 - Google Recaptcha** for more details)
9. for Mmonit to work, you will need a Licence Key - see **Global Variables** later in this Chapter for how to get it and where to put it.
10. cd to the aws directory
11. run ./master/master.sh

OK, so you just finished your first deploy: what to do next?

1. test the website using the ELB domain name printed at the end of master.sh
2. if you have connected DNS, test with your real domain

name

3. test the Admin Interface with ./credentials/connectadmin.sh
4. SSH to your new boxes with ./credentials/connectssh.sh web1 (or web2 etc)
5. SSH to the Admin Server with ./credentials/connectssh.sh admin

Running master.sh for Production

This process is largely similar to the previous section except that all steps must take place on the Secure Laptop.

1. prepare the Secure Laptop (see **Secure Laptop** later in this chapter)
2. copy the aws folder with data to the Secure Laptop via clean USB key
3. all the next steps must be executed on the Secure Laptop
4. create an AWS Account for Production (with MFA) and only ever access this account from the Secure Laptop
5. if your are rerunning the master script, ensure all AWS resources are deleted (from the AWS Console you will need to visit VPC, EC2, RDS, IAM, SES and SNS) and delete things in the right order (start with any EC2 instances and RDS, the VPC is last). A script is provided (see **Deleting All Assets** later in this chapter).
6. install AWS CLI with your Production Account (see **Installing AWS CLI** later in this chapter)
7. configure AWS CLI (see **Installing AWS CLI** later in this chapter)
8. edit aws/master/vars.sh (see **Global Variables** later in this chapter)
9. you will likely need a secure email account, so create one at Gmail (with MFA) and only ever access this account from the Secure Laptop
10. create your SSL Supplier Account and Valid SSL Certificate on the Secure Laptop and copy the supplied SSL files to aws/ami/elb/validssl
11. edit aws/master/vars.sh to reflect the SSL files you have

12. for the demo site provided, we are using Google Recaptcha, so you will need to create keys for a Google Recaptcha Account and then edit credentials/recaptcha.sh and copy in your private and public keys (do this on the Secure Laptop) (see **Chapter 10 - Google Recaptcha** for more details)
13. for Mmonit to work, you will need a Licence Key - see **Global Variables** later in this Chapter for how to get it and where to put it.
14. cd to the aws directory
15. run ./master/master.sh
16. start a secure DNS account (I like Misk.com), transfer in the domain and only ever access this account from the Secure Laptop
17. follow the instructions at the end of the master script for setting up DNS and your email TXT record

Installing AWS CLI

On Mac OSX, you can install the AWS CLI (Command Line Interface) with a few commands in Terminal:

```
sudo easy_install pip
sudo pip install awscli
```

Next, open your .profile file with:

```
sudo vi ~/.profile
```

Paste in the following 2 lines at the bottom:

```
export LC_ALL=en_US.UTF-8
export LANG=en_US.UTF-8
```

(press 'i' to insert, paste with command-V, press Escape, save with :wq)

Download your root credentials file from the AWS Console (Click your name top right and select 'Security Credentials', then select 'Access Keys (Access Key ID and Secret Access Key)', Create New Access Key and Download). Amazon plaster warnings that you should not do this and instead use an IAM user. However, you would need an IAM user with full permissions anyway, which is the same thing. Once your system is up and running, you should definitely use IAM Users to control fine grain access to AWS resources.

Next (in Terminal):

```
aws configure
```

and paste in your Access Key ID and Secret Access Key from the credentials file you just downloaded. You should set your default region here too, eg eu-west-1, and set the Default output format to json.

Restart your Terminal Window. That's it. The aws command will now work from any Terminal Window.

Global Variables

Because the deployment scripts run into several thousand lines, we need to be very organised. The most obvious requirement is that any global configuration options should be stored in one file and shared by all other scripts. God forbid we should have to trawl through all our files if we want to change an instance type or a deployment zone! The main configuration file is as follows:

[aws/master/vars.sh]

```
#!/bin/bash

# check aws for regions, zones and pricing
deployregion=eu-west-1
deployzone=eu-west-1a
deployzone2=eu-west-1b

# the fully qualified path to the aws directory
basedir=/Users/ccerri/Desktop/aws

# these directories point to your development environment
# currently they point to the aws/development folder
# you should change them to your specific dev folders
# webdir would refer to your apache2 directory (ie contains htdocs
```

```
and phpinclude)
# you might share the apache folder on a server and use
/Volumes/apache2
webdir=$basedir/development/website
admindir=$basedir/development/website/htdocs/admin
javadir=$basedir/development/java
databasedir=$basedir/development/database

# location of the sshknowhosts file for your user account
sshknownhosts=/Users/ccerri/.ssh/known_hosts

# database config
# the instance type to use (different from ec2 instance types)
rdsinstancetype=db.m3.medium
# in GB
rdsvolumesize=40
# 1=use multi-az, 0=don't
rdsusemultiaz=0
# name for your db subnet group
dbsubnetgroupname=MYDBSUBNETGROUP
# description for said db subnet group
dbsubnetgroupdesc=MYDBSUBNETGROUPDESC
# name for your db parameter group
dbpgname=MYDBPG
# description for said parameter group
dbpgdesc=MYDBPGDESC
# name of the rds instance
dbinstancename=MYDBINSTANCE
# name for your db
dbname=MYDB

# this may change so find the latest from the aws console
# Amazon Linux AMI, HVM
baseami=ami-aa8f28dd
# use this instance type for the temporary shared image server
sharedinstancetype=m1.small
# in GB, subsequent servers can be larger, but not smaller
sharedebsvolumesize=20

# the instance type for the admin server
admininstancetype=m1.small

# the instance type for each webphp server
webphpinstancetype=m1.small

# size of admin server ebs volume in GB
adminebsvolumesize=100

# size of webphp server ebs volume in GB
webphpebsvolumesize=20

# name for your vpc
vpcname=MYVPC

# name for your elb
elbname=MYELB

# 1=use self-signed ELB SSL cert 0=use valid cert
elbselfsigned=1
```

```
# ELB SSL Certificate name (for both self-signed and valid)
elbcertname=MYELBCERT

# valid certificate for ELB (production)
# these files need to be put in aws/ami/elb/validssl
# filename of your .key file as provided by your Certificate
Authority
elbvalidcertkeyfile=www_yourdomain_com.key
# filename of your .crt file as provided by your Certificate
Authority
elbvalidcertcertfile=www_yourdomain_com.crt
# filename of your intermediate .crt file as provided by your
Certificate Authority, eg DigiCert
elbvalidcertinterfile=DigiCertCA.crt

# number of webphp servers to make
numwebs=2

# your domain name
webdomain=www.yourdomain.com

# email address to send from
# must be valid as needs to be verified
emailsendfrom=donotreply@yourdomain.com
```

The only variables you really need to change (or it won't work) are: basedir, sshknownhosts and emailsendfrom. The first two tell the scripts where they are. If you plonk the aws folder on your Mac desktop, you'll only need to change 'ccerri' to your username - do a right-click Get Info if necessary. 'emailsendfrom' is needed because the script will send an email to this address for verification because the SNS setup needs a verified email address. For other values, you will need to adapt the values to suit your circumstances, but it will work if you don't change anything.

You can select the instance size for the base image (Shared Image), the Admin Server and the Webphp Servers. The base image is a temporary construct, so you can pick something quite low end (such as m1.small). Using t1.micro is a little slow but not impossible. The Admin Server type will depend on how many web servers you are running. A c3.medium will handle several c3.medium web servers, but if you are launching 5 or more you may want to consider upping the Admin Server instance type to a c3.large or more.

The main load on the Admin Server is the centralised logging. You will need to do load testing for your application if you want to determine realistic load values before launch. Otherwise, you can measure performance after launch and if necessary upgrade the Admin Server as required.

For your in-house installation only, you will need to edit aws/development/website/phpincludes/globalvariables.php by entering in-house development Google Recaptcha Keys (see **Chapter 10 - Google Recaptcha**). Otherwise, the Public Website won't let you Sign Up.

For AWS Development, you should set up your Google Recaptcha Account, then insert the keys into the aws/credentials/recaptcha.sh file.

For AWS Production, you should set up your Google Recaptcha Account from the Secure Laptop, then edit the file aws/credentials/recaptcha.sh so that the keys never leave the Secure Laptop (except to your servers).

For Mmonit to work successfully on the Admin Server, in aws/ami/admin/server_template.xml you will need to paste in your licence key. These keys change, so if you want a 30 day trial, you will need to find and download the linux-x64 package from https://mmonit.com/download/ and open it up. Navigate to the conf folder and open the server.xml file. Copy the trial licence from the bottom of the page (the entire Licence tag) and paste into the server_template.xml file near the bottom. If you purchase a licence, paste that in instead. Mmonit will not work unless you do this.

Migrating Data

Copying and preparing data from your in-house Development Environment to any AWS Environment is vital. In development in-house, you can share the Admin and Public Websites on a single installation, but on AWS these are split (we don't want a publicly accessible Admin Site, however secure). We also want to minify our Javascript and CSS to make it quicker to download and harder to decipher. All this happens in the aws/data/makedata.sh script. Note that the only permanent file in the data directory is this script - everything else should be recreatable from your development files. **See Chapter 13 - Preparing Assets** for more details.

Passwords

You will need a large number of passwords, so we need to automate the process for storing and using them. We use a script to create a passwords script which can be included by whatever needs them:

[aws/credentials/makepasswords.sh]

```
#!/bin/bash

# create password file

# passwords are used like this
# password1=rds mainuser password
# password2=admin server root user
# password3=admin server ec2-user
# password4=adminrw sql user password
# password5=webphprw sql user password
# password6=javamail sql user password
# password7=sns sql user password
# password8=web1 root user
# password9=web1 ec2-user
# password10=web2 root user
# password11=web2 ec2-user
# password12=web3 root user
# password13=web3 ec2-user
# password14=web4 root user
# password15=web4 ec2-user
# password16=web5 root user
# password17=web5 ec2-user
# password18=web6 root user
# password19=web6 ec2-user
# password20=aeskey for php sessions

# check dir
where=$(pwd)
where="${where: -3}"
if test "$where" = "aws"; then
 echo "running from correct directory"
else
 echo "must be run from aws directory with
./credentials/makepasswords.sh"
 exit
fi
```

```
# include global variables
. ./master/vars.sh

cd $basedir/credentials

# save old passwords just in case
now=$(date +"%m_%d_%Y")
mv passwords.sh oldpasswords/passwords_$now.sh

# start the passwords script
echo "#!/bin/bash" > passwords.sh

echo "rds mainuser password (max 16)"
newpassword=$(openssl rand -base64 10)
newpassword=$(echo $newpassword | tr '/' '0')
echo "password1=$newpassword" >> passwords.sh

for (( i=2; i<=20; i++ ))
do
        # randomly discard some passwords
        randdiscard=$[1+$[RANDOM%10]]
        echo "next password $randdiscard"
        for (( j=1; j<=$randdiscard; j++ ))
        do
                newpassword=$(openssl rand -base64 33)
                echo "discarded 1"
        done
        newpassword=$(openssl rand -base64 33)
        newpassword=$(echo $newpassword | tr '/' '0')
        echo "password$i=$newpassword" >> passwords.sh
done

# make the generated script executable
chmod +x passwords.sh

cd $basedir
```

This creates a file which will look something like this:

[aws/snippets/snippet_passwordsexample.sh]

```
#!/bin/bash
password1=R+nFaj0E2mrYmQ==
password2=qDGp45nyOYFKlgXpcQY4NOVUpx9VhHSb5aIY3+ynBwMJ
password3=RMNJenT9dYRCASYRr9Nk4V9LKSbUWMGz0Jh2IbR4hEQJ
password4=XsCTaqx2XW7dtF1EOzNgq3AersiIpO9gadDYBvWfet98
password5=EPkVeEa8c6Tb15U7L3+2tp+xKG2F+JkG6xbM3dDwbp0B
password6=Bu0ivYnTbCSPBDpX0QI7xQxyDA0ARw8aNv5bAAf8RrME
password7=IxHCruZDowBkyRFpTyXnwxXguNvz+0MWkqOlwWm6n8X0
password8=OGDgXyAZw0fzv6vXiPi7kOTsbtcpsxZebSRcX13SF2aC
password9=TddI5TdZIq0f0FSKNJLd7jpYJF0u7yqyAyksSVSw2hzy
password10=NbaYKBAqp4LTuqFP5NgoPikvmslvRAcLo6nUin5H4gMQ
password11=fdEw0SjfoC+74lhxCA5cOauW9rcFzIIcxBs2XbxQWj2r
password12=WzffIwIW9KDQO7kk+DKRqNtj9vTX6uUVy9MdbpYvj2Ez
password13=ov0tkKaa8svmTB8QCooHo740tgyrxa3mSq2wcxTeffGa
password14=V74uML0prn3QRrJe0i7sJNQTNA127zHQDGcMg2fPUqLx
password15=OHdwuU0PrVnUax3tZvwnOR+3dSW7aLR1E2S0iUypmZoN
```

```
password16=jQiBWHeTRDS23Iu9YoevvHzBOmgzUPLT9pYa7mUpimsA
password17=SEEAnIUTTf0+E07Py4eEkEbdeIIGck5K0NyhLHcPMMR5
password18=wzLBGSQWZt5oX+C3oT2U0caLNDilGjCxxjqYeQkA2GGo
password19=GzYQ6i18IvuPQd2N9zST5adIEyOub0hKUzmKQRzubyQA
password20=M1Wpc41uClRDQIHw5dJZWsVO0YtYNWTHI1HtsO703RzH
```

This file is normally found at aws/credentials/passwords.sh, but does not exist until you run makepasswords.sh, so an example is shown. Now we have a good supply of highly secure passwords, utterly uncrackable, and we can use them in scripts by including passwords.sh as needed.

Secure Laptop

The importance of a secure environment when running these scripts cannot be over-emphasised. When you sign in to the AWS Console on the Internet, you have some protection with MFA (Multi-Factor Authentication), but with AWS CLI all your credentials are on the system and if a hacker compromised you they would have full control over your servers.

Because we are using Linux, a Mac laptop is highly recommended. The Mac bash shell is the same as the Linux one (for our purposes), so you can test commands from your Mac. In addition, Macs are much more secure than most other platforms and also rather pleasant on the eyes. A Linux environment would also work. And if you feel confident you can secure a Windows installation - go for it! I say Laptop because laptops feel inherently more secure than desktops. You can put a laptop in a safe. It's quite hard to take them apart. And so on.

Here are some steps you should take to secure a Mac Laptop for this purpose:

Administrator Account

Use a very long and difficult password for the Administrator Account, something like a phrase with numbers interspersed, at least 30 or 40 characters. From this account you need to create your day to day account with heavy restrictions.

Install Chrome Browser

You will need this for Admin Server Access.

Users and Groups

From your Administrator Account, go to Users and Groups in Settings. Turn off the Guest Account. Add a new account with a long password, at least 20 characters. For this new user uncheck 'Allow user to administer this computer' and turn on Parental Controls.

Parental Controls

For your new user, on the Apps Tab, check Limit Applications. Don't allow App Store Apps. From the list of available apps, select the absolute minimum you will need: Calculator, Chrome, ksadmin, Mission Control, Safari and TextEdit; from the Utilities, select only Terminal.

On the Web Tab, select 'Allow access to only these websites', and add in any websites you will need. The first will be AWS at aws.amazon.com, and then any others such as your Domain Name Provider, Gmail and any other services which need to be secure.

What we mean by secure is this: there is no point having hyper-security on your AWS and servers if your DNS account can be hacked, as this could compromise your Application in a major way. Similarly, if you use a provider such as GAuthify for MFA, this account also needs to be secure. All these peripheral service accounts should be created from your Secure Laptop and should never be used from any other computer.

Do not add in things like Google (for searching) or your personal email account or similar. This laptop is not for development, not for reading emails, not for updating your FB page! Only access things that need to be secured, only access those secure services from the laptop and don't ever be tempted to open up access to potential threats for the sake of convenience. Then it will be impossible for you to download a key-logger or other malware, which would be a disaster for your organisation.

Secure Settings

Always 'Click the lock to prevent further changes'. Also, in Terminal, turn on 'Secure Keyboard Entry' under the Terminal menu option.

Security and Privacy

From the Security and Privacy Settings panel, select 'Require password IMMEDIATELY after sleep or screensaver begins'. Turn on FileVault to encrypt your drive and set a recovery key. Only the Administrator Account should be able to to unlock the disk.

On the Firewall Tab, enable the firewall and in Firewall Options enable 'Block All Incoming Connections' and 'Enable Stealth Mode'.

Other Services

Don't set up anything else, such as iCloud, your Apple ID, or Sharing. You should set up Time Machine (a good way to do this is to an SD Card) and Encrypt Backups. To copy files to the Secure Laptop, you should use a USB stick, not file sharing. And preferably a new USB stick at that.

General Use

Now sign out of the Administrator Account and sign back in as your new user. Day to day, you will use this account. Minimise signing in as the Administrator. On the rare occasions that you need to add a new website (because it is a secure service) or make a new App available you can do this from the new account by typing the Administrator Password.

Storing Passwords

Because you are using long and complex passwords, you should write them down. You are using FileVault and other measures which mean that if you do lose access you really won't be able to fix it. And if you lose access to your Secure Laptop, you will lose access to all your servers, which could be a disaster. So, contrary to popular opinion, write your passwords down on one sheet of paper and then secure that sheet, in a safe, under a floorboard or with your organisation's secure storage facility.

Connecting to the Network

It is preferable to use an encrypted Wireless Connection rather than a cable connection. However, if other users are sharing this connection, they will have the access keys. So, try to use a dedicated wifi network where you are the only connected user. Avoid crowded hotspots with lots of other users.

Deploying from AWS

There is a further option for deploying your web cloud application: do it from an AWS box. This involves setting up a temporary AWS server, uploading the deployment scripts and running them. You will probably then tear down the server (assuming everything works).

Because this solution is intended for use on any platform (Windows included), there is little point scripting this exercise. Rather, here are the required steps via the AWS Console.

This is the initial setup of AWS and your aws folder:

1. start an AWS Account (or use your Development or Production Account)
2. download your root credentials file from the AWS Console (Click your name top right and select 'Security Credentials', then select 'Access Keys (Access Key ID and Secret Access Key)', Create New Access Key and Download) and save the file somewhere outside the aws folder (we don't want to upload these credentials to the cloud). Note that you can't do this from the linux box because you don't have a browser.
3. edit aws/master/vars.sh (see **Global Variables** earlier in this chapter)
4. in aws/master/vars.sh change basedir to '/home/ec2-user/aws'
5. in aws/master/vars.sh change sshknownhosts to '/home/ec2-user/.ssh/known_hosts'
6. if you are using a valid SSL, copy the supplied SSL files to aws/ami/elb/validssl
7. edit aws/master/vars.sh to reflect the SSL files you have
8. for the demo site provided, we are using Google Recaptcha, so you will need to create keys for a Google Recaptcha Account and then edit credentials/recaptcha.sh and copy in your private and public keys (see **Chapter 10 - Google Recaptcha** for more details)
9. for Mmonit, download a Licence Key and paste into aws/ami/admin/server_template.xml (see **Global Variables** earlier in this Chapter)
10. once you are happy with your aws folder, cd to the aws folder and create a zip of its contents with:

```
zip -R aws '*'
```

All new AWS accounts must use a VPC so there is a checklist to complete. For our cloud application we use a new VPC, but for this deployment server we will use the default VPC. You can delete the default VPC eventually, but you need to contact AWS to reinstate it and as it's free you might as well leave it, just in case you need it one day.

On a new AWS Account, this is configured for you, so you don't need to change anything. But, in case you deleted things, here is what you need to do:

1. sign in to the AWS Console and go to VPC
2. in 'Subnets', make sure you have at least one Subnet, if you don't add one. Choose a Name tag, select your default VPC (normally starts with 172.31) and Availability Zone can be No Preference. For the CIDR Block, use 172.31.1.0/24, but note that if your VPC default subnet is X.Y.0.0/Z you should use X.Y.1.0/A where A<Z.
3. in 'Route Tables', make sure you have at least one Route Table. If you don't, add one. Choose a Name tag and select the default VPC (starts with 172.31).
4. in 'Internet Gateways', make sure you have at least one Internet Gateway. If you don't, add one. Choose a Name tag.
5. Last, you need to connect everything up. Go to 'Route Tables', select the Route Table and at the bottom of the page, select 'Routes'. If you see a route from '0.0.0.0/0' to your Internet Gateway (starts with igw-), you are done. Otherwise, you need to add a route from your Internet Gateway to your subnet, so click 'Edit' and add a record with Destination 0.0.0.0/0 and Target igw-***** (if you start typing 'igw' a pop-down will appear, just click it). Then 'Save'.

Now that your VPC is correctly configured, you can launch an instance:

1. click EC2 in the AWS Console, then 'Instances'
2. click 'Launch Instance'
3. select the top AMI - 'Amazon Linux AMI (HVM)'

4. select an instance type (t2.micro is free but a bit slow, you may want to go with t2.small)
5. click 'Next: Configure Instance Details'
6. ensure 'Network' refers to your default subnet (172.31.0.0/16)
7. ensure 'Subnet' refers to your 172.31.1.0/24 subnet (actually any subnet will do)
8. 'Auto-assign Public IP' should be 'Enable'
9. click 'Next: Add Storage'
10. click 'Next: Tag Instance'
11. click 'Next: Configure Security Group'
12. select 'Create a new Security Group' and call it 'deploy'
13. SSH is already enabled, just change the Source to 'My IP'
14. click 'Review and Launch'
15. click 'Launch'
16. in the Key popup, select 'Create a new key pair' and set Key pair name to 'deploy'
17. click 'Download Key Pair' and put the file in the aws/credentials folder and rename it to 'deploy.pem' (from deploy.pem.txt)
18. click 'Launch Instance'
19. click 'View Instances' and wait for your new instance to be 'running'

Now the fun part - uploading the zip, preparing the server and running the scripts. If you are using a bash terminal, the commands are provided below. On other platforms where bash is unavailable, you'll need a SSH/SCP client such as WinSCP or PuTTY.

1. Unnecessary for Windows. For bash, Set permissions on the SSH key (deploy.pem) by 'cd'ing to the aws directory and running:

```
chmod 600 credentials/deploy.pem
```

2. Upload the zip you created earlier to the new box by connecting to your box with your SSH/SCP app as user ec2-user, with the deploy.pem key and the Public IP of your box. In bash, form the aws directory run:

```
scp -i credentials/deploy.pem aws.zip ec2-user@<Public IP>:
```

(type yes if asked and don't forget the ':' after the Public IP!)

3. SSH to the box, using the user ec2-user, the Public IP assigned to the instance and the deploy.pem key you downloaded. In a bash environment, from the aws directory, use:

```
ssh -i credentials/deploy.pem ec2-user@<Public IP>
```

(type yes if asked)

4. note that if nothing happens or you can't connect it's probably your Security Group - go back to AWS Console > EC2 > Security Groups > deploy > Inbound and check that MyIP is correct or reset it.
5. you should now have a command line on your box
6. get super user power with:

```
sudo su
```

7. configure aws (manually as 'aws configure' doesn't work on an AWS box...):

[aws/snippets/snippet_linuxawsconfigure.sh]

```
mkdir ~/.aws
echo [default] > ~/.aws/config
echo aws_access_key_id=<your AWS ACCESS KEY ID> >>
~/.aws/config
echo aws_secret_access_key=<your AWS SECRET ACCESS KEY> >>
~/.aws/config
echo region=<your REGION> >> ~/.aws/config
echo output=json >> ~/.aws/config
```

(note that you need to replace <your AWS ACCESS KEY ID> and your <AWS SECRET ACCESS KEY> with the values from the rootkey.txt file containing your root credentials. Also <your REGION> with your region, eg eu-west-1. Don't leave the enclosing < and > characters in!)

8. install expect with:

```
yum install -y expect
```

9. unzip the archive to an aws folder:

[aws/snippets/snippet_linuxunpackaws.sh]

```
mkdir aws
mv aws.zip aws
cd aws
unzip aws.zip
rm -f aws.zip
```

10. run the master script:

```
cd /home/ec2-user/aws
./master/master.sh
```

11. that's it! You should now either terminate the deploy instance, or at the very least close the SSH ingress in the deploy Security Group.

Once the scripts complete and you have checked the results, you can delete associated resources.

Now do you see the advantage of scripts?

Deleting All Assets

… is not as simple as you might think. Many assets need to be disassociated first. And assets with dependent assets also can't be deleted. Here is a script which deletes everything we make in the master script (if you change things, you will probably need to edit this as well):

[aws/master/delete.sh]

```
#!/bin/bash

# delete all aws assets
```

```
read -p "DELETE ALL AWS ASSETS? <Y/N> " prompt
if [[ $prompt == "y" || $prompt == "Y" || $prompt == "yes" ||
$prompt == "Yes" ]]
then
  echo "PROCEEDING..."
else
  exit
fi

# check dir
where=$(pwd)
where="${where: -3}"
if test "$where" = "aws"; then
 echo "running from correct directory"
else
 echo "must be run from aws directory with ./master/delete.sh"
 exit
fi

# include global variables
. ./master/vars.sh

# terminate instances
instances=$(aws ec2 describe-instances --output text --query
'Reservations[*].Instances[*].InstanceId')
echo instances=$instances
aws ec2 terminate-instances --instance-ids $instances

# terminate rds (with no final snapshot)
aws rds delete-db-instance --db-instance-identifier $dbinstancename
--skip-final-snapshot

# terminate elb
aws elb delete-load-balancer --load-balancer-name $elbname

# delete the ssl cert
aws iam delete-server-certificate --server-certificate-name
$elbcertname

# wait for instances (or subsequent deletes will fail)
echo -n "waiting for instances termination"
while state=$(aws ec2 describe-instances --output text --query
'Reservations[*].Instances[*].State.Name'); [[ $state == *shutting*
]]; do
 echo -n . ; sleep 5;
done; echo " $state"

# wait for rds (or subsequent deletes will fail)
echo -n "waiting for database termination"
while state=$(aws rds describe-db-instances --output text --query
'DBInstances[*].DBInstanceStatus'); [[ $state == deleting ]]; do
 echo -n . ; sleep 5;
done; echo " $state"

# delete rds parameter group
aws rds delete-db-parameter-group --db-parameter-group-name
$dbpgname

# delete rds subnet group
aws rds delete-db-subnet-group --db-subnet-group-name
```

AWS Scripted   48

```
$dbsubnetgroupname

# delete sns topics
topicarns=$(aws sns list-topics --output text --query
'Topics[*].TopicArn')
topicarnarr=$(echo $topicarns | tr " " "\n")
for i in $topicarnarr
do
 echo found topic $i
 aws sns delete-topic --topic-arn $i
done

# delete ses email identity
aws ses delete-identity --identity $emailsendfrom

# delete iam sesuser
aws iam delete-user-policy --user-name sesuser --policy-name
SESAccess
sesuserkey=$(aws iam list-access-keys --user-name sesuser --output
text --query 'AccessKeyMetadata[*].AccessKeyId')
aws iam delete-access-key --access-key $sesuserkey --user-name
sesuser
aws iam delete-user --user-name sesuser

# deregister image
bslami_id=$(aws ec2 describe-images --filters
'Name=name,Values=Basic Secure Linux' --output text --query
'Images[*].ImageId')
echo bslami_id=$bslami_id
aws ec2 deregister-image --image-id $bslami_id

# delete snapshots
snapshot_ids=$(aws ec2 describe-snapshots --owner-ids self --output
text --query 'Snapshots[*].SnapshotId')
echo snapshot_ids=$snapshot_ids
for snapshot_id in $snapshot_ids
do
 echo "deleting snapshot $snapshot_id"
 aws ec2 delete-snapshot --snapshot-id $snapshot_id
done

# delete key pairs
aws ec2 delete-key-pair --key-name basic
aws ec2 delete-key-pair --key-name admin
aws ec2 delete-key-pair --key-name web1
aws ec2 delete-key-pair --key-name web2
aws ec2 delete-key-pair --key-name web3
aws ec2 delete-key-pair --key-name web4
aws ec2 delete-key-pair --key-name web5
aws ec2 delete-key-pair --key-name web6

# release elastic ips
eip=$(aws ec2 describe-addresses --output text --query
'Addresses[*].AllocationId')
echo eip=$eip
eiparr=$(echo $eip | tr " " "\n")
for i in $eiparr
do
 echo found eip $i
 aws ec2 release-address --allocation-id $i
```

```
done

# delete vpc
# from the console (VPC), this can be done in one operation, but
not from the cli...
vpc_id=$(aws ec2 describe-vpcs --filters Name=tag-
key,Values=vpcname --filters Name=tag-value,Values=$vpcname
--output text --query 'Vpcs[*].VpcId')
echo vpc_id=$vpc_id

# delete igw
igw_id=$(aws ec2 describe-internet-gateways --output text --query
'InternetGateways[*].InternetGatewayId')
aws ec2 detach-internet-gateway --internet-gateway-id $igw_id
--vpc-id $vpc_id
aws ec2 delete-internet-gateway --internet-gateway-id $igw_id

# delete subnets
subnet_id=$(aws ec2 describe-subnets --filters Name=vpc-
id,Values=$vpc_id --filters Name=tag-key,Values=subnet --filters
Name=tag-value,Values=1 --output text --query
'Subnets[*].SubnetId')
echo subnet_id=$subnet_id
aws ec2 delete-subnet --subnet-id $subnet_id
subnet_id=$(aws ec2 describe-subnets --filters Name=vpc-
id,Values=$vpc_id --filters Name=tag-key,Values=subnet --filters
Name=tag-value,Values=2 --output text --query
'Subnets[*].SubnetId')
echo subnet_id=$subnet_id
aws ec2 delete-subnet --subnet-id $subnet_id

# delete security groups...
# first get all the ids
adminsg_id=$(aws ec2 describe-security-groups --filters Name=tag-
key,Values=sgname --filters Name=tag-value,Values=adminsg --output
text --query 'SecurityGroups[*].GroupId')
echo adminsg_id=$adminsg_id
dbsg_id=$(aws ec2 describe-security-groups --filters Name=tag-
key,Values=sgname --filters Name=tag-value,Values=dbsg --output
text --query 'SecurityGroups[*].GroupId')
echo dbsg_id=$dbsg_id
elbsg_id=$(aws ec2 describe-security-groups --filters Name=tag-
key,Values=sgname --filters Name=tag-value,Values=elbsg --output
text --query 'SecurityGroups[*].GroupId')
echo elbsg_id=$elbsg_id
web1sg_id=$(aws ec2 describe-security-groups --filters Name=tag-
key,Values=sgname --filters Name=tag-value,Values=web1sg --output
text --query 'SecurityGroups[*].GroupId')
echo web1sg_id=$web1sg_id
web2sg_id=$(aws ec2 describe-security-groups --filters Name=tag-
key,Values=sgname --filters Name=tag-value,Values=web2sg --output
text --query 'SecurityGroups[*].GroupId')
echo web2sg_id=$web2sg_id
web3sg_id=$(aws ec2 describe-security-groups --filters Name=tag-
key,Values=sgname --filters Name=tag-value,Values=web3sg --output
text --query 'SecurityGroups[*].GroupId')
echo web3sg_id=$web3sg_id
web4sg_id=$(aws ec2 describe-security-groups --filters Name=tag-
key,Values=sgname --filters Name=tag-value,Values=web4sg --output
text --query 'SecurityGroups[*].GroupId')
```

```
echo web4sg_id=$web4sg_id
web5sg_id=$(aws ec2 describe-security-groups --filters Name=tag-
key,Values=sgname --filters Name=tag-value,Values=web5sg --output
text --query 'SecurityGroups[*].GroupId')
echo web5sg_id=$web5sg_id
web6sg_id=$(aws ec2 describe-security-groups --filters Name=tag-
key,Values=sgname --filters Name=tag-value,Values=web6sg --output
text --query 'SecurityGroups[*].GroupId')
echo web6sg_id=$web6sg_id
# remove all rules from adminsg
aws ec2 revoke-security-group-ingress --group-id $adminsg_id
--protocol tcp --port 514 --source-group $web1sg_id
aws ec2 revoke-security-group-ingress --group-id $adminsg_id
--protocol tcp --port 8080 --source-group $web1sg_id
aws ec2 revoke-security-group-ingress --group-id $adminsg_id
--protocol tcp --port 514 --source-group $web2sg_id
aws ec2 revoke-security-group-ingress --group-id $adminsg_id
--protocol tcp --port 8080 --source-group $web2sg_id
aws ec2 revoke-security-group-ingress --group-id $adminsg_id
--protocol tcp --port 514 --source-group $web3sg_id
aws ec2 revoke-security-group-ingress --group-id $adminsg_id
--protocol tcp --port 8080 --source-group $web3sg_id
aws ec2 revoke-security-group-ingress --group-id $adminsg_id
--protocol tcp --port 514 --source-group $web4sg_id
aws ec2 revoke-security-group-ingress --group-id $adminsg_id
--protocol tcp --port 8080 --source-group $web4sg_id
aws ec2 revoke-security-group-ingress --group-id $adminsg_id
--protocol tcp --port 514 --source-group $web5sg_id
aws ec2 revoke-security-group-ingress --group-id $adminsg_id
--protocol tcp --port 8080 --source-group $web5sg_id
aws ec2 revoke-security-group-ingress --group-id $adminsg_id
--protocol tcp --port 514 --source-group $web6sg_id
aws ec2 revoke-security-group-ingress --group-id $adminsg_id
--protocol tcp --port 8080 --source-group $web6sg_id
# remove all rules from dbsg
aws ec2 revoke-security-group-ingress --group-id $dbsg_id
--protocol tcp --port 3306 --source-group $adminsg_id
aws ec2 revoke-security-group-ingress --group-id $dbsg_id
--protocol tcp --port 3306 --source-group $web1sg_id
aws ec2 revoke-security-group-ingress --group-id $dbsg_id
--protocol tcp --port 3306 --source-group $web2sg_id
aws ec2 revoke-security-group-ingress --group-id $dbsg_id
--protocol tcp --port 3306 --source-group $web3sg_id
aws ec2 revoke-security-group-ingress --group-id $dbsg_id
--protocol tcp --port 3306 --source-group $web4sg_id
aws ec2 revoke-security-group-ingress --group-id $dbsg_id
--protocol tcp --port 3306 --source-group $web5sg_id
aws ec2 revoke-security-group-ingress --group-id $dbsg_id
--protocol tcp --port 3306 --source-group $web6sg_id
# remove all rules from elbsg
aws ec2 revoke-security-group-ingress --group-id $elbsg_id
--protocol tcp --port 80 --cidr 0.0.0.0/0
aws ec2 revoke-security-group-ingress --group-id $elbsg_id
--protocol tcp --port 443 --cidr 0.0.0.0/0
# remove all rules from web1sg
aws ec2 revoke-security-group-ingress --group-id $web1sg_id
--protocol tcp --port 80 --source-group $elbsg_id
aws ec2 revoke-security-group-ingress --group-id $web1sg_id
--protocol tcp --port 443 --source-group $elbsg_id
aws ec2 revoke-security-group-ingress --group-id $web1sg_id
```

```
--protocol tcp --port 2812 --source-group $adminsg_id
# remove all rules from web2sg
aws ec2 revoke-security-group-ingress --group-id $web2sg_id
--protocol tcp --port 80 --source-group $elbsg_id
aws ec2 revoke-security-group-ingress --group-id $web2sg_id
--protocol tcp --port 443 --source-group $elbsg_id
aws ec2 revoke-security-group-ingress --group-id $web2sg_id
--protocol tcp --port 2812 --source-group $adminsg_id
# remove all rules from web3sg
aws ec2 revoke-security-group-ingress --group-id $web3sg_id
--protocol tcp --port 80 --source-group $elbsg_id
aws ec2 revoke-security-group-ingress --group-id $web3sg_id
--protocol tcp --port 443 --source-group $elbsg_id
aws ec2 revoke-security-group-ingress --group-id $web3sg_id
--protocol tcp --port 2812 --source-group $adminsg_id
# remove all rules from web4sg
aws ec2 revoke-security-group-ingress --group-id $web4sg_id
--protocol tcp --port 80 --source-group $elbsg_id
aws ec2 revoke-security-group-ingress --group-id $web4sg_id
--protocol tcp --port 443 --source-group $elbsg_id
aws ec2 revoke-security-group-ingress --group-id $web4sg_id
--protocol tcp --port 2812 --source-group $adminsg_id
# remove all rules from web5sg
aws ec2 revoke-security-group-ingress --group-id $web5sg_id
--protocol tcp --port 80 --source-group $elbsg_id
aws ec2 revoke-security-group-ingress --group-id $web5sg_id
--protocol tcp --port 443 --source-group $elbsg_id
aws ec2 revoke-security-group-ingress --group-id $web5sg_id
--protocol tcp --port 2812 --source-group $adminsg_id
# remove all rules from web6sg
aws ec2 revoke-security-group-ingress --group-id $web6sg_id
--protocol tcp --port 80 --source-group $elbsg_id
aws ec2 revoke-security-group-ingress --group-id $web6sg_id
--protocol tcp --port 443 --source-group $elbsg_id
aws ec2 revoke-security-group-ingress --group-id $web6sg_id
--protocol tcp --port 2812 --source-group $adminsg_id
# finally delete sgs
aws ec2 delete-security-group --group-id $adminsg_id
aws ec2 delete-security-group --group-id $dbsg_id
aws ec2 delete-security-group --group-id $elbsg_id
aws ec2 delete-security-group --group-id $web1sg_id
aws ec2 delete-security-group --group-id $web2sg_id
aws ec2 delete-security-group --group-id $web3sg_id
aws ec2 delete-security-group --group-id $web4sg_id
aws ec2 delete-security-group --group-id $web5sg_id
aws ec2 delete-security-group --group-id $web6sg_id

# now we can finally delete the vpc
# all remaining assets are also deleted (eg route table, default
security group)
aws ec2 delete-vpc --vpc-id $vpc_id

# tags are deleted automatically when associated resource dies

# now delete some files which are useless
cd $basedir
rm -f credentials/*.pem
rm -f credentials/passwords.sh
rm -f credentials/sesuser_AccessKeyId
rm -f credentials/sesuser_SecretAccessKey
```

```
rm -f credentials/smtp.sh
rm -f ami/elb/ssl/cert.pem
rm -f ami/elb/ssl/key.pem
rm -f ami/elb/ssl/server.crt
rm -f ami/elb/ssl/server.csr
rm -f ami/elb/ssl/server.key
rm -f ami/elb/ssl/server.key.org

echo "all deleted"
```

As you can see, the process is... interesting.

SSH KnownHosts

You will notice that in all our scripts we delete the SSH KnownHosts file. This file stores access keys for SSH and warns if a key changes. However, the security provided is minimal since the checks only apply to subsequent connection attempts. So, if you are the victim of a Man-in-the-Middle attack when you first launch, and then reconnect with the Man listening in again, SSH KnownHosts checks won't save you. The reason we remove the file is that ssh interrupts our scripts with requests for confirmation.

It is true that if the access key changes after the first connection attempt, SSH KnownHosts would detect this. However, this vulnerability is mitigated by the fact that we need to explicitly open up ports in Security Groups to allow access to SSH on any of our boxes. This is separate from our SSH keys and by using the CIDR notation to allow access only to our own IP we effectively block a Man-in-the-Middle attack.

In addition, by removing the password-less 'sudo su' option on our boxes and requiring a strong password, even if your SSH keys are stolen, a hacker could not get access.

Chapter 3 - AWS VPC

VPC Script

Basic network configuration in AWS is handled by a VPC (Virtual Private Cloud). Here, you define your subnets, gateways and DNS settings. This script needs to be called first, before any EC2 instances are launched, because EC2 instances (and ELBs) are launched into this VPC. The VPC underpins the whole endeavour, but once created you don't really need to worry about it. You will, however, be referring to it almost everywhere, ie getting its ID, getting its subnets etc.

The steps are as follows:

1. create the VPC with a master subnet of 10.0.0.0/16 (we can then create further subnets within this subnet)
2. enable DNS support (needed by ModSecurity)
3. tag the VPC
4. wait for the VPC to be ready
5. create an Internet Gateway (to allow access to the Internet)
6. attach the Internet Gateway to the VPC
7. identify the Route Table for the VPC
8. create 2 subnets within the VPC, one in deployment zone 1 and one in deployment zone 2 (we need this for RDS Multi-AZ deployment)
9. tag and associate these new subnets with the VPC Route Table
10. create a route from the Route Table to the Internet Gateway

Here is the full script:

[aws/ami/vpc/make.sh]

```
#!/bin/bash

# makes a vpc
```

```
# check dir
where=$(pwd)
where="${where: -3}"
if test "$where" = "aws"; then
 echo "running from correct directory"
else
 echo "must be run from aws directory with ./ami/vpc/make.sh"
 exit
fi

# include global variables
. ./master/vars.sh

# make a new vpc with a master 10.0.0.0/16 subnet
vpc_id=$(aws ec2 create-vpc --cidr-block 10.0.0.0/16 --output text
--query 'Vpc.VpcId')
echo vpc_id=$vpc_id

# enable dns support or modsecurity wont let apache start...
aws ec2 modify-vpc-attribute --vpc-id $vpc_id --enable-dns-support
aws ec2 modify-vpc-attribute --vpc-id $vpc_id --enable-dns-
hostnames

# tag the vpc
aws ec2 create-tags --resources $vpc_id --tags
Key=vpcname,Value=$vpcname

# wait for the vpc
echo -n "waiting for vpc..."
while state=$(aws ec2 describe-vpcs --filters Name=tag-
key,Values=vpcname --filters Name=tag-value,Values=$vpcname
--output text --query 'Vpcs[*].State'); test "$state" = "pending";
do
 echo -n . ; sleep 3;
done; echo " $state"

# create an internet gateway (to allow access out to the internet)
igw=$(aws ec2 create-internet-gateway --output text --query
'InternetGateway.InternetGatewayId')
echo igw=$igw

# attach the igw to the vpc
echo attaching igw
aws ec2 attach-internet-gateway --internet-gateway-id $igw --vpc-id
$vpc_id

# get the route table id for the vpc (we need it later)
rtb_id=$(aws ec2 describe-route-tables --filters Name=vpc-
id,Values=$vpc_id --output text --query
'RouteTables[*].RouteTableId')
echo rtb_id=$rtb_id

# create our main subnets
# we use 10.0.0.0/24 as our main subnet and 10.0.10.0/24 as a
backup for multi-az rds
subnet_id=$(aws ec2 create-subnet --vpc-id $vpc_id --cidr-block
10.0.0.0/24 --availability-zone $deployzone --output text --query
'Subnet.SubnetId')
echo subnet_id=$subnet_id
# tag this subnet
```

```
aws ec2 create-tags --resources $subnet_id --tags
Key=subnet,Value=1
# associate this subnet with our route table
aws ec2 associate-route-table --subnet-id $subnet_id --route-table-
id $rtb_id
# now the 10.0.10.0/24 subnet in our secondary deployment zone
subnet_id=$(aws ec2 create-subnet --vpc-id $vpc_id --cidr-block
10.0.10.0/24 --availability-zone $deployzone2 --output text --query
'Subnet.SubnetId')
echo subnet_id=$subnet_id
# tag this subnet
aws ec2 create-tags --resources $subnet_id --tags
Key=subnet,Value=2
# associate this subnet with our route table
aws ec2 associate-route-table --subnet-id $subnet_id --route-table-
id $rtb_id

# create a route out from our route table to the igw
echo creating route from igw
aws ec2 create-route --route-table-id $rtb_id --gateway-id $igw
--destination-cidr-block 0.0.0.0/0

# done
echo vpc setup done
```

Chapter 4 - AWS RDS

Initial Setup

Deploying an RDS Instance can take a little longer than a standard EC2 instance, so we split the process up and do other things while we wait for the database (such as making the Linux Shared Image).

There are a few steps to set up an RDS instance:

1. create an RDS DB Subnet Group which spans both our subnets (10.0.0.0/24 and 10.0.10.0/24)
2. create the security group which will control access to the database instance
3. create a DB Parameter Group to turn on Slow Query Logging and set the trigger time at 1 second
4. launch the RDS instance (multi-AZ or not as defined by rdsusemultiaz in aws/master/vars.sh)

Note over time the minimum recommended version of MySQL might change (as of writing it is 5.6.21). You should check this by attempting to launch a database in the AWS Console and noting the available versions (you don't actually need to launch a database). Then change the mysqlversion variable in the script below.

This is the main script:

[aws/ami/rds/make.sh]

```
#!/bin/bash

# makes an rds database
# database is populated in admin server setup

# check dir
where=$(pwd)
where="${where: -3}"
if test "$where" = "aws"; then
 echo "running from correct directory"
```

```
else
  echo "must be run from aws directory with ./ami/rds/make.sh"
  exit
fi

# include global variables
. ./master/vars.sh

cd $basedir

# include passwords
source credentials/passwords.sh

# create an rds db subnet group which spans both our subnets
(10.0.0.0/24 and 10.0.10.0/24)
vpc_id=$(aws ec2 describe-vpcs --filters Name=tag-
key,Values=vpcname --filters Name=tag-value,Values=$vpcname
--output text --query 'Vpcs[*].VpcId')
echo vpc_id=$vpc_id
subnet_ids=$(aws ec2 describe-subnets --filters Name=vpc-
id,Values=$vpc_id --output text --query 'Subnets[*].SubnetId')
echo subnet_ids=$subnet_ids
aws rds create-db-subnet-group --db-subnet-group-name
$dbsubnetgroupname --db-subnet-group-description $dbsubnetgroupdesc
--subnet-ids $subnet_ids

# create a vpc security group
# db sg will control access to the database
sg_id=$(aws ec2 create-security-group --group-name dbsg
--description "rds database security group" --vpc-id $vpc_id
--output text --query 'GroupId')
echo sg_id=$sg_id
# tag it
aws ec2 create-tags --resources $sg_id --tags Key=sgname,Value=dbsg
# get its id
vpcdbsg_id=$(aws ec2 describe-security-groups --filters Name=tag-
key,Values=sgname --filters Name=tag-value,Values=dbsg --output
text --query 'SecurityGroups[*].GroupId')
echo vpcdbsg_id=$vpcdbsg_id

# we want to log slow queries and set the trigger time to be 1
second
# any query taking more than 1 second will be logged
echo making db parameter group
aws rds create-db-parameter-group --db-parameter-group-name
$dbpgname --db-parameter-group-family MySQL5.6 --description
$dbpgdesc
aws rds modify-db-parameter-group --db-parameter-group-name
$dbpgname --parameters
ParameterName=slow_query_log,ParameterValue=1,ApplyMethod=immediate
aws rds modify-db-parameter-group --db-parameter-group-name
$dbpgname --parameters
ParameterName=long_query_time,ParameterValue=1,ApplyMethod=immediat
e

# create the rds instance
# you can't specify the private ip address for an rds instance, but
they tend to be in the 200s...

# the mysql version can change (if AWS force an upgrade for
```

```
security reasons)
# enter the required mysql version here
# (attempt to launch an instance in the console to see minimum
version)
mysqlversion=5.6.21

if (($rdsusemultiaz > 0)); then

  # multi-az : can't use --availability-zone with --multi-az
  aws rds create-db-instance --db-instance-identifier
$dbinstancename --db-instance-class $rdsinstancetype --db-name
$dbname --engine MySQL --engine-version $mysqlversion --port 3306
--allocated-storage $rdsvolumesize --no-auto-minor-version-upgrade
--db-parameter-group-name $dbpgname --master-username mainuser
--master-user-password $password1 --backup-retention-period 14
--no-publicly-accessible --region $deployregion --multi-az --vpc-
security-group-ids $vpcdbsg_id --db-subnet-group-name
$dbsubnetgroupname

else

  # no multi-az
  aws rds create-db-instance --db-instance-identifier
$dbinstancename --db-instance-class $rdsinstancetype --db-name
$dbname --engine MySQL --engine-version $mysqlversion --port 3306
--allocated-storage $rdsvolumesize --no-auto-minor-version-upgrade
--db-parameter-group-name $dbpgname --master-username mainuser
--master-user-password $password1 --backup-retention-period 14
--no-publicly-accessible --region $deployregion --availability-zone
$deployzone --vpc-security-group-ids $vpcdbsg_id --db-subnet-group-
name $dbsubnetgroupname

fi

echo database started, use make2.sh to check for completion

cd $basedir
```

Wait for Completion

Let the database cook - it normally takes about 10 minutes. You should now execute the Linux Shared Image scripts (which takes a while), as is done in the aws/master/master.sh script.

This script waits for the database to be ready:

[aws/ami/rds/make2.sh]

```
#!/bin/bash

# waits for completion of rds database

# check dir
```

```
where=$(pwd)
where="${where: -3}"
if test "$where" = "aws"; then
 echo "running from correct directory"
else
 echo "must be run from aws directory with ./ami/rds/make2.sh"
 exit
fi

# include global variables
. ./master/vars.sh

cd $basedir

# wait for the db state to be available
echo -n "waiting for db"
while state=$(aws rds describe-db-instances --db-instance-
identifier $dbinstancename --output text --query
'DBInstances[*].DBInstanceStatus'); test "$state" != "available";
do
 echo -n . ; sleep 3;
done; echo " $state"

# this is the address, or endpoint, for the db
dbendpoint=$(aws rds describe-db-instances --db-instance-identifier
$dbinstancename --output text --query
'DBInstances[*].Endpoint.Address')
echo dbendpoint=$dbendpoint

cd $basedir

echo "database ALIVE"
```

Data Installation

The database is installed from the Admin Server (which is the most secure EC2 instance on our farm). Normal mysql commands are used. This is because there is no public access to the RDS server, nor do you want to enable this massive security hole. So we load the database creation scripts to the Admin Server and run them from there. See **Chapter 13 - Uploading a new database** for upload scripts and **Chapter 11 - MySQL Database** for sql database scripts.

Chapter 5 - Linux Shared Image

Setting up the Server

The Shared Image is a version of the Amazon Linux AMI beefed up with security enhancements. This image is used as the base for the Admin Server and our Webphp Servers. It's better to separate the linux security aspect of the servers from the application security - hence this Shared Image. We could just apply the code below to any server we build, but it would involve code duplication, which is to be avoided, and is much slower (when, for instance, you are launching 5 Webphp Servers). The Shared Image is also a good starting point for any further servers you may wish to build. In addition, Amazon releases new AMIs and/or updates them, so, given a project lifetime of several years, it is sensible to have our own, unchanging image.

The first choice you will need to make is what base image to use. All the scrips in this book are based on the Amazon Linux AMI. However, there are 2 choices: HVM (Hardware Virtual Machine) or PV (Paravirtual). Generally, PV is considered to have better performance, since there is less connection to hardware. However, some people have reported Networking Issues with PV. Amazon actually recommend HVM because Enhanced Networking is enabled on HVM. You should use HVM unless you really know what you are doing. All scripts in this book are tested on HVM Images.

To find the latest image identifiers, sign in to the AWS Console, go to EC2 and select 'Launch Instance'. You will be presented with a list of possible AMIs - the HVM tends to be at the top and the PV a page down. Copy the AMI Identifier (eg ami-748e2903) and put this in the aws/master/vars.sh file in the baseami variable. Note that this is necessary because AMIs change over time.

Note that when creating the Shared Image, the EBS Volume Size (eg 20GB) can be increased in subsequent servers launched from the image, but not reduced, so don't make it 200GB if you want your web servers to have only 20GB drives.

Note also that we only use EBS storage and ignore what AWS terms 'ephemeral' storage.

Making an Image

The process for making the Shared Image is broadly as follows:

1. make the instance
2. update security
3. update SSH
4. update YUM
5. run some security checks
6. make an Image
7. terminate the instance and associated resources

This is the main script to build the Shared Image:

[aws/ami/shared/make.sh]

```
#!/bin/bash

# makes a secure linux box image, hardened
# ssh on 38142
# XGB EBS root volume

# check dir
where=$(pwd)
where="${where: -3}"
if test "$where" = "aws"; then
 echo "running from correct directory"
else
 echo "must be run from aws directory with ./ami/shared/make.sh"
 exit
fi

# include global variables
. ./master/vars.sh

# a complex string needed to specify EBS volume size
bdm=[{\"DeviceName\":\"/dev/sda1\",\"Ebs\":{\"VolumeSize\":
$sharedebsvolumesize}}]
echo bdm=$bdm

# hosts change, we don't need this
```

```
rm -f $sshknownhosts

cd $basedir

# get our ip from amazon
myip=$(curl http://checkip.amazonaws.com/)
echo myip=$myip

# make a new keypair
echo "making keypair"
rm credentials/basic.pem
aws ec2 delete-key-pair --key-name basic
aws ec2 create-key-pair --key-name basic --query 'KeyMaterial'
--output text > credentials/basic.pem
chmod 600 credentials/basic.pem
echo "keypair made"

# make a security group
vpc_id=$(aws ec2 describe-vpcs --filters Name=tag-
key,Values=vpcname --filters Name=tag-value,Values=$vpcname
--output text --query 'Vpcs[*].VpcId')
echo vpc_id=$vpc_id
sg_id=$(aws ec2 create-security-group --group-name basicsg
--description "basic security group" --vpc-id $vpc_id --output text
--query 'GroupId')
echo sg_id=$sg_id
# tag it
aws ec2 create-tags --resources $sg_id --tags
Key=sgname,Value=basicsg
vpcbasicsg_id=$(aws ec2 describe-security-groups --filters
Name=tag-key,Values=sgname --filters Name=tag-value,Values=basicsg
--output text --query 'SecurityGroups[*].GroupId')
echo vpcbasicsg_id=$vpcbasicsg_id
# allow SSH in on port 22 from our ip only
aws ec2 authorize-security-group-ingress --group-id $vpcbasicsg_id
--protocol tcp --port 22 --cidr $myip/32

# get our main subnet id
subnet_id=$(aws ec2 describe-subnets --filters Name=vpc-
id,Values=$vpc_id --filters Name=tag-key,Values=subnet --filters
Name=tag-value,Values=1 --output text --query
'Subnets[*].SubnetId')
echo subnet_id=$subnet_id

# make the instance on 10.0.0.9
instance_id=$(aws ec2 run-instances --image $baseami --key basic
--security-group-ids $vpcbasicsg_id --placement
AvailabilityZone=$deployzone --instance-type $sharedinstancetype
--block-device-mapping $bdm --region $deployregion --subnet-id
$subnet_id --private-ip-address 10.0.0.9 --associate-public-ip-
address --output text --query 'Instances[*].InstanceId')
echo instance_id=$instance_id

# wait for it
echo -n "waiting for instance"
while state=$(aws ec2 describe-instances --instance-ids
$instance_id --output text --query
'Reservations[*].Instances[*].State.Name'); test "$state" =
"pending"; do
 echo -n . ; sleep 3;
```

```
done; echo " $state"

# get the new instance's public ip address
ip_address=$(aws ec2 describe-instances --instance-ids $instance_id
--output text --query
'Reservations[*].Instances[*].PublicIpAddress')
echo ip_address=$ip_address

# wait for ssh to work
echo -n "waiting for ssh"
while ! ssh -i credentials/basic.pem -o ConnectTimeout=60 -o
BatchMode=yes -o StrictHostKeyChecking=no ec2-user@$ip_address >
/dev/null 2>&1 true; do
 echo -n . ; sleep 3;
done; echo " ssh ok"

# send required files
echo "transferring files"
scp -i credentials/basic.pem ami/shared/secure.sh ec2-
user@$ip_address:
scp -i credentials/basic.pem ami/shared/check.sh ec2-
user@$ip_address:
scp -i credentials/basic.pem ami/shared/sshd_config ec2-
user@$ip_address:
scp -i credentials/basic.pem ami/shared/yumupdate.sh ec2-
user@$ip_address:
echo "transferred files"

# run the secure script
echo "running secure.sh"
ssh -i credentials/basic.pem -t ec2-user@$ip_address sudo
./secure.sh
echo "finished secure.sh"

# now ssh is on 38142
echo "adding port 38142 to sg"
aws ec2 authorize-security-group-ingress --group-id $vpcbasicsg_id
--protocol tcp --port 38142 --cidr $myip/32
echo "sg updated"

# instance is rebooting, wait for ssh again
echo -n "waiting for ssh"
while ! ssh -i credentials/basic.pem -p 38142 -o ConnectTimeout=60
-o BatchMode=yes -o StrictHostKeyChecking=no ec2-user@$ip_address >
/dev/null 2>&1 true; do
 echo -n . ; sleep 3;
done; echo " ssh ok"

# run a check script, you should check this output
echo "running check.sh"
ssh -i credentials/basic.pem -p 38142 -t -o ConnectTimeout=60 -o
BatchMode=yes -o StrictHostKeyChecking=no ec2-user@$ip_address sudo
./check.sh
echo "finished check.sh"

# make the image
echo "creating image"
image_id=$(aws ec2 create-image --instance-id $instance_id --name
"Basic Secure Linux" --description "Basic Secure Linux AMI"
--output text --query 'ImageId')
```

```
echo image_id=$image_id

# wait for the image
echo -n "waiting for image"
while state=$(aws ec2 describe-images --image-id $image_id --output
text --query 'Images[*].State'); test "$state" = "pending"; do
 echo -n . ; sleep 3;
done; echo " $state"

# terminate the instance
aws ec2 terminate-instances --instance-ids $instance_id

# wait for termination
echo -n "waiting for instance termination"
while state=$(aws ec2 describe-instances --instance-ids
$instance_id --output text --query
'Reservations[*].Instances[*].State.Name'); test "$state" !=
"terminated"; do
 echo -n . ; sleep 3;
done; echo " $state"

# delete the key
echo deleting key
rm credentials/basic.pem
aws ec2 delete-key-pair --key-name basic

# delete the security group
echo deleting security group
aws ec2 delete-security-group --group-id $vpcbasicsg_id

cd $basedir

echo "done - Image made; Key, Security Group and Instance deleted"
```

The new SSH config is hardened and changes the SSH port to 38142. This is the new SSH configuration:

[aws/ami/shared/sshd_config]

```
# ssh config file
# the main change is using port 38142
# otherwise, we turn off anything we don't need

Port 38142

Protocol 2

SyslogFacility AUTHPRIV
LogLevel INFO

PermitRootLogin no
PermitRootLogin forced-commands-only
AuthorizedKeysFile        .ssh/authorized_keys
HostbasedAuthentication no
IgnoreRhosts yes
PasswordAuthentication no
ChallengeResponseAuthentication no
```

```
AllowUsers ec2-user

UsePAM yes

X11Forwarding yes
PrintLastLog yes
UsePrivilegeSeparation sandbox

AcceptEnv LANG LC_CTYPE LC_NUMERIC LC_TIME LC_COLLATE LC_MONETARY
LC_MESSAGES
AcceptEnv LC_PAPER LC_NAME LC_ADDRESS LC_TELEPHONE LC_MEASUREMENT
AcceptEnv LC_IDENTIFICATION LC_ALL LANGUAGE
AcceptEnv XMODIFIERS

Subsystem       sftp    /usr/libexec/openssh/sftp-server
```

We do a YUM update, remove unwanted services and schedule a daily update. This is the new YUM daily update script:

[aws/ami/shared/yumupdate.sh]

```
#!/bin/bash
# script to do a daily YUM update
# copy to /etc/cron.daily/
YUM=/usr/bin/yum
$YUM -y -R 120 -d 0 -e 0 update yum
$YUM -y -R 10 -e 0 -d 0 update
```

This is a script uploaded to the new box which displays a few security checks (everything is ok):

[aws/ami/shared/check.sh]

```
#!/bin/bash

# script to check some linux security issues

echo "some linux security checks"

echo "You should only see one line as follows:
root:x:0:0:root:/root:/bin/bash"
awk -F: '($3 == "0") {print}' /etc/passwd

#echo "press a key"
#read -n 1 -s

# check network listeners
echo "net listeners"
netstat -tulpn

#echo "press a key"
#read -n 1 -s
```

```
# Disable Unwanted SUID and SGID Binaries
# All SUID/SGID bits enabled file can be misused when the SUID/SGID
executable has a security problem or bug
# All local or remote user can use such file. It is a good idea to
find all such files. Use the find command as follows:
# See all set user id files:
echo "Disable Unwanted SUID and SGID Binaries"
find / -perm +4000

#echo "press a key"
#read -n 1 -s

echo "See all group id files"
find / -perm +2000

#echo "press a key"
#read -n 1 -s

echo "World-Writable Files"
# Anyone can modify world-writable file resulting into a security
issue
# Use the following command to find all world writable and sticky
bits set files:
find / -xdev -type d \( -perm -0002 -a ! -perm -1000 \) -print

#echo "press a key"
#read -n 1 -s

echo "Noowner Files"
# Files not owned by any user or group can pose a security problem
# Just find them with the following command which do not belong to
a valid user and a valid group
find / -xdev \( -nouser -o -nogroup \) -print

#echo "press a key"
#read -n 1 -s

echo "deleting ec2-user files"

rm -f /home/ec2-user/*
ls
```

Original Files

The configuration files above have been edited and most
comments removed for clarity and succinctness. You can find the
original unedited files in the aws/ami/shared/original folder. The
locations for these files are as follows:

1. sshd_config (SSH) (on a new AWS box)

   /etc/ssh/sshd_config

Building from the Image

When aws/ami/shared/make.sh has finished, our new AMI will be ready to work from. You can see it in AWS Console under EC2 > AMIs.

To use this AMI to launch an instance we need to get its identifier:

```
bslami_id=$(aws ec2 describe-images --filters
'Name=name,Values=Basic Secure Linux' --output text --query
'Images[*].ImageId')
echo bslami_id=$bslami_id
```

You can then use this AMI in future instance launches:

```
aws ec2 run-instances --image $bslami_id ...
```

Changing Passwords

The default AWS installation uses keys to allow SSH into the box and more importantly, the password-less ability to do sudo or sudo su (which gives full root permissions). Given that we use AWS Security Groups to open and close SSH ports as and when needed, this is pretty secure: a hacker would need to compromise your AWS account, open up ports and steal your .pem key files. However, some of our servers accept request from the Internet and are potentially vulnerable, so it is a good idea to disable the password-less sudo option. You can do this by executing the following on the AWS box:

```
echo "ec2-user ALL = ALL" > /etc/sudoers.d/cloud-init
```

Now that we have disabled this feature, we need to sudo with a password, so we need scripts to change the password to something we know. For this we use 2 expect scripts, one for root and one for ec2-user:

Change password for root (note SED***SED items are replaced with real values):

[aws/ami/shared/chp_root.sh]

```
#!/usr/bin/expect
# used when we set up boxes to change the password for root
spawn passwd root
expect "New password:"
send "SED-ROOT-PASS-SED\n";
expect "new password:"
send "SED-ROOT-PASS-SED\n";
interact
```

Change password for ec2-user (note SED***SED items are replaced with real values):

[aws/ami/shared/chp_ec2-user.sh]

```
#!/usr/bin/expect
# used when we set up boxes to change the password for ec2-user
spawn passwd ec2-user
expect "New password:"
send "SED-EC2-USER-PASS-SED\n";
expect "new password:"
send "SED-EC2-USER-PASS-SED\n";
interact
```

If you are not familiar with expect, it is a nifty tool which allows direct scripting of the command line. The main commands are 'spawn' (execute a command), 'expect' (wait for output on the command line), 'send' (type something) and 'interact' (execute the script). An expect script is recognised by the '#!/usr/bin/expect' first line. We use expect extensively to change passwords, sign into boxes or create SSL certificates.

Note that you need to install expect with YUM before using it:

```
yum install -y expect
```

and (as it is potentially a security threat) remove it when you have finished:

```
yum erase -y expect
```

For each aws server instance we have passwords allocated in the aws/credentials/passwords.sh file. When the box is being made, we retrieve those passwords, sed them into the above two scripts, upload them to the new server, install expect, run the scripts and erase expect. You can see this in the creation scripts for the Admin Server and for Webphp Servers.

Chapter 6 - AWS SES

The Problem with Cloud Email

Amazon have obviously had a lot of problems with Spammers. Over the years, their instances have been used to send a lot of spam. With their free tier, you could start an account, launch a few servers and send millions of emails without paying a penny!

For this reason, if you try to send email from any of your EC2 instances direct to the Internet, you will almost certainly be flagged as Spam. Obviously, this is completely unacceptable as you will lose half your customers who won't find your Email Address Verification notification. It also looks very bad if emails you send are Marked as Spam by Gmail or the like.

There is a way around this: AWS SES (Simple Email Service)... however there is nothing simple about setting this up, and I suspect Amazon have done this on purpose to discourage on the fly spammers.

Amazon also requires you to have a system in place to handle Complaint and Bounce notifications. This means setting SNS up. It also means that if a user marks your email as spam, you should take note of this and not send any more emails to that user. If you ignore notifications, Amazon are likely to revoke your email sending privileges.

AWS Procedures

To get SES working you need to jump through hoops.

Phase 1:

1. create an SES user and set the correct policy

2. get the user's credentials
3. create an SMTP password (with a java class)
4. verify an email address

Phase 2:

1. set up SNS
2. set up Bounce and Complaint feeds
3. link SES to SNS
4. disable feedback forwarding

You will then also need to:

1. at your preferred DNS Registrar, add a TXT record to yourdomain.com containing: include:amazonses.com
2. request full email sending Production Access from Amazon at http://aws.amazon.com/ses/fullaccessrequest/

Phase 1 is done in the aws/email/make.sh script, Phase 2 in the aws/email/make2.sh script. The reason these scripts are separated is that you need to verify you email address for the SNS to work. SNS also needs to call PHP files on your servers, so your web servers must be running. But we also need the file aws/credentials/smtp.sh to have been created to upload our JavaMail Server. Also note that SNS won't work with self-signed certificates, and your DNS needs to be set up and working. A way round this is to use your ELB domain name without SSL for SNS notifications. But if you have valid SLL and your domain CNAME is set up, you can edit make2.sh to reflect this (change the scriptshost and protocol variables).

Setup Scripts

SES script part 1 (requires java):

[aws/ami/email/make.sh]

```
#!/bin/sh
```

```
# interactive script to set up SES user and smtp credentials
# ses regions are limited
# creates file credentials/smtp.sh
# which is needed by upload/java/upload.sh

# check dir
where=$(pwd)
where="${where: -3}"
if test "$where" = "aws"; then
 echo "running from correct directory"
else
 echo "must be run from aws directory with ./ami/email/make.sh"
 exit
fi

# include global variables
. ./master/vars.sh

cd $basedir

# this function allows us to extract data from a json string
function jsonval {
        temp=`echo $json | sed 's/\\\\\//\//g' | sed 's/[{}]//g' |
awk -v k="text" '{n=split($0,a,","); for (i=1; i<=n; i++) print
a[i]}' | sed 's/\"\:\"/\|/g' | sed 's/[\,]/ /g' | sed 's/\"//g' |
grep -w $prop | cut -d":" -f2| sed -e 's/^ *//g' -e 's/ *$//g'`
    echo ${temp##*|}
        }

# make ses user
echo creating aws ses user
aws iam create-user --user-name sesuser
# the ses user can send raw email
policy={\"Version\":\"2012-10-17\",\"Statement\":
[{\"Effect\":\"Allow\",\"Action\":\"ses:SendRawEmail\",\"Resource\"
:\"*\"}]}
echo policy=$policy
echo $policy > temppolicy
# attach the policy to the user
aws iam put-user-policy --user-name sesuser --policy-name SESAccess
--policy-document file://temppolicy
rm -f temppolicy

# we need to get 2 values from this returned data but can only call
the function once
# hence the laborious jsonval method
json=$(aws iam create-access-key --user-name sesuser)

# get key id
prop='AccessKeyId'
AccessKeyId=`jsonval`

# get secret key
prop='SecretAccessKey'
SecretAccessKey=`jsonval`

# save these values as they can't be redownloaded
cd $basedir
echo $AccessKeyId > credentials/sesuser_AccessKeyId
echo $SecretAccessKey > credentials/sesuser_SecretAccessKey
```

AWS Scripted

```
# the smtp password needs to be generated from the secret access
key
# we need java to do this
echo making smtp password with java
cd $basedir/ami/email/pgen
smtppass=$(java -cp . SesSmtpCredentialGenerator $SecretAccessKey)

# write smtp credentials to a file we can use later
echo writing smtp.sh
cd $basedir/credentials
rm -f smtp.sh
# not all regions support SES, check
http://docs.aws.amazon.com/ses/latest/DeveloperGuide/regions.html
echo "#!/bin/bash" > smtp.sh
echo "smtp_server=email-smtp.$deplyregion.amazonaws.com" >> smtp.sh
echo "smtp_port=25" >> smtp.sh
echo "smtp_user=$AccessKeyId" >> smtp.sh
echo "smtp_pass=$smtppass" >> smtp.sh
echo "" >> smtp.sh
chmod +x smtp.sh

# we need to verify the email identity of the sending email so we
can attach the sns feeds to the ses notifications
# you will receive an email, do what it says
aws ses verify-email-identity --email-address $emailsendfrom
--region $deployregion
echo email to verify identity sent to $emailsendfrom please click
link in email

cd $basedir
```

SES script part 2 (requires working website and verified email):

[aws/ami/email/make2.sh]

```
#!/bin/bash

# interactive script to set up SES and SNS for email sending
# must be run after the website is running
# ses regions are limited
# we link to the elb name and don't use SSL (it needs to be valid)

# check dir
where=$(pwd)
where="${where: -3}"
if test "$where" = "aws"; then
 echo "running from correct directory"
else
 echo "must be run from aws directory with ./ami/email/make.sh"
 exit
fi

# include global variables
. ./master/vars.sh

cd $basedir
```

```
# address of elb
elbdns=$(aws elb describe-load-balancers --load-balancer-names
$elbname --output text --query
'LoadBalancerDescriptions[*].DNSName')
echo $elbdns

# where sns looks for your bounce and complaint scripts
# you can change this to your real domain name and https if you
have set up your CNAME record and have valid SSL
scriptshost=$elbdns
echo scriptshost=$scriptshost
protocol=http
echo protocol=$protocol

# check the website is running
# elb.htm should return ok
elbokaddr=$protocol://$scriptshost/elb.htm
echo $elbokaddr
echo -n "waiting for website"
while elbok=$(curl $elbokaddr); test "$elbok" != "ok"; do
 echo -n . ; sleep 3;
done; echo " $elbok"

# check email has been verified
# needed to attach ses feeds to sns topics
echo -n "waiting for verification of $emailsendfrom (click link in
email)"
while verified=$(aws ses get-identity-verification-attributes
--identities "$emailsendfrom" --region $deployregion --output text
--query
'VerificationAttributes."'$emailsendfrom'".VerificationStatus');
test "$verified" != "Success"; do
 echo -n . ; sleep 3;
done; echo " $elbok"

echo "creating SNS Topics (Bounce and Complaint)"

# this is the bounced email topic
bouncesnsarn=$(aws sns create-topic --name EmailBounce --output
text --query 'TopicArn' --region $deployregion)
echo "bouncesnsarn=$bouncesnsarn"

# subscribe to the script on your webserver
echo "pointing to bounce receiver url"
aws sns subscribe --topic-arn $bouncesnsarn --protocol $protocol
--notification-endpoint $protocol://$scriptshost/sns/bounce.php
--region $deployregion

# this is the complained email topic
complaintsnsarn=$(aws sns create-topic --name EmailComplaint
--output text --query 'TopicArn' --region $deployregion)
echo complaintsnsarn=$complaintsnsarn

# subscribe to the script on your webserver
echo "pointing to complaint receiver url"
aws sns subscribe --topic-arn $complaintsnsarn --protocol $protocol
--notification-endpoint $protocol://$scriptshost/sns/complaint.php
--region $deployregion
```

```
# attach ses feeds to sns topics
echo "attaching sns to ses feeds"
aws ses set-identity-notification-topic --identity $emailsendfrom
--notification-type Bounce --sns-topic $bouncesnsarn --region
$deployregion
aws ses set-identity-notification-topic --identity $emailsendfrom
--notification-type Complaint --sns-topic $complaintsnsarn --region
$deployregion

# we don't want an email every time (but you might)
echo "disable feedback forwarding"
aws ses set-identity-feedback-forwarding-enabled --identity
$emailsendfrom --no-forwarding-enabled --region $deployregion

echo SES SNS done
echo test by sending to success@simulator.amazonses.com
echo or bounce@simulator.amazonses.com
echo or complaint@simulator.amazonses.com
echo or suppressionlist@simulator.amazonses.com
echo then request production access at
http://aws.amazon.com/ses/fullaccessrequest/

echo "if testing, you need to verify those emails (send or receive)
until you get production access"

cd $basedir
```

Java SMTP Generator Class

Wow! To make an SMTP password to access SES, you need to do some pretty heavy cryptography. Using the SES user key wont work.

The line in aws/ami/email/make.sh which does this is:

```
smtppass=$(java -cp . SesSmtpCredentialGenerator $SecretAccessKey)
```

The java source for this class is as follows:

[aws/ami/email/pgen/SesSmtpCredentialGenerator.java]

```
import javax.crypto.Mac;
import javax.crypto.spec.SecretKeySpec;
import javax.xml.bind.DatatypeConverter;

public class SesSmtpCredentialGenerator {

        private static final String MESSAGE = "SendRawEmail"; //
Used to generate the HMAC signature. Do not modify.
        private static final byte VERSION =  0x02; // Version
number. Do not modify.
```

```java
        // <AWS secret access key>
        public static void main(String[] args) {

                // Get the AWS secret access key from environment
variable AWS_SECRET_ACCESS_KEY.
                String key = args[0];
                if (key == null) {
                        System.out.println("Error: Cannot find
environment variable AWS_SECRET_ACCESS_KEY.");
                        System.exit(0);
                }

                // Create an HMAC-SHA256 key from the raw bytes of
the AWS secret access key.
                SecretKeySpec secretKey = new
SecretKeySpec(key.getBytes(), "HmacSHA256");

                try {
                        // Get an HMAC-SHA256 Mac instance and
initialize it with the AWS secret access key.
                        Mac mac = Mac.getInstance("HmacSHA256");
                        mac.init(secretKey);

                        // Compute the HMAC signature on the input
data bytes.
                        byte[] rawSignature =
mac.doFinal(MESSAGE.getBytes());

                        // Prepend the version number to the
signature.
                        byte[] rawSignatureWithVersion = new
byte[rawSignature.length + 1];
                        byte[] versionArray = {VERSION};
                        System.arraycopy(versionArray, 0,
rawSignatureWithVersion, 0, 1);
                        System.arraycopy(rawSignature, 0,
rawSignatureWithVersion, 1, rawSignature.length);

                        // To get the final SMTP password, convert
the HMAC signature to base 64.
                        String smtpPassword =
DatatypeConverter.printBase64Binary(rawSignatureWithVersion);
                        System.out.println(smtpPassword);
                }
                catch (Exception ex) {
                        System.out.println("Error generating SMTP
password: " + ex.getMessage());
                }

        }

    }
```

A complied .class file is provided for your convenience.

SNS Notifications with PHP

SNS requires you to provide a script which can confirm a subscription and receive notifications. The same script is called to Subscribe and then to receive messages.

The email bounce PHP script is as follows:

[aws/development/website/htdocs/sns/bounce.php]

```php
<?php

    // called by aws sns with json payload for subscribe sns or
bounced email
    // can't be called on the dev environment

    if($_SERVER['REQUEST_METHOD'] != 'POST')
        exit;

    $post = file_get_contents('php://input');

    require_once('../../phpinclude/snsverify.php');
    if(!verify_sns($post, $_SERVER['AWS_DEPLOYREGION'],
$_SERVER['AWS_ACCOUNT'], array('EmailBounce')))
        exit;

    $msg = json_decode($post, true);

    if ($msg['Type'] == 'SubscriptionConfirmation') {
        // need to visit SubscribeURL
        $surl=$msg['SubscribeURL'];
        $curlOptions = array (
                CURLOPT_URL => $surl,
                CURLOPT_VERBOSE => 1,
                CURLOPT_RETURNTRANSFER => 1,
                CURLOPT_SSL_VERIFYPEER => TRUE,
                CURLOPT_SSL_VERIFYHOST => 2
                );
        $ch = curl_init();
        curl_setopt_array($ch, $curlOptions);
        $response = curl_exec($ch);
        if (curl_errno($ch)) {
                $errors = curl_error($ch);
                curl_close($ch);
                echo $errors;
                }
        else  {
                curl_close($ch);
                echo $response;
                }
        exit;
        }

    elseif ($msg['Type'] == 'Notification') {
```

```php
                // init db
                $global_is_dev="0";
                include '../../phpinclude/db.php';
                // check if resend and data already stored
                dbconnect(0);
                $messageid=$msg['MessageId'];
                $sql=doSQL("select count(*) as tot from
snsnotifications where messageid=?", $messageid) or die ("error1");
                $tot=0;
                if (!is_array($sql))
                        $tot=0;
                else {
                        $tot=$sql[0]['tot'];
                        $tot=($tot=="")?0:$tot;
                        }
                if ($tot>0)
                        exit;
                // new message
                $subject="";
                if (isset($msg['Subject']))
                        $subject=$msg['Subject'];
                $message="";
                if (isset($msg['Message']))
                        $message=$msg['Message'];

                $result = json_decode($message, true);
                if ($result['notificationType']=="Bounce") {
                        if ($result['bounce']
['bounceType']=="Permanent") {
                                $emailaddr=$result['bounce']
['bouncedRecipients'][0]['emailAddress'];
                                doSQL("insert into snsnotifications
(messageid, subject, message, email) values (?, ?, ?, ?);",
$messageid, $subject, $message, $emailaddr) or die ("error2");
                                $nid=$db->insert_id;
                                doSQL("update users set
emailbounce=? where email=?;", $nid, $emailaddr) or die ("error3");
                                exit;
                                }
                        }

                // if we get here nothing has been inserted to
snsnotifications, insert for posterity
                doSQL("insert into snsnotifications (messageid,
subject, message, email) values (?, ?, ?, ?);", $messageid,
$subject, $message, "") or die ("error4");

                }
?>
```

The email complaint PHP script is as follows:

[aws/development/website/htdocs/sns/complaint.php]

```php
<?php
        // called by aws sns with json payload for subscribe sns or
```

```
complaint email
        // can't be called on the dev environment

        if($_SERVER['REQUEST_METHOD'] != 'POST')
                exit;

        $post = file_get_contents('php://input');

        require_once('../../phpinclude/snsverify.php');
        if(!verify_sns($post, $_SERVER['AWS_DEPLOYREGION'],
$_SERVER['AWS_ACCOUNT'], array('EmailComplaint')))
                exit;

        $msg = json_decode($post, true);

        if ($msg['Type'] == 'SubscriptionConfirmation') {
                // need to visit SubscribeURL
                $surl=$msg['SubscribeURL'];
                $curlOptions = array (
                        CURLOPT_URL => $surl,
                        CURLOPT_VERBOSE => 1,
                        CURLOPT_RETURNTRANSFER => 1,
                        CURLOPT_SSL_VERIFYPEER => TRUE,
                        CURLOPT_SSL_VERIFYHOST => 2
                        );
                $ch = curl_init();
                curl_setopt_array($ch, $curlOptions);
                $response = curl_exec($ch);
                if (curl_errno($ch)) {
                        $errors = curl_error($ch);
                        curl_close($ch);
                        echo $errors;
                        }
                else  {
                        curl_close($ch);
                        echo $response;
                        }
                exit;
                }

        elseif ($msg['Type'] == 'Notification') {
                // init db
                $global_is_dev="0";
                include '../../phpinclude/db.php';
                // check if resend and data already stored
                dbconnect(0);
                $messageid=$msg['MessageId'];
                $sql=doSQL("select count(*) as tot from
snsnotifications where messageid=?", $messageid) or die ("error1");
                $tot=0;
                if (!is_array($sql))
                        $tot=0;
                else {
                        $tot=$sql[0]['tot'];
                        $tot=($tot=="")?0:$tot;
                        }
                if ($tot>0)
                        exit;
                // new message
                $subject="";
```

```
            if (isset($msg['Subject']))
                    $subject=$msg['Subject'];
            $message="";
            if (isset($msg['Message']))
                    $message=$msg['Message'];

            $result = json_decode($message, true);
            if ($result['notificationType']=="Complaint") {
                    $emailaddr=$result['complaint']
['complainedRecipients'][0]['emailAddress'];
                    doSQL("insert into snsnotifications
(messageid, subject, message, email) values (?, ?, ?, ?);",
$messageid, $subject, $message, $emailaddr) or die ("error2");
                    $nid=$db->insert_id;
                    doSQL("update users set emailcomplaint=?
where email=?;", $nid, $emailaddr) or die ("error3");
                    exit;
                    }

            // if we get here nothing has been inserted to
snsnotifications, insert for posterity
            doSQL("insert into snsnotifications (messageid,
subject, message, email) values (?, ?, ?, ?);", $messageid,
$subject, $message, "") or die ("error4");

            }
?>
```

The SNS scripts use some shared functions:

[aws/development/website/phpinclude/snsverify.php]

```
<?php

/* Adapted from:

   http://sns-public-
resources.s3.amazonaws.com/Verifying_Message_Signatures_4_26_10.pdf
   https://forums.aws.amazon.com/thread.jspa?threadID=45518

   Verify SNS JSON message against Amazon certificate. Following
message types can be verified:
        * SubscriptionConfirmation
        * Notification

   Region, account and one of topics[] must match the contents of
the "TopicArn" included
   in the message. Also, SigningCertURL's domain must end in
".amazonaws.com".

   Joni /2011
*/

function verify_sns($message, $region, $account, $topics) {
        $msg = json_decode($message);
        // Check that region, account and topic match
        $topicarn = explode(':', $msg->TopicArn);
```

```
        if ($topicarn[3] != $region || $topicarn[4] != $account
|| !in_array($topicarn[5], $topics))
                return false;
        $_region = $topicarn[3];
        $_account = $topicarn[4];
        $_topic = $topicarn[5];

        // Check that the domain in message ends with
'.amazonaws.com'
        if(!endswith(get_domain_from_url($msg->SigningCertURL),
'.amazonaws.com'))
                return false;

        // Load certificate and extract public key from it
        $surl=$msg->SigningCertURL;
        $curlOptions = array (
                CURLOPT_URL => $surl,
                CURLOPT_VERBOSE => 1,
                CURLOPT_RETURNTRANSFER => 1,
                CURLOPT_SSL_VERIFYPEER => TRUE,
                CURLOPT_SSL_VERIFYHOST => 2
                );
        $ch = curl_init();
        curl_setopt_array($ch, $curlOptions);
        $cert = curl_exec($ch);
        $pubkey = openssl_get_publickey($cert);
        if(!$pubkey)
                return false;

        // Generate a message string for comparison in Amazon-
specified format
        $text = "";
        if($msg->Type == 'Notification') {
                $text .= "Message\n";
                $text .= $msg->Message . "\n";
                $text .= "MessageId\n";
                $text .= $msg->MessageId . "\n";
                if (isset($msg->Subject)) {
                        if ($msg->Subject != "") {
                                $text .= "Subject\n";
                                $text .= $msg->Subject . "\n";
                                }
                        }
                $text .= "Timestamp\n";
                $text .= $msg->Timestamp . "\n";
                $text .= "TopicArn\n";
                $text .= $msg->TopicArn . "\n";
                $text .= "Type\n";
                $text .= $msg->Type . "\n";
                }
        elseif($msg->Type == 'SubscriptionConfirmation') {
                $text .= "Message\n";
                $text .= $msg->Message . "\n";
                $text .= "MessageId\n";
                $text .= $msg->MessageId . "\n";
                $text .= "SubscribeURL\n";
                $text .= $msg->SubscribeURL . "\n";
                $text .= "Timestamp\n";
                $text .= $msg->Timestamp . "\n";
                $text .= "Token\n";
```

```php
                $text .= $msg->Token . "\n";
                $text .= "TopicArn\n";
                $text .= $msg->TopicArn . "\n";
                $text .= "Type\n";
                $text .= $msg->Type . "\n";
                }
        else
                return false;

        // Get a raw binary message signature
        $signature = base64_decode($msg->Signature);

        // ..and finally, verify the message
        if(openssl_verify($text, $signature, $pubkey,
OPENSSL_ALGO_SHA1))
                return true;

        return false;
        }

// http://stackoverflow.com/questions/619610/whats-the-most-
efficient-test-of-whether-a-php-string-ends-with-another-string
function endswith($string, $test) {
        $strlen = strlen($string);
        $testlen = strlen($test);
        if ($testlen > $strlen) return false;
        return substr_compare($string, $test, -$testlen) === 0;
        }

// http://codepad.org/NGlABcAC
function get_domain_from_url( $url, $max_node_count = 0 ) {
        $return_value='';
        $max_node_count=(int)$max_node_count;
        $url_parts=parse_url((string)$url);

if(is_array($url_parts)&&isset($url_parts['host'])&&strlen((string)
$url_parts['host'])>0) {
                $return_value=(string)$url_parts['host'];
                if($max_node_count>0) {
                        $host_parts=explode('.',$return_value);
                        $return_parts=array();
                        for($i=$max_node_count;$i>0;$i--) {

$current_node=array_pop($host_parts);

if(is_string($current_node)&&$current_node!=='')

$return_parts[]=$current_node;
                                else
                                        break;
                                }
                        if(count($return_parts)>0)

$return_value=implode('.',array_reverse($return_parts));
                        else
                                $return_value='';
                        }
                }
        return $return_value;
        }
```

```
?>
```

Ideally, we would like to put this script on our secure Admin Server, but there are impediments: you may not be using a valid SSL cert; more importantly, we don't want to open up the Admin Server to the public Internet. It would be helpful if Amazon restricted the IP addresses of the servers making SNS calls and published these, but unfortunately they do not. Hence we need to put the SNS PHP scripts on our public servers. The scripts are, however, very secure as they cryptographically validate the data sent from Amazon before doing any database interaction.

Note that these scripts need to know the AWS Deploy Region and the AWS Account Number. These are both placed into the httpd.conf file for each Webphp Server and read with the PHP global server variables $_SERVER['AWS_DEPLOYREGION'] and $_SERVER['AWS_ACCOUNT']. Deploy Region is a variable defined in the aws/master/vars.sh file. But getting your AWS Account Number programmatically is a little harder, given no explicit function to do so. We use the following script and 'source' it in when we need it:

[aws/credentials/account.sh]

```
#!/bin/sh

# aws account number
# available from Aws > Name > My Account
# used by SNS verify message
# create a dummy user, get the Account Identifier from the ARN,
delete the user

arn=$(aws iam create-user --user-name getaccount --output text
--query 'User.Arn')
aws_account=$(echo $arn | cut -d ":"  -f 5)
echo aws_account=$aws_account
aws iam delete-user --user-name getaccount
```

Sending Email

There are several ways to send email from a PHP script. However, sending mails direct (via the mail() function or similar) has various problems.

1. it can take a few seconds (or more on a busy system), which means a delay in loading the page for the user
2. it could fail, and you don't have a resend option
3. you are susceptible to sending multiple mails, eg if the user presses refresh on a badly designed script
4. you probably want to save the email in a database, so you'll need to do a database insert anyway
5. before sending the email, you'll want to check things like whether the email recipient has complained before (or Amazon may revoke your sending privileges)

Therefore, the best way to send email is via the database. Simply do an insert into the sendemails table and use something like the JavaMail server (see **Chapter 12 - Java Servers**) to complete the operation.

Here is an example sendmail function in PHP:

[aws/snippets/snippet_sendemail.php]

```
function sendemail($nuserID, $nto, $nsubject, $nmessage) {
        // check verified and not bouncer or complainer
        $result=doSQL("select emailbounce, emailcomplaint from
users where userID=?;", $nuserID) or do_std_err("Error getting mail
details");
        if (!is_array($result))
                do_std_err("Error getting mail details");
        if ($result[0]['emailbounce']>0)
                do_std_err("Email has Bounced previous emails");
        if ($result[0]['emailcomplaint']>0)
                do_std_err("Email has Complained about previous
emails");
        // send
        $emsg=$nmessage."\n\nThanks\n";
        $result=doSQL("insert into sendemails (userID, sendto,
sendfrom, sendsubject, sendmessage) values (?, ?, ?, ?, ?)",
$nuserID, $nto, "donotreply@yourdomain.com", $nsubject, $emsg) or
do_std_err("Error sending mail");
        }

// example call
sendemail(1, "recipient@somedomain.com", "this is the subject",
"this is the message");
```

Obviously, you should edit this function to reflect your specific requirements. For example, you might wish to check that the sending user has verified his email, or you might place a daily limit on emails sent. Given that you will probably send emails from several places in your application, it's a good idea to avoid code duplication and use a shared function to do it.

Chapter 7 - AWS ELB

ELB Advantages

First and foremost, Elastic Load Balancers are cheap relative to an EC2 instance, about half the cost of an EC2 Instance.

Second, ELBs are very reliable, and they are supported by a comprehensive failover structure, so once again they trump EC2 instances (unless you are willing to pay for 2 instances to load balance with one as a failover).

Third, SSL is not only much easier to install, but is also handled for you. HTTPS requests can be terminated on the ELB and forwarded to your web servers as HTTP! This reduces load on the web servers substantially, but does need some handling on the PHP side (see **Chapter 10 - Handling SSL**).

Lastly, ELBs allow you to provide a truly resilient application by running several web servers. Session management is a little more complicated (see **Chapter 10 - Sessions on a Multi-Server System**) but given that web servers are the most likely failure points in the system, it is worth it.

ELBs handle the monitoring of your servers via a regular HTTP call (eg every 5 seconds), and automatically stop routing traffic to unresponsive servers.

Regarding Session Stickiness, the functionality provided which routes any given user to the same server for repeated requests, this has not been implemented. The main reason is that you would need to plan for a failure of this system, eg a user is redirected to a new server because of a timeout or similar, and hence store session variables in a database anyway, so the functionality is much more complex. You would need to save session variables to a database and keep them in PHP session variables. Hence, the preferred approach is truly 'any web server will do'. The overhead of a database read per PHP call to fetch session variables is acceptable (given a fast indexed database query) and the occasional database update is negligible.

SSL Certificates

Either a self-signed or a valid certificate can be used for the SSL installation on the ELB. You should use a self-signed certificate for your AWS Development Environment, so as not to expose your SSL Key. However, see **Chapter 2 - Running master.sh for Development** for more discussion.

The provided code (in aws/ami/elb/make.sh and aws/ami/elb/ssl/) can handle both self-signed certificates (generated for you automatically) or valid certificates.

To use a self-signed certificate:

1. in aws/master/vars.sh set elbselfsigned to 1
2. in aws/master/vars.sh set elbcertname to a name for your certificate (of your choosing)
3. edit ssl1.sh, ssl2.sh, ssl3.sh in aws/ami/elb/ssl to fit your organisation
4. that's it

To use a valid certificate:

1. in aws/master/vars.sh set elbselfsigned to 0
2. in aws/master/vars.sh set elbcertname to a name for your certificate (of your choosing)
3. put the three files provided by your Certificate Authority in the folder aws/ami/elb/validssl (there should be <yourdomain>.crt, <yourdomain>.key and an Intermediate Certificate file, normally <yourprovider>.crt)
4. in aws/master/vars.sh set the variables elbvalidcertkeyfile, elbvalidcertcertfile and elbvalidcertinterfile to reflect these files
5. NOTE: you should really do this on your Secure Laptop

If you want the SNS callbacks to work with SSL, you need to use a valid SSL certificate.

ELB Script

This script generates SSL credentials (for self-signed) or uses valid ones and makes an ELB:

[aws/ami/elb/make.sh]

```
#!/bin/bash

# makes an elb
# elbselfsigned (in aws/master/vars.sh) decides if self-signed or
valid cert is used

# check dir
where=$(pwd)
where="${where: -3}"
if test "$where" = "aws"; then
 echo "running from correct directory"
else
 echo "must be run from aws directory with ./ami/admin/make.sh"
 exit
fi

# include global variables
. ./master/vars.sh

echo "launching ELB"

echo "check ELB does not exist"
exists=$(aws elb describe-load-balancers --load-balancer-names
$elbname --output text --query
'LoadBalancerDescriptions[*].LoadBalancerName' 2>/dev/null)

if test "$exists" = $elbname; then
 echo "ELB already exists = exiting"
 exit
else
 echo "ELB not found - proceeding"
fi

if (($elbselfsigned == 1)); then

echo "making self-signed ssl"

# sleeps are needed or it won't work
cd $basedir/ami/elb/ssl
rm -f cert.pem
rm -f key.pem
rm -f server.crt
rm -f server.csr
```

```
rm -f server.key
rm -f server.key.org
echo deleted old files
./ssl1.sh
./ssl2.sh
cp server.key server.key.org
./ssl3.sh
openssl x509 -req -days 365 -in server.csr -signkey server.key -out
server.crt
sleep 15
cp server.key key.pem
openssl x509 -inform PEM -in server.crt > cert.pem
sleep 15
aws iam delete-server-certificate --server-certificate-name
$elbcertname
sleep 15
sslarn=$(aws iam upload-server-certificate --server-certificate-
name $elbcertname --certificate-body file://cert.pem --private-key
file://key.pem --output text --query
'ServerCertificateMetadata.Arn')
echo sslarn=$sslarn

else

echo "using valid ssl"

# read the valid SSL cert and upload to iam
echo "using valid ssl"
cd $basedir/ami/elb/validssl
cert=$(cat $elbvalidcertcertfile)
echo loaded cert
key=$(cat $elbvalidcertkeyfile)
echo loaded key
inter=$(cat $elbvalidcertinterfile)
echo loaded inter
echo deleting previous certificate
aws iam delete-server-certificate --server-certificate-name
$elbcertname
echo uploading certificate
sslarn=$(aws iam upload-server-certificate --server-certificate-
name $elbcertname --certificate-body "$cert" --private-key "$key"
--certificate-chain "$inter" --output text --query
'ServerCertificateMetadata.Arn')
echo sslarn=$sslarn

fi

# let the cert cook
sleep 5

# make a security group to control access to the elb
echo "making sg"
vpc_id=$(aws ec2 describe-vpcs --filters Name=tag-
key,Values=vpcname --filters Name=tag-value,Values=$vpcname
--output text --query 'Vpcs[*].VpcId')
echo vpc_id=$vpc_id
sg_id=$(aws ec2 create-security-group --group-name elbsg
--description "elb security group" --vpc-id $vpc_id --output text
--query 'GroupId')
echo sg_id=$sg_id
```

```
# tag it
aws ec2 create-tags --resources $sg_id --tags
Key=sgname,Value=elbsg
# get its id
vpcelbsg_id=$(aws ec2 describe-security-groups --filters Name=tag-
key,Values=sgname --filters Name=tag-value,Values=elbsg --output
text --query 'SecurityGroups[*].GroupId')
echo vpcelbsg_id=$vpcelbsg_id
# allow 80, 443 from anywhere into the elb
aws ec2 authorize-security-group-ingress --group-id $vpcelbsg_id
--protocol tcp --port 80 --cidr 0.0.0.0/0
aws ec2 authorize-security-group-ingress --group-id $vpcelbsg_id
--protocol tcp --port 443 --cidr 0.0.0.0/0
echo "elbsg made"

# get our vpc subnets
subnet_ids=$(aws ec2 describe-subnets --filters Name=vpc-
id,Values=$vpc_id --output text --query 'Subnets[*].SubnetId')
echo subnet_ids=$subnet_ids

# create an elb
# it listens for http on 80 and https on 443 and forwards both to
80 http (no SSL)
# you can tell if the request came in on SLL with
$_SERVER['HTTP_X_FORWARDED_PROTO'] (should be "https") in PHP
aws elb create-load-balancer --load-balancer-name $elbname
--listener
LoadBalancerPort=80,InstancePort=80,Protocol=http,InstanceProtocol=
http
LoadBalancerPort=443,InstancePort=80,Protocol=https,InstanceProtoco
l=http,SSLCertificateId=$sslarn --security-groups $vpcelbsg_id
--subnets $subnet_ids --region $deployregion

# set the elb health check
aws elb configure-health-check --load-balancer-name $elbname
--health-check
Target=HTTP:80/elb.htm,Interval=10,Timeout=5,UnhealthyThreshold=2,H
ealthyThreshold=2

# show the elb address
elbdns=$(aws elb describe-load-balancers --load-balancer-names
$elbname --output text --query
'LoadBalancerDescriptions[*].DNSName')
echo elbdns=$elbdns

cd $basedir

echo "elb created"
```

For self signed certificates we use 3 expect scripts:

[aws/ami/elb/ssl/ssl1.sh]

```
#!/usr/bin/expect
spawn openssl genrsa -des3 -out server.key 1024
expect "Enter pass phrase for server.key:"
send "somepassword7372638\n";
```

```
expect "Enter pass phrase for server.key:"
send "somepassword7372638\n";
interact
```

[aws/ami/elb/ssl/ssl2.sh]

```
#!/usr/bin/expect
spawn openssl req -new -key server.key -out server.csr
expect ":"
send "somepassword7372638\n"
expect ":"
send "GB\n"
expect ":"
send "London\n"
expect ":"
send "London\n"
expect ":"
send "Your Company\n"
expect ":"
send "WWW\n"
expect ":"
send "www.yourwebsite.com\n"
expect ":"
send "youremail at yourcompany dot com\n"
expect ":"
send "\n"
expect ":"
send "\n"
interact
```

[aws/ami/elb/ssl/ssl3.sh]

```
#!/usr/bin/expect
spawn openssl rsa -in server.key.org -out server.key
expect ":"
send "somepassword7372638\n"
interact
```

Obviously, you can change values as you require. However, if you change the password 'somepassword7372638' make sure you change it in all three files.

The ELB needs a file to call on each Webphp Server and we are using /elb.htm which is a very simple file:

[aws/development/website/htdocs/elb.htm]

```
ok
```

Connecting DNS

Your ELB or ELBs will come with a DNS name from Amazon, which can be used for testing. To access your website with a domain name, simply create a CNAME record for www which points to the Amazon provided address. You should not use the IP address of the ELB as this could change.

Note about WebSockets

There is much confusion on the Internet about WebSockets and ELB. Don't Panic! It works!

In the same way that you set up a route into your ELB for SSL on port 443 and send it to your EC2 instances on 80, you can configure a similar WebSockets port (eg on port 8887) and the ELB will respect future requests and send them to the same server the initial request was on. Note that the ELB Protocol is 'SSL' and the Instance Protocol is 'TCP'.

If you think about it, this makes sense because the WebSockets protocol starts with an HTTP(S) request which then becomes a socket to socket connection - the ELB would be violating the fundamental rules of sockets if it redirected your request somewhere else! This means that you can run a WebSocket Server on each web server. ELB will select one at random for the initial connection and then all future requests will go to that same server. Initially, I was worried that the ELB would continue to split data amongst the servers, which obviously wouldn't work because the socket connection is open to one Java WebSocket server only. But thankfully, this doesn't happen.

One of the advantages of a WebSockets server is that you can stream data very quickly to clients. So with a WebSockets Chat Server, when a message is posted, it can be relayed almost instantly to other listening clients, without polling a database. However, this only works if you run a single WebSockets Server, and this makes your application vulnerable to failure.

So if you want resilience, you will have to forgo database-less retransmission. Take a Chat Server, for example. If someone sends a new chat message to server 1, server 2 does not know about this, so server 1 must save to the database and server 2 must poll the database for new messages to send to clients listening in on server 2.

Another ELB advantage is that you can write, for example, a Java WS Server which does not use SSL. But your front end application can use SSL WebSockets because the ELB will terminate the SSL for you and forward the request unencrypted. This is also important because you will get SSL error messages if you are on an SSL web page and try to WebSocket to a non-SSL endpoint, or to an SSL endpoint on a different domain.

To enable a WebSocket route, you need to allow a new port into the ELB with:

```
aws ec2 authorize-security-group-ingress --group-id $vpcelbsg_id
--protocol tcp --port 8887 --cidr 0.0.0.0/0
```

and you need to change the 'aws elb create-load-balancer' command to:

```
aws elb create-load-balancer --load-balancer-name $elbname
--listener
LoadBalancerPort=80,InstancePort=80,Protocol=http,InstanceProtocol=
http
LoadBalancerPort=443,InstancePort=80,Protocol=https,InstanceProtoco
l=http,SSLCertificateId=$sslarn
LoadBalancerPort=8887,InstancePort=8887,Protocol=ssl,InstanceProtoc
ol=tcp,SSLCertificateId=$sslarn --security-groups $vpcelbsg_id
--subnets $subnet_ids --region $deployregion
```

You will also need to allow port 8887 into your web servers and install a WebSocket Server of your design on each web server.

Chapter 8 - Admin Server

The main function of the Admin Server is Centralised Logging - you don't want to be picking through 17 different web server log files now do you? However, we can also use it for many other helpful and necessary functions, such as scheduled files, JavaMail Server, Mmonit, PHPMyAdmin and LogAnalyzer.

In terms of security, this is a highly secure server. The best security for an Internet server is not to be connected to the Internet. Hence, we only open up access as and when needed. Otherwise, it is effectively 'offline' and only accessible from our other instances on very restricted ports.

We also use the Admin Server to host our JavaMail Server which forwards mail from the database to AWS SES.

Admin Website

We host a useful website on the Admin Server which provides system information, diagnostics and testing facilities. You will probably want to expand on the functionality as required by your Application.

The provided site includes: simple access to log files; an At A Glance overview of logs; email testing; access to the MySQL slow query table; and phpinfo().

The password for the admin website is admin. You can change this in the aws/development/website/admin/signin2.php file.

Note that in the development folder, or on your in-house development platform, the Admin Website is merged with the main website, and available at /admin/. This greatly simplifies the web server setup for your development environment. However, when we migrate data (with the aws/data/makedata.sh script), the Admin Website is separated off and runs independently. The

Admin Website is not hosted on the Webphp Servers for security reasons.

One of the main uses for an Admin Server would be a Contact Management system. You will no doubt need to allow access to others in your organisation to contact submissions, so you should consider building a dedicated Contact Management server, based on the Admin Server, but stripped down (ie drop Centralised Logging, PHPMyAdmin, LogAnalyzer and Mmonit). You could use a script very similar to aws/credentials/connectadmin.sh to allow access.

Centralised Logging and LogAnalyzer

Centralised Logging is achieved with rsyslog. Each Webphp Server sends Apache Error and Access Logs to local logging (syslog local4 and local6) and then forwards these logs to the Admin Server. The Admin Server collates these logs into single files. One advantage of rsyslog is that messages are stored if not transmitted. This means that even if your Admin Server goes down for a few minutes, you won't lose logs. This can be useful if you need to upgrade your Admin Server.

The relevant lines in the Webphp Server httpd.conf are:

[aws/snippets/snippet_httpdlogging.conf]

```
ErrorLog syslog:local4

LogLevel warn
LogFormat "%h %l %u %t \"%r\" %>s %b \"%{Referer}i\" \"%{User-
Agent}i\"" combined
LogFormat "%h %l %u %t \"%r\" %>s %b" common
LogFormat "%{Referer}i -> %U" referer
LogFormat "%{User-agent}i" agent

SetEnvIf Request_URI "^/elb\.htm$" dontlog
SetEnvIf Request_URI ".(js|css|jpg|ico|png|gif|ttf|woff|svg|eot|
pem|wav|txt)$" dontlog

CustomLog "|/usr/bin/logger -t httpd -p local6.info" combined env=!
dontlog
```

The first line sends the Apache Error Log to syslog local4 logging. The next LogLevel and LogFormat lines are standard configurations to set formatting (unchanged). The SetEnvIf lines are interesting. Together with the 'env=!dontlog' at the end of the last line, this turns off logging for the ELB heartbeat file and for all files that end in the extensions js, css, jpg, etc. You can customise this as required, but I have generally found that logging 'support files' is pretty useless and really you just want the .php files to be logged. This also cuts your log file size by about 90%! The last line sends the Apache Access Log to local6 with the tag 'httpd'.

Here is how these Apache configurations are picked up in the Webphp rsyslog.conf file:

[aws/snippets/snippet_webphprsyslog.conf]

```
# httpd error sends on local4

$WorkDirectory /var/lib/rsyslog # where to place spool files
$ActionQueueFileName fwdRule1 # unique name prefix for spool files
$ActionQueueMaxDiskSpace 1g   # 1gb space limit (use as much as
possible)
$ActionQueueSaveOnShutdown on # save messages to disk on shutdown
$ActionQueueType LinkedList   # run asynchronously
$ActionResumeRetryCount -1    # infinite retries if host is down
local4.* @@SEDadminhostSED:514

# httpd access sends on local6 (with tag)

$WorkDirectory /var/lib/rsyslog # where to place spool files
$ActionQueueFileName fwdRule2 # unique name prefix for spool files
$ActionQueueMaxDiskSpace 1g   # 1gb space limit (use as much as
possible)
$ActionQueueSaveOnShutdown on # save messages to disk on shutdown
$ActionQueueType LinkedList   # run asynchronously
$ActionResumeRetryCount -1    # infinite retries if host is down
local6.* @@SEDadminhostSED:514
```

The two blocks set up some options (such as where and how to store logs if they can't be sent), but the real action is in the 'local4.* @@SEDadminhostSED:514' which is 'sed'ed to 'local4.* @@10.0.0.10:514' and this is what forwards the logs to the Admin Server on port 514. Remember, local4 is receiving the Apache Error Log and local6 the Access Log.

On the Admin Server, the relevant rsyslog configuration is slightly different:

[aws/snippets/snippet_adminrsyslog.conf]

```
local4.* /var/log/webhttpderr.log
local4.* ~

:msg, contains, "\"-\" 408 - \"-\""  ~
:msg, contains, "Apache (internal dummy connection)"  ~

:syslogtag, isequal, "httpd:" /var/log/webhttpd.log
:syslogtag, isequal, "httpd:" ~
```

Here, the first line saves local4 messages (Error Logs sent by all the Webphp Servers) to the /var/log/webhttpderr.log file. The next line (with the ~) tells rsyslog to do no further processing on the message (if it is to local4). The next line drops an annoying hit we get from the ELB, an HTTP 408, probably a second heartbeat check. We also drop logs generated by Apache's own internal checks. The penultimate line checks if the log message is tagged with 'httpd' (remember our Apache Access Log are so tagged) and saves it to /var/log/webhttpd.log if so. The last line drops any messages tagged 'httpd', so no further processing.

It is truly interesting to see the interplay of services that make Centralised Logging work: the Webphp httpd.conf settings, then the Webphp rsyslog settings, then the Admin rsyslog settings. Also, don't forget that ports need to be opened up in AWS Security Groups to make all the communication possible.

LogAnalyzer (from Adiscon) is a free and useful mini-website which allows you to browse logs. You should have a more comprehensive strategy for downloading logs and analysing them out of the cloud, but LogAnalyzer allows you to see real-time logs for troubleshooting and it is very much friendlier than 'cat' or 'tail'.

Monit and Mmonit

Monit is a wonderful service which looks after your running daemons and notifies you if there are changes. It is free and runs on all your servers, including the Admin Server. You can also use it to run security checks (eg if filesystems change), although we don't do that here.

Mmonit is a central mini-website which allows you to monitor all your monit instances, and centralises email notifications. Mmonit is not free, but is well worth the price (you can see these at **https://mmonit.com/shop/**). As of writing, 129 Euros for the 10 server package should not dent your budget too much. You don't need Mmonit - it is possible to configure each monit instance to send notification emails. But there is nothing more satisfying that signing into Mmonit and seeing that big green circle telling you all systems are go. It also provides useful metrics for all your servers.

Once you have deployed to AWS, you will need to configure Mmonit. Here's how:

1. sign in with username admin and password swordfish
2. admire the big green circle... you will come to love it
3. click Admin > Alerts
4. click Mail Servers
5. click the Add New "+"
6. enter 127.0.0.1
7. port 25
8. status should be 'OK'
9. click Rules
10. click the Add New "+"
11. enter a name, like 'alerter' and Enter
12. select 'send mail to the following address' in the action drop down
13. enter your email address (the address for notifications)
14. click the orange Save
15. that's it, consider yourself notified

There are a few other configurations for Mmonit - they are all pretty easy to understand, so take a look around and experiment a bit. You'll probably want to change the admin password. Also note that Mmonit (so configured) uses the default Linux sendmail to send emails, so it's likely you'll get messages in your Spam folder. Unspam them - Gmail learns pretty quick.

PHPMyAdmin

PHPMyAdmin is the de facto standard in MySQL remote database administration. It is extremely comprehensive and gives you full access to your RDS database.

Scheduled Tasks

Scheduled Tasks need to be run on the Admin Server, not on individual web servers. Cron is used for this. As an example, we email some At A Glance Server log files every 6 hours:

```
line="1 0,6,12,18 * * * wget --no-check-certificate -O - -q
https://localhost/sched/ataglance.php | /usr/bin/logger -t
ataglance -p local6.info"
(crontab -u root -l; echo "$line" ) | crontab -u root -
```

We pipe the output of the PHP call to rsyslog with the tag 'ataglance' (see aws/ami/admin/rsyslog.conf) and it is available in LogAnalyzer.

Elastic IP

Technically, we don't really need to attach an Elastic IP to the Admin Server. The self-signed SSL cert will work (for encrypting) whatever the domain we create it with is. However, this is a good opportunity to showcase some EIP code. Also, should you wish to connect a valid SSL certificate and DNS, you can link direct to the EIP, which is probably easier than linking to the Instance Public DNS. In terms of communications internal to our network, everything talks to 10.0.0.10, which is the static private IP we assign to the Admin Server.

Building the Server

The automated deployment scripts for the Admin Server are pretty complex, comprising 14 files in all. The core script is aws/ami/admin/make.sh which brings it all together.

Before running the script you should check the following:

1. in aws/ami/admin/install_admin_template.sh you should review the SSL self-signed certificate generation routines and change any values as required for your situation (however, it will work without any changes).
2. in aws/ami/admin/server_template.xml you will need to paste in your Mmonit licence key. These keys change, so if you want a 30 day trial, you need to download the linux-x64 package from https://mmonit.com/download/ and open it up. Navigate to the conf folder and open the server.xml file. Copy the trial licence from the bottom of the page (the entire Licence tag) and paste into the server_template.xml file. If you purchase a licence, paste that in instead. Mmonit will not work unless you do this.

Here is the script which makes the Admin Server and and associated security group, then edits required files, uploads them to the new server and runs the Admin Server install script:

[aws/ami/admin/make.sh]

```
#!/bin/bash

# makes an admin box, from linux hardened image
# ssh on 38142
# includes: rsyslog receiver for all logs; admin website;
loganalyzer; mmonit; javaMail
# admin box needs an elastic ip address for the self-signed SSL
cert

# check dir
where=$(pwd)
where="${where: -3}"
if test "$where" = "aws"; then
 echo "running from correct directory"
else
 echo "must be run from aws directory with ./ami/admin/make.sh"
 exit
fi

# include global variables
. ./master/vars.sh

# EBS volume size specifier
```

```
bdm=[{\"DeviceName\":\"/dev/sda1\",\"Ebs\":{\"VolumeSize\":
$adminebsvolumesize}}]
echo bdm=$bdm

# we don't need this
rm -f $sshknownhosts

cd $basedir

echo "building admin"

echo "check admin not exist"
exists=$(aws ec2 describe-key-pairs --key-names admin --output text
--query 'KeyPairs[*].KeyName' 2>/dev/null)

if test "$exists" = "admin"; then
 echo "key admin already exists = exiting"
 #exit
else
 echo "key admin not found - proceeding"
fi

cd $basedir

# include passwords
source credentials/passwords.sh
rootpass=$password2
ec2pass=$password3

# get our ip from amazon
myip=$(curl http://checkip.amazonaws.com/)
echo myip=$myip

# make keypair
rm credentials/admin.pem
aws ec2 delete-key-pair --key-name admin
aws ec2 create-key-pair --key-name admin --query 'KeyMaterial'
--output text > credentials/admin.pem
chmod 600 credentials/admin.pem
echo "keypair admin made"

# make security group
vpc_id=$(aws ec2 describe-vpcs --filters Name=tag-
key,Values=vpcname --filters Name=tag-value,Values=$vpcname
--output text --query 'Vpcs[*].VpcId')
echo vpc_id=$vpc_id
sg_id=$(aws ec2 create-security-group --group-name adminsg
--description "admin security group" --vpc-id $vpc_id --output text
--query 'GroupId')
echo sg_id=$sg_id
# tag it
aws ec2 create-tags --resources $sg_id --tags
Key=sgname,Value=adminsg
# get its id
vpcadminsg_id=$(aws ec2 describe-security-groups --filters
Name=tag-key,Values=sgname --filters Name=tag-value,Values=adminsg
--output text --query 'SecurityGroups[*].GroupId')
echo vpcadminsg_id=$vpcadminsg_id
# allow ssh
aws ec2 authorize-security-group-ingress --group-id $vpcadminsg_id
```

```
--protocol tcp --port 38142 --cidr $myip/32
echo "adminsg made"

# get the main subnet
subnet_id=$(aws ec2 describe-subnets --filters Name=vpc-
id,Values=$vpc_id --filters Name=tag-key,Values=subnet --filters
Name=tag-value,Values=1 --output text --query
'Subnets[*].SubnetId')
echo subnet_id=$subnet_id

# get the shared image id
bslami_id=$(aws ec2 describe-images --filters
'Name=name,Values=Basic Secure Linux' --output text --query
'Images[*].ImageId')
echo bslami_id=$bslami_id

# make the instance
instance_id=$(aws ec2 run-instances --image $bslami_id --placement
AvailabilityZone=$deployzone --key admin --security-group-ids
$vpcadminsg_id --instance-type $admininstancetype --block-device-
mapping $bdm --region $deployregion --subnet-id $subnet_id
--private-ip-address 10.0.0.10 --output text --query
'Instances[*].InstanceId')
echo instance_id=$instance_id

# wait for it
echo -n "waiting for instance"
while state=$(aws ec2 describe-instances --instance-ids
$instance_id --output text --query
'Reservations[*].Instances[*].State.Name'); test "$state" =
"pending"; do
 echo -n . ; sleep 3;
done; echo " $state"

# find an unused eip or make one
eip=$(aws ec2 describe-addresses --output text --query
'Addresses[*].PublicIp')
echo eip=$eip

useeip=
eiparr=$(echo $eip | tr " " "\n")
for i in $eiparr
do
 echo found eip $i
 eipinsid=$(aws ec2 describe-addresses --filters Name=public-
ip,Values=$i --output text --query 'Addresses[*].InstanceId')
 echo eip $i instanceid $eipinsid
 if test -z "$eipinsid"; then
  useeip=$i
 fi
done

# check if eip found, otherwise make one
if test -z "$useeip"; then
        echo "no eip, allocate one"
        useeip=$(aws ec2 allocate-address --output text --query
'PublicIp')
fi

# associate eip with admin instance
```

AWS Scripted   105

```
aws ec2 associate-address --instance-id $instance_id --public-ip
$useeip
echo "associated eip with admin instance"

# get adminhost private ip
adminhost=$(aws ec2 describe-instances --filters Name=key-
name,Values=admin --output text --query
'Reservations[*].Instances[*].PrivateIpAddress')
echo adminhost=$adminhost

# ipaddress is new eib address
ip_address=$(aws ec2 describe-instances --instance-ids $instance_id
--output text --query
'Reservations[*].Instances[*].PublicIpAddress')
echo ip_address=$ip_address

# allow access to rds database
echo "allowing access to rds database"
vpcdbsg_id=$(aws ec2 describe-security-groups --filters Name=tag-
key,Values=sgname --filters Name=tag-value,Values=dbsg --output
text --query 'SecurityGroups[*].GroupId')
echo vpcdbsg_id=$vpcdbsg_id
aws ec2 authorize-security-group-ingress --group-id $vpcdbsg_id
--source-group $vpcadminsg_id --protocol tcp --port 3306

# get the database address
dbendpoint=$(aws rds describe-db-instances --db-instance-identifier
$dbinstancename --output text --query
'DBInstances[*].Endpoint.Address')

cd $basedir

# remove old files
rm -f ami/admin/install_admin.sh
rm -f ami/admin/httpd.conf
rm -f ami/admin/config.inc.php
rm -f ami/admin/chp_ec2-user.sh
rm -f ami/admin/chp_root.sh
rm -f ami/admin/server.xml

# sed data files

sed "s/SEDadminpublicipSED/$ip_address/g"
ami/admin/install_admin_template.sh > ami/admin/install_admin.sh
chmod +x ami/admin/install_admin.sh

sed -e "s/SEDdbhostSED/$dbendpoint/g" -e "s/SEDdbnameSED/$dbname/g"
-e "s/SEDdbpass_adminrwSED/$password4/g"
ami/admin/httpd_template.conf > ami/admin/httpd.conf

sed -e "s/SEDdbhostSED/$dbendpoint/g" -e "s/SEDdbmainuserpassSED/
$password1/g" ami/admin/config_inc_template.php >
ami/admin/config.inc.php

sed "s/SED-EC2-USER-PASS-SED/$ec2pass/g" ami/shared/chp_ec2-user.sh
> ami/admin/chp_ec2-user.sh
chmod +x ami/admin/chp_ec2-user.sh

sed "s/SED-ROOT-PASS-SED/$rootpass/g" ami/shared/chp_root.sh >
ami/admin/chp_root.sh
```

```
chmod +x ami/admin/chp_root.sh

sed -e "s/SEDadminpublicipSED/$ip_address/g" -e
"s/SEDadminprivateipSED/$adminhost/g" ami/admin/server_template.xml
> ami/admin/server.xml

# wait for ssh
echo -n "waiting for ssh"
while ! ssh -i credentials/admin.pem -p 38142 -o ConnectTimeout=60
-o BatchMode=yes -o StrictHostKeyChecking=no ec2-user@$ip_address >
/dev/null 2>&1 true; do
 echo -n . ; sleep 3;
done; echo " ssh ok"

# send files
echo "transferring files"
scp -i credentials/admin.pem -P 38142 ami/admin/httpd.conf ec2-
user@$ip_address:
scp -i credentials/admin.pem -P 38142 ami/admin/monit.conf ec2-
user@$ip_address:
scp -i credentials/admin.pem -P 38142 ami/admin/rsyslog.conf ec2-
user@$ip_address:
scp -i credentials/admin.pem -P 38142 ami/admin/config.php ec2-
user@$ip_address:
scp -i credentials/admin.pem -P 38142 ami/admin/config.inc.php ec2-
user@$ip_address:
scp -i credentials/admin.pem -P 38142 ami/admin/server.xml ec2-
user@$ip_address:
scp -i credentials/admin.pem -P 38142 ami/admin/install_admin.sh
ec2-user@$ip_address:
scp -i credentials/admin.pem -P 38142 ami/admin/chp_ec2-user.sh
ec2-user@$ip_address:
scp -i credentials/admin.pem -P 38142 ami/admin/chp_root.sh ec2-
user@$ip_address:
scp -i credentials/admin.pem -P 38142 ami/admin/logrotatehttp ec2-
user@$ip_address:
scp -i credentials/admin.pem -P 38142 ami/admin/mmonit-3.2.1-linux-
x64.tar.gz ec2-user@$ip_address:
scp -i credentials/admin.pem -P 38142 ami/admin/loganalyzer-
3.6.5.tar.gz ec2-user@$ip_address:
scp -i credentials/admin.pem -P 38142 ami/admin/launch_javaMail.sh
ec2-user@$ip_address:
echo "transferred files"

# remove generated files
rm -f ami/admin/install_admin.sh
rm -f ami/admin/httpd.conf
rm -f ami/admin/config.inc.php
rm -f ami/admin/chp_ec2-user.sh
rm -f ami/admin/chp_root.sh
rm -f ami/admin/server.xml

# run the install script
echo "running install_admin.sh"
ssh -i credentials/admin.pem -p 38142 -t -o ConnectTimeout=60 -o
BatchMode=yes -o StrictHostKeyChecking=no ec2-user@$ip_address sudo
./install_admin.sh
echo "finished install_admin.sh"

# close the ssh port
```

```
echo "removing ssh access from sg"
aws ec2 revoke-security-group-ingress --group-id $vpcadminsg_id
--protocol tcp --port 38142 --cidr $myip/32

cd $basedir

# done
echo "admin done - needs upload"
```

The install script which is uploaded and run on the Admin Server is as follows (note SED***SED items are replaced with real values):

[aws/ami/admin/install_admin_template.sh]

```
#!/bin/bash

yum -y install mysql php php-soap php-bcmath php-mysql php-mbstring
php-imap php-mcrypt openssl mod_ssl httpd

cd /home/ec2-user

# install httpd.conf
cp -f httpd.conf /etc/httpd/conf/httpd.conf
chown root:root /etc/httpd/conf/httpd.conf
chmod 400 /etc/httpd/conf/httpd.conf

# setup admin site
rm -f -R /var/www/cgi-bin
rm -f -R /var/www/error
rm -f -R /var/www/icons
rm -f -R /var/www/html/*

# install phpMyAdmin
yum --enablerepo=epel install -y phpmyadmin
cp -r /usr/share/phpMyAdmin /var/www/html/phpmyadmin
rm -f /etc/httpd/conf.d/phpMyAdmin.conf
cd /home/ec2-user
cp -f config.inc.php /etc/phpMyAdmin/config.inc.php
chown root:apache /etc/phpMyAdmin
chmod 750 /etc/phpMyAdmin
chown root:apache /etc/phpMyAdmin/config.inc.php
chmod 750 /etc/phpMyAdmin/config.inc.php

# install loganalyser
cd /home/ec2-user
#wget http://download.adiscon.com/loganalyzer/loganalyzer-
3.6.5.tar.gz
tar -xvf loganalyzer-3.6.5.tar.gz
cd loganalyzer-3.6.5
cp -r src /var/www/html/loganalyzer
cd /home/ec2-user
cp config.php /var/www/html/loganalyzer/config.php

# grant read access to log files
chmod 604 /var/log/messages
```

AWS Scripted   108

```
chmod 604 /var/log/maillog

# install monit
yum install -y monit
# configure monit
cd /home/ec2-user
cp -f monit.conf /etc/monit.conf
# start at boot
chkconfig --levels 2345 monit on

# turn off autostart services (monit handles them)
chkconfig --levels 2345 ntpd off
chkconfig --levels 2345 sshd off
chkconfig --levels 2345 httpd off

# install mmonit
mkdir /mmonit
cd /home/ec2-user
cp mmonit-3.2.1-linux-x64.tar.gz /mmonit
cd /mmonit
#wget http://mmonit.com/dist/mmonit-3.2-linux-x64.tar.gz
tar -xvf mmonit-3.2.1-linux-x64.tar.gz
rm -f mmonit-3.2.1-linux-x64.tar.gz
cd /home/ec2-user
rm -f /mmonit/mmonit-3.2.1/conf/server.xml
mv server.xml /mmonit/mmonit-3.2.1/conf/server.xml
# to start (but handled by monit)
#cd mmonit-3.2
#./bin/mmonit

# configure rsyslog
cd /home/ec2-user
cp -f rsyslog.conf /etc/rsyslog.conf
chown root:root /etc/rsyslog.conf
chmod 400 /etc/rsyslog.conf

# set webroot permissions
find /var/www/html -type d -exec chown apache:apache {} +
find /var/www/html -type d -exec chmod 500 {} +
find /var/www/html -type f -exec chown apache:apache {} +
find /var/www/html -type f -exec chmod 400 {} +

# remove ec2-user no password from sshed with key feature
echo "ec2-user ALL = ALL" > /etc/sudoers.d/cloud-init

# install expect
yum install -y expect

# update root and ec2-user passwords
cd /home/ec2-user
./chp_ec2-user.sh
./chp_root.sh

# make ssl

cd /home/ec2-user

echo "#!/usr/bin/expect -f" > expect.sh
echo "set timeout -1" >> expect.sh
echo "spawn openssl genrsa -des3 -out server.key 1024" >> expect.sh
```

```
echo "expect \":\"" >> expect.sh
echo "send \"somepasswordssl382594\n\"" >> expect.sh
echo "expect \":\"" >> expect.sh
echo "send \"somepasswordssl382594\n\"" >> expect.sh
echo "interact" >> expect.sh
chmod +x expect.sh
./expect.sh
rm expect.sh

echo "#!/usr/bin/expect -f" > expect.sh
echo "set timeout -1" >> expect.sh
echo "spawn openssl req -new -key server.key -out server.csr" >>
expect.sh
echo "expect \":\"" >> expect.sh
echo "send \"somepasswordssl382594\n\"" >> expect.sh
echo "expect \":\"" >> expect.sh
echo "send \"GB\n\"" >> expect.sh
echo "expect \":\"" >> expect.sh
echo "send \"London\n\"" >> expect.sh
echo "expect \":\"" >> expect.sh
echo "send \"London\n\"" >> expect.sh
echo "expect \":\"" >> expect.sh
echo "send \"YOURCOMPANY\n\"" >> expect.sh
echo "expect \":\"" >> expect.sh
echo "send \"YOURCOMPANY Admin\n\"" >> expect.sh
echo "expect \":\"" >> expect.sh
echo "send \"SEDadminpublicipSED\n\"" >> expect.sh
echo "expect \":\"" >> expect.sh
echo "send \"youremail@yourdomain.com\n\"" >> expect.sh
echo "expect \":\"" >> expect.sh
echo "send \"\n\"" >> expect.sh
echo "expect \":\"" >> expect.sh
echo "send \"\n\"" >> expect.sh
echo "interact" >> expect.sh
chmod +x expect.sh
./expect.sh
rm expect.sh

cp server.key server.key.org

echo "#!/usr/bin/expect -f" > expect.sh
echo "set timeout -1" >> expect.sh
echo "spawn openssl rsa -in server.key.org -out server.key" >>
expect.sh
echo "expect \":\"" >> expect.sh
echo "send \"somepasswordssl382594\n\"" >> expect.sh
echo "interact" >> expect.sh
chmod +x expect.sh
./expect.sh
rm expect.sh

openssl x509 -req -days 3650 -in server.csr -signkey server.key
-out server.crt

mkdir -p /etc/httpd/ssl
cp server.crt /etc/httpd/ssl/ssl.crt
cp server.key /etc/httpd/ssl/ssl.key
rm -f /etc/httpd/conf.d/ssl.conf

yum erase -y expect
```

AWS Scripted

```
# do ssl for mmonit
cat server.key > /mmonit/mmonit-3.2.1/conf/mmonit.pem
cat server.crt >> /mmonit/mmonit-3.2.1/conf/mmonit.pem

# add php sched files
line="1 0,6,12,18 * * * wget --no-check-certificate -O - -q
https://localhost/sched/ataglance.php | /usr/bin/logger -t
ataglance -p local6.info"
(crontab -u root -l; echo "$line" ) | crontab -u root -
echo php scheduled files crontabbed

# logrotate
cd /home/ec2-user
mv logrotatehttp /etc/logrotate.d/logrotatehttp
chown root:root /etc/logrotate.d/logrotatehttp
chmod 644 /etc/logrotate.d/logrotatehttp
mkdir -p /var/log/old
chown root:root /var/log/old
chmod 700 /var/log/old

# javaMail - make new dirs for java files and logs, copy launch
files there and set permissions

mkdir /java

mkdir /java/javamail
mv /home/ec2-user/launch_javaMail.sh
/java/javamail/launch_javaMail.sh

chown root:root /java
chmod 700 /java
find /java -type d -exec chown root:root {} +
find /java -type d -exec chmod 700 {} +
find /java -type f -exec chown root:root {} +
find /java -type f -exec chmod 700 {} +

rm -f -R /home/ec2-user/*

echo "deleted files from /home/ec2-user"

reboot
```

The httpd.conf for apache on the Admin Server is as follows (note SED***SED items are replaced with real values):

[aws/ami/admin/httpd_template.conf]

```
ServerTokens Prod
ServerRoot "/etc/httpd"
PidFile run/httpd.pid
Timeout 30
#LimitRequestBody 4096
#LimitRequestFields 50
#LimitRequestFieldSize 256
KeepAlive On
MaxKeepAliveRequests 500
```

```
KeepAliveTimeout 30
<IfModule prefork.c>
StartServers        8
MinSpareServers     5
MaxSpareServers    20
ServerLimit       256
MaxClients        256
MaxRequestsPerChild  10000
</IfModule>
<IfModule worker.c>
StartServers        4
MaxClients        300
MinSpareThreads    25
MaxSpareThreads    75
ThreadsPerChild    25
MaxRequestsPerChild  10000
</IfModule>

Listen 443
#ChrootDir /jail

LoadModule authz_host_module modules/mod_authz_host.so
LoadModule include_module modules/mod_include.so
LoadModule log_config_module modules/mod_log_config.so
LoadModule logio_module modules/mod_logio.so
LoadModule env_module modules/mod_env.so
LoadModule ext_filter_module modules/mod_ext_filter.so
LoadModule mime_magic_module modules/mod_mime_magic.so
LoadModule expires_module modules/mod_expires.so
LoadModule deflate_module modules/mod_deflate.so
LoadModule headers_module modules/mod_headers.so
LoadModule usertrack_module modules/mod_usertrack.so
LoadModule setenvif_module modules/mod_setenvif.so
LoadModule mime_module modules/mod_mime.so
LoadModule status_module modules/mod_status.so
LoadModule vhost_alias_module modules/mod_vhost_alias.so
LoadModule negotiation_module modules/mod_negotiation.so
LoadModule dir_module modules/mod_dir.so
LoadModule actions_module modules/mod_actions.so
LoadModule speling_module modules/mod_speling.so
LoadModule alias_module modules/mod_alias.so
LoadModule substitute_module modules/mod_substitute.so
LoadModule rewrite_module modules/mod_rewrite.so
LoadModule cache_module modules/mod_cache.so
LoadModule suexec_module modules/mod_suexec.so
LoadModule disk_cache_module modules/mod_disk_cache.so
LoadModule cgi_module modules/mod_cgi.so
LoadModule version_module modules/mod_version.so
LoadModule ssl_module modules/mod_ssl.so

Include conf.d/*.conf

User apache
Group apache

ServerAdmin youremail@yourdomain.com
ServerName admin.yourdomain.com:443
UseCanonicalName Off
DocumentRoot "/var/www/html"
```

```
SSLEngine on
SSLCertificateFile /etc/httpd/ssl/ssl.crt
SSLCertificateKeyFile /etc/httpd/ssl/ssl.key

<Directory />
    Options None
    AllowOverride None
        Order Deny,Allow
        Deny from all
</Directory>
<Directory "/var/www/html">
    Options None
    AllowOverride None
    <Limit GET POST>
        Order allow,deny
        Allow from all
    </Limit>
    <LimitExcept GET POST>
        Order deny,allow
        Deny from all
    </LimitExcept>
</Directory>

<IfModule mod_userdir.c>
    UserDir disabled
</IfModule>

AccessFileName .htaccess
<Files ~ "^\.ht">
    Order allow,deny
    Deny from all
    Satisfy All
</Files>

TypesConfig /etc/mime.types

DefaultType text/plain

<IfModule mod_mime_magic.c>
    MIMEMagicFile conf/magic
</IfModule>

HostnameLookups Off

#ErrorLog logs/error_log
ErrorLog syslog:local5
LogLevel warn
LogFormat "%h %l %u %t \"%r\" %>s %b \"%{Referer}i\" \"%{User-
Agent}i\"" combined
LogFormat "%h %l %u %t \"%r\" %>s %b" common
LogFormat "%{Referer}i -> %U" referer
LogFormat "%{User-agent}i" agent

#CustomLog logs/access_log combined
CustomLog "|/usr/bin/logger -t adminhttpd -p local6.info" combined

ServerSignature Off

LanguagePriority en
ForceLanguagePriority Prefer Fallback
```

AWS Scripted

```
AddDefaultCharset UTF-8
AddType application/x-compress .Z
AddType application/x-gzip .gz .tgz

BrowserMatch "Mozilla/2" nokeepalive
BrowserMatch "MSIE 4\.0b2;" nokeepalive downgrade-1.0 force-
response-1.0
BrowserMatch "RealPlayer 4\.0" force-response-1.0
BrowserMatch "Java/1\.0" force-response-1.0
BrowserMatch "JDK/1\.0" force-response-1.0

BrowserMatch "Microsoft Data Access Internet Publishing Provider"
redirect-carefully
BrowserMatch "MS FrontPage" redirect-carefully
BrowserMatch "^WebDrive" redirect-carefully
BrowserMatch "^WebDAVFS/1.[0123]" redirect-carefully
BrowserMatch "^gnome-vfs/1.0" redirect-carefully
BrowserMatch "^XML Spy" redirect-carefully
BrowserMatch "^Dreamweaver-WebDAV-SCM1" redirect-carefully

SetEnv DBHOST SEDdbhostSED
SetEnv DBPORT 3306
SetEnv DBNAME SEDdbnameSED
SetEnv DBUSER_adminrw adminrw
SetEnv DBPASS_adminrw SEDdbpass_adminrwSED
```

The LogAnalyzer config file is as follows:

[aws/ami/admin/config.php]

```php
<?php
/*

********************************************************************
**
        * LogAnalyzer - http://loganalyzer.adiscon.com
        *
------------------------------------------------------------------
        * Main Configuration File
        *
        * -> Configuration need variables for the Database
connection
        *
        * Copyright (C) 2008-2010 Adiscon GmbH.
        *

********************************************************************
**
*/

// --- Avoid directly accessing this file!
if ( !defined('IN_PHPLOGCON') ) {
        die('Hacking attempt');
        exit;
        }

$CFG['UserDBEnabled'] = false;
```

```
$CFG['UserDBServer'] = 'localhost';
$CFG['UserDBPort'] = 3306;
$CFG['UserDBName'] = 'loganalyzer';
$CFG['UserDBPref'] = 'logcon_';
$CFG['UserDBUser'] = 'root';
$CFG['UserDBPass'] = '';
$CFG['UserDBLoginRequired'] = false;
$CFG['UserDBAuthMode'] = 0;

$CFG['LDAPServer'] = '127.0.0.1';
$CFG['LDAPPort'] = 389;
$CFG['LDAPBaseDN'] = 'CN=Users,DC=domain,DC=local';
$CFG['LDAPSearchFilter'] = '(objectClass=user)';
$CFG['LDAPUidAttribute'] = 'sAMAccountName';
$CFG['LDAPBindDN'] = 'CN=Searchuser,CN=Users,DC=domain,DC=local';
$CFG['LDAPBindPassword'] = 'Password';

$CFG['MiscShowDebugMsg'] = 0;
$CFG['MiscDebugToSyslog'] = 0;
$CFG['MiscShowDebugGridCounter'] = 0;
$CFG["MiscShowPageRenderStats"] = 1;
$CFG['MiscEnableGzipCompression'] = 1;
$CFG['MiscMaxExecutionTime'] = 60;
$CFG['DebugUserLogin'] = 0;

$CFG['PrependTitle'] = "";
$CFG['ViewUseTodayYesterday'] = 1;
$CFG['ViewMessageCharacterLimit'] = 0;
$CFG['ViewStringCharacterLimit'] = 0;
$CFG['ViewEntriesPerPage'] = 100;
$CFG['ViewEnableDetailPopups'] = 0;
$CFG['ViewDefaultTheme'] = "default";
$CFG['ViewDefaultLanguage'] = "en";
$CFG['ViewEnableAutoReloadSeconds'] = 0;

$CFG['SearchCustomButtonCaption'] = "I'd like to feel sad";
$CFG['SearchCustomButtonSearch'] = "error";

$CFG['EnableContextLinks'] = 0;
$CFG['EnableIPAddressResolve'] = 0;
$CFG['SuppressDuplicatedMessages'] = 0;
$CFG['TreatNotFoundFiltersAsTrue'] = 0;
$CFG['PopupMenuTimeout'] = 3000;
$CFG['PhplogconLogoUrl'] = "";
$CFG['InlineOnlineSearchIcons'] = 1;
$CFG['UseProxyServerForRemoteQueries'] = "";
$CFG['HeaderDefaultEncoding'] = ENC_ISO_8859_1;

$CFG['InjectHtmlHeader'] = "";
$CFG['InjectBodyHeader'] = "";
$CFG['InjectBodyFooter'] = "";

$CFG['DefaultViewsID'] = "";

$CFG['Search'][] = array ( "DisplayName" => "Syslog Warnings and
Errors", "SearchQuery" => "filter=severity
%3A0%2C1%2C2%2C3%2C4&search=Search" );
$CFG['Search'][] = array ( "DisplayName" => "Syslog Errors",
"SearchQuery" => "filter=severity%3A0%2C1%2C2%2C3&search=Search" );
$CFG['Search'][] = array ( "DisplayName" => "All messages from the
```

```
last hour", "SearchQuery" => "filter=datelastx
%3A1&search=Search" );
$CFG['Search'][] = array ( "DisplayName" => "All messages from last
12 hours", "SearchQuery" => "filter=datelastx%3A2&search=Search" );
$CFG['Search'][] = array ( "DisplayName" => "All messages from last
24 hours", "SearchQuery" => "filter=datelastx%3A3&search=Search" );
$CFG['Search'][] = array ( "DisplayName" => "All messages from last
7 days", "SearchQuery" => "filter=datelastx%3A4&search=Search" );
$CFG['Search'][] = array ( "DisplayName" => "All messages from last
31 days", "SearchQuery" => "filter=datelastx%3A5&search=Search" );

$CFG['Charts'][] = array ( "DisplayName" => "Top Hosts",
"chart_type" => CHART_BARS_HORIZONTAL, "chart_width" => 400,
"chart_field" => SYSLOG_HOST, "maxrecords" => 10, "showpercent" =>
0, "chart_enabled" => 1 );
$CFG['Charts'][] = array ( "DisplayName" => "SyslogTags",
"chart_type" => CHART_CAKE, "chart_width" => 400, "chart_field" =>
SYSLOG_SYSLOGTAG, "maxrecords" => 10, "showpercent" => 0,
"chart_enabled" => 1 );
$CFG['Charts'][] = array ( "DisplayName" => "Severity Occurences",
"chart_type" => CHART_BARS_VERTICAL, "chart_width" => 400,
"chart_field" => SYSLOG_SEVERITY, "maxrecords" => 10, "showpercent"
=> 1, "chart_enabled" => 1 );
$CFG['Charts'][] = array ( "DisplayName" => "Usage by Day",
"chart_type" => CHART_CAKE, "chart_width" => 400, "chart_field" =>
SYSLOG_DATE, "maxrecords" => 10, "showpercent" => 1,
"chart_enabled" => 1 );

$CFG['DiskAllowed'][] = "/var/log/";

$CFG['DefaultSourceID'] = 'Source1';

$CFG['Sources']['Source1']['ID'] = 'Source1';
$CFG['Sources']['Source1']['Name'] = 'Syslog';
$CFG['Sources']['Source1'][!ViewID'] = 'SYSLOG';
$CFG['Sources']['Source1']['SourceType'] = SOURCE_DISK;
$CFG['Sources']['Source1']['LogLineType'] = 'syslog';
$CFG['Sources']['Source1']['DiskFile'] = '/var/log/messages';

$CFG['Sources']['Source2']['ID'] = 'Source2';
$CFG['Sources']['Source2']['Name'] = 'Admin Httpd Error';
$CFG['Sources']['Source2']['ViewID'] = 'SYSLOG';
$CFG['Sources']['Source2']['SourceType'] = SOURCE_DISK;
$CFG['Sources']['Source2']['LogLineType'] = 'syslog';
$CFG['Sources']['Source2']['DiskFile'] =
'/var/log/adminhttpderr.log';

$CFG['Sources']['Source3']['ID'] = 'Source3';
$CFG['Sources']['Source3']['Name'] = 'Web Httpd Error';
$CFG['Sources']['Source3']['ViewID'] = 'SYSLOG';
$CFG['Sources']['Source3']['SourceType'] = SOURCE_DISK;
$CFG['Sources']['Source3']['LogLineType'] = 'syslog';
$CFG['Sources']['Source3']['DiskFile'] =
'/var/log/webhttpderr.log';

$CFG['Sources']['Source4']['ID'] = 'Source4';
$CFG['Sources']['Source4']['Name'] = 'JavaMail';
$CFG['Sources']['Source4']['ViewID'] = 'SYSLOG';
$CFG['Sources']['Source4']['SourceType'] = SOURCE_DISK;
$CFG['Sources']['Source4']['LogLineType'] = 'syslog';
```

```php
$CFG['Sources']['Source4']['DiskFile'] = '/var/log/javamail.log';

$CFG['Sources']['Source5']['ID'] = 'Source5';
$CFG['Sources']['Source5']['Name'] = 'Admin Httpd';
$CFG['Sources']['Source5']['ViewID'] = 'WEBLOG';
$CFG['Sources']['Source5']['SourceType'] = SOURCE_DISK;
$CFG['Sources']['Source5']['LogLineType'] = 'syslog';
$CFG['Sources']['Source5']['DiskFile'] = '/var/log/adminhttpd.log';
$CFG['Sources']['Source5']['MsgParserList'] = "apache2";

$CFG['Sources']['Source6']['ID'] = 'Source6';
$CFG['Sources']['Source6']['Name'] = 'Web Httpd';
$CFG['Sources']['Source6']['ViewID'] = 'WEBLOG';
$CFG['Sources']['Source6']['SourceType'] = SOURCE_DISK;
$CFG['Sources']['Source6']['LogLineType'] = 'syslog';
$CFG['Sources']['Source6']['DiskFile'] = '/var/log/webhttpd.log';
$CFG['Sources']['Source6']['MsgParserList'] = "apache2";

$CFG['Sources']['Source7']['ID'] = 'Source7';
$CFG['Sources']['Source7']['Name'] = 'PHP At A Glance';
$CFG['Sources']['Source7']['ViewID'] = 'SYSLOG';
$CFG['Sources']['Source7']['SourceType'] = SOURCE_DISK;
$CFG['Sources']['Source7']['LogLineType'] = 'syslog';
$CFG['Sources']['Source7']['DiskFile'] = '/var/log/ataglance.log';

?>
```

The PHPMyAdmin config file is as follows (note SED***SED items are replaced with real values):

[aws/ami/admin/config_inc_template.php]

```php
<?php
/**
 * phpMyAdmin configuration file, you can use it as base for the
manual
 * configuration.
 */

$cfg['blowfish_secret'] = '';

$i = 0;

$i++;
$cfg['Servers'][$i]['host']          = 'SEDdbhostSED';
$cfg['Servers'][$i]['port']          = '3306';
$cfg['Servers'][$i]['socket']        = '';
$cfg['Servers'][$i]['connect_type']  = 'tcp';
$cfg['Servers'][$i]['extension']     = 'mysqli';
$cfg['Servers'][$i]['compress']      = FALSE;
$cfg['Servers'][$i]['controluser']   = '';
$cfg['Servers'][$i]['controlpass']   = '';
$cfg['Servers'][$i]['auth_type']     = 'config';
$cfg['Servers'][$i]['user']          = 'mainuser';
$cfg['Servers'][$i]['password']      = 'SEDdbmainuserpassSED';
$cfg['Servers'][$i]['only_db']       = '';
$cfg['Servers'][$i]['hide_db']       = '';
```

```
$cfg['Servers'][$i]['verbose']       = '';
$cfg['Servers'][$i]['pmadb']         = '';
$cfg['Servers'][$i]['bookmarktable'] = '';
$cfg['Servers'][$i]['relation']      = '';
$cfg['Servers'][$i]['table_info']    = '';
$cfg['Servers'][$i]['table_coords']  = '';
$cfg['Servers'][$i]['pdf_pages']     = '';
$cfg['Servers'][$i]['column_info']   = '';
$cfg['Servers'][$i]['history']       = '';
$cfg['Servers'][$i]['verbose_check'] = TRUE;
$cfg['Servers'][$i]['AllowRoot']     = TRUE;
$cfg['Servers'][$i]['AllowDeny']['order'] = '';
$cfg['Servers'][$i]['AllowDeny']['rules'] = array();
$cfg['Servers'][$i]['AllowNoPassword'] = FALSE;
$cfg['Servers'][$i]['designer_coords'] = '';
$cfg['Servers'][$i]['bs_garbage_threshold'] = 50;
$cfg['Servers'][$i]['bs_repository_threshold'] = '32M';
$cfg['Servers'][$i]['bs_temp_blob_timeout'] = 600;
$cfg['Servers'][$i]['bs_temp_log_threshold'] = '32M';

$cfg['UploadDir'] = '/var/lib/phpMyAdmin/upload';
$cfg['SaveDir']   = '/var/lib/phpMyAdmin/save';

$cfg['PmaNoRelation_DisableWarning'] = TRUE;
?>
```

The Monit config file is as follows:

[aws/ami/admin/monit.conf]

```
# monit for admin

set daemon   10

set logfile syslog facility log_daemon

set eventqueue
        basedir /var/monit

set mmonit http://monit:monit@127.0.0.1:8080/collector

set httpd port 2812
    use address localhost
        allow monit:monit

# mmonit
check process mmonit with pidfile /mmonit/mmonit-
3.2.1/logs/mmonit.pid
   start program = "/mmonit/mmonit-3.2.1/bin/mmonit" as uid root
and gid root
   stop program = "/mmonit/mmonit-3.2.1/bin/mmonit stop" as uid
root and gid root

# javaMail
check process javaMail with pidfile /java/javamail/javaMail.pid
        start = "/java/javamail/launch_javaMail.sh start"
        stop = "/java/javamail/launch_javaMail.sh stop"
```

```
# ntp
check process ntpd with pidfile /var/run/ntpd.pid
        start program = "/etc/init.d/ntpd start"
        stop  program = "/etc/init.d/ntpd stop"
        if failed host 127.0.0.1 port 123 type udp then alert
        if 5 restarts within 5 cycles then timeout

# ssh
check process sshd with pidfile /var/run/sshd.pid
        start program  "/etc/init.d/sshd start"
        stop program  "/etc/init.d/sshd stop"

# apache
check process apache with pidfile /var/run/httpd/httpd.pid
    start program = "/etc/init.d/httpd start" with timeout 60
seconds
    stop program  = "/etc/init.d/httpd stop"

check system localhost
    if loadavg (1min) > 4 then alert
    if loadavg (5min) > 2 then alert
    if memory usage > 75% then alert
    if swap usage > 25% then alert
    if cpu usage (user) > 70% then alert
    if cpu usage (system) > 30% then alert
    if cpu usage (wait) > 20% then alert

include /etc/monit.d/*
```

The Mmonit config file is as follows (note SED***SED items are replaced with real values) (note also you need to edit and put your purchased Mmonit key in the Licence tag at the end of the file):

[aws/ami/admin/server_template.xml]

```
<?xml version="1.0" encoding="UTF-8"?>

<Server>
   <Service>
       <Connector address="*" port="8080" processors="10" />
       <Engine name="mmonit" defaultHost="localhost"
fileCache="10MB">
           <Realm url="sqlite:///db/mmonit.db?
synchronous=normal&heap_limit=8000&foreign_keys=on&journal_mode=wal
"
               minConnections="5"
               maxConnections="25"
               reapConnections="300" />
           <ErrorLogger directory="logs" fileName="error.log"
rotate="month" />
           <Host name="localhost" appBase=".">
               <Logger directory="logs" fileName="mmonit.log"
rotate="month" timestamp="true" />
               <Context path="" docBase="docroot"
sessionTimeout="1800" maxActiveSessions="1024"
```

```
saveSessions="true" />
                <Context path="/collector"
docBase="docroot/collector" />
          </Host>
        </Engine>
        <Connector address="SEDadminprivateipSED" port="8443"
processors="10" secure="true" />
        <Engine name="SEDadminpublicipSED"
defaultHost-"SEDadminpublicipSED" fileCache="10MB">
            <Realm url="sqlite:///db/mmonit.db?
synchronous=normal&heap_limit=8000&foreign_keys=on&journal_mode=wal
"
                minConnections="5"
                maxConnections="25"
                reapConnections="300" />
            <ErrorLogger directory="logs" fileName="error.log"
rotate="month" />
            <Host name="SEDadminpublicipSED" appBase="."
address="SEDadminprivateipSED" certificate="conf/mmonit.pem">
                <Logger directory="logs" fileName="mmonit.log"
rotate="month" timestamp="true" />
                <Context path="" docBase="docroot"
sessionTimeout="1800" maxActiveSessions="1024"
saveSessions="true" />
                <Context path="/collector"
docBase="docroot/collector" />
            </Host>
        </Engine>
    </Service>

<License owner="Paste your licence here, replace the whole Licence
Tag, owner is required">
</License>

</Server>
```

The rsyslog conf file:

[aws/ami/admin/rsyslog.conf]

```
# rsyslog for admin server

$ModLoad imuxsock
$ModLoad imklog
$ModLoad imudp
$UDPServerRun 514
$ModLoad imtcp
$InputTCPServerRun 514

$ActionFileDefaultTemplate RSYSLOG_TraditionalFileFormat

$umask 0000
$FileCreateMode 0666

:syslogtag, isequal, "javamail:" /var/log/javamail.log
:syslogtag, isequal, "javamail:" ~
```

```
:syslogtag, isequal, "adminhttpd:" /var/log/adminhttpd.log
:syslogtag, isequal, "adminhttpd:" ~

:syslogtag, isequal, "ataglance:" /var/log/ataglance.log
:syslogtag, isequal, "ataglance:" ~

# admin httpd error log
local5.* /var/log/adminhttpderr.log
local5.* ~

# web httpd error log
#local4.* /var/log/webhttpderr.log;myFormat
local4.* /var/log/webhttpderr.log
local4.* ~

:msg, contains, "\"-\" 408 - \"-\""  ~
:msg, contains, "Apache (internal dummy connection)"  ~

:syslogtag, isequal, "httpd:" /var/log/webhttpd.log
:syslogtag, isequal, "httpd:" ~

*.info;mail.none;authpriv.none;cron.none
/var/log/messages

authpriv.*
/var/log/secure

mail.*
-/var/log/maillog

cron.*
/var/log/cron

*.emerg                                                    *

uucp,news.crit
/var/log/spooler

local7.*
/var/log/boot.log

$IncludeConfig /etc/rsyslog.d/*.conf
```

The logrotate script to rotate log files likely to be large:

[aws/ami/admin/logrotatehttp]

```
/var/log/webhttpd.log /var/log/webhttpderr.log {
    daily
    rotate 90
    olddir /var/log/old
    missingok
    sharedscripts
    postrotate
        service rsyslog restart
    endscript
    nocompress
```

```
}
```

The JavaMail launch script which links to Monit:

[aws/ami/admin/launch_javaMail.sh]

```
#!/bin/bash

case $1 in
 start)
  cd /java/javamail
  echo $$ > javaMail.pid;
  exec 2>&1 java -jar javaMail.jar |/usr/bin/logger -t javamail -p
local3.info
  ;;
 stop)
  pid1=$(ps axf | grep "java -jar javaMail.jar" | grep -v grep |
awk '{print $1}')
  pid2=$(ps axf | grep "/usr/bin/logger -t javamail -p local3.info"
| grep -v grep | awk '{print $1}')
  pid3=$(ps axf | grep "/bin/bash /java/javamail/launch_javaMail.sh
start" | grep -v grep | awk '{print $1}')
  kill $pid1
  sleep 2
  kill $pid2
  kill $pid3
  ;;
 *)
  echo "usage: launch_javaMail.sh {start|stop}" ;;
esac
exit 0
```

We also sed, upload and run the two password change expect scripts for root and ec2-user accounts. You can find these in **Chapter 5 - Changing Passwords**.

There are 2 other files: loganalyzer-3.6.5.tar.gz and mmonit-3.2.1-linux-x64.tar.gz which could be downloaded from the Internet by the scripts but unfortunately, these versions change and we can't get the latest versions programmatically. Also, old versions tend not to be downloadable. Hence, we hard code a version and provide the install bundle. Because Mmonit uses a Licence Key, even for the trial version, you may need to update to the latest Mmonit version. If you do, you will need to edit files in the aws/ami/admin/ folder to reflect this (and copy the new mmonit tar.gz into the aws/ami/admin/ folder.

You can find more details on uploading required files to the Admin

Server and Remote Access in **Chapter 13 - Deploying Assets** and **Chapter 14 - Remote Access**.

Original Files

The configuration files above have been edited and most comments removed for clarity and succinctness. You can find the original unedited files in the aws/ami/admin/original folder. The locations for these files are as follows:

1. httpd.conf (Apache)

   run: yum -y install httpd php (on a new AWS box)

   /etc/httpd/conf/httpd.conf

2. config_inc.php (PHPMyAdmin)

   install Apache (item 1)

   run: yum --enablerepo=epel install -y phpmyadmin (on a new AWS box)

   /etc/httpd/conf.d/phpMyAdmin.conf

3. config.sample.php (LogAnalyzer)

   unzip the bundle (loganalyzer-3.6.5.tar.gz)

   src/include/config.sample.php

4. monit.conf (Monit)

   run: yum -y install monit (on a new AWS box)

   /etc/monit.conf

5. rsyslog.conf (Rsyslog)

on a new AWS box

/etc/rsyslog.conf

6. server.xml (Mmonit)

unzip the bundle (mmonit-3.2.1-linux-x64.tar.gz)

conf/server.xml

Admin Website Source Code

The Admin Website is a simple demonstration of basic Administration Tasks. You will no doubt want to expand it, including, for instance, Contact Management, Sales Statistics or User Metrics. The source code listings follow.

Provides a list of log files, their size and links for more details for each log.

[aws/development/website/htdocs/admin/alllogs.php]

```php
<?php require "init.php";?>

<html>
<head>
        <link href="admstyle.css" type="text/css" rel="stylesheet">
</head>
<body>

<center>

<br><h2>All Logs</h2>
<table border=1 cellspacing=0 cellpadding=5>
        <tr bgcolor='cccccc'><td>log</td><td
colspan="5">Action</td></tr>
<?php

        $logdir="/var/log/";
        $logs=array("messages", "maillog", "adminhttpderr.log",
"webhttpderr.log", "javamail.log", "adminhttpd.log",
"webhttpd.log", "ataglance.log");

        $oscil=0;
        // show a listing of the logs
        foreach ($logs as $log) {
                $output = shell_exec('ls -lart '.$logdir.$log.'
```

```
2>&1');
                echo "<tr bgcolor='#".
(($oscil==0)?'ffffff':'eeeeee')."'>";
                echo "<td><pre>".$output."</pre></td>";
                echo "<td><a href='alllogsview.php?t=all&log=".
$log."'>View All</a></td>";
                echo "<td><a href='alllogsview.php?t=100&log=".
$log."'>Tail 100</a></td>";
                echo "<td><a href='alllogsview.php?t=500&log=".
$log."'>Tail 500</a></td>";
                echo "</tr>";
                $oscil=($oscil==0)?1:0;
                }
?>
</table>

<br><br>

</center>

</body>
</html>
```

Called from alllogs.php, gives more detail on a particular log file.

[aws/development/website/htdocs/admin/alllogsview.php]

```
<?php require "init.php";?>

<html>
<head>
        <link href="admstyle.css" type="text/css" rel="stylesheet">
</head>
<body>

<center>

<?php
        $logdir="/var/log/";
        $log=$_GET['log'];
        $type=$_GET['t'];
?>

<br><h2>All Logs View</h2>
<table border=1 cellspacing=0 cellpadding=5>
        <tr bgcolor='cccccc'><td>log: <?php echo $logdir.$log;?> <a
href="alllogs.php">Back</a></td></tr>

<?php
        // print the log file as requested
        if ($type=="all")
                $output = shell_exec('cat '.$logdir.$log.' 2>&1');
        else if ($type=="100")
                $output = shell_exec('tail -n 100 '.$logdir.$log.'
2>&1');
        else if ($type=="500")
                $output = shell_exec('tail -n 500 '.$logdir.$log.'
```

```
2>&1');
        echo "<tr><td><pre>".$output."</pre></td></tr>";
?>
</table>

<br><br>

</center>

</body>
</html>
```

Shows a list of log files and the latest log entries. Similar code is used for the At A Glance scheduled page example.

[aws/development/website/htdocs/admin/ataglance.php]

```
<?php require "init.php";?>

<html>
<head>
        <link href="admstyle.css" type="text/css" rel="stylesheet">
</head>
<body>

<center>

<br><h2>At A Glance</h2>

<table border=1 cellspacing=0 cellpadding=5>
<?php

        $logdir="/var/log/";
        $logs=array("messages", "maillog", "adminhttpderr.log",
"webhttpderr.log", "javamail.log", "adminhttpd.log",
"webhttpd.log", "ataglance.log");

        $oscil=0;
        // show details about each log file
        foreach ($logs as $log) {
                $output = shell_exec('ls -lart '.$logdir.$log.'
2>&1');
                echo "<tr bgcolor='#".
(($oscil==0)?'ffffff':'eeeeee')."'>";
                echo "<td><pre>".$output."</pre></td>";
                echo "</tr>";
                $oscil=($oscil==0)?1:0;
                $output = shell_exec('tail -n 5 '.$logdir.$log.'
2>&1');
                echo "<tr bgcolor='#".
(($oscil==0)?'ffffff':'eeeeee')."'>";
                echo "<td><pre>".$output."</pre></td>";
                echo "</tr>";
                $oscil=($oscil==0)?1:0;
                }
?>
</table>
```

```
<br><br>

</center>

</body>
</html>
```

Allows you to send a test email to check your JavaMail, SES and SNS settings.

[aws/development/website/htdocs/admin/email.php]

```
<?php require "init.php";?>

<html>
<head>
        <link href="admstyle.css" type="text/css" rel="stylesheet">
</head>
<body>

<center>

<br><h2>Send Test Email</h2>

<form action="email2.php" method="get">

        Sending from <?php echo $global_sendemailfrom;?>

        <br><br>

        To:
        <select name="predef">
                <option
value="success@simulator.amazonses.com">success@simulator.amazonses
.com
                <option
value="bounce@simulator.amazonses.com">bounce@simulator.amazonses.c
om
                <option
value="complaint@simulator.amazonses.com">complaint@simulator.amazo
nses.com
                <option
value="suppressionlist@simulator.amazonses.com">suppressionlist@sim
ulator.amazonses.com
        </select>

        <br><br>

        or: <input type="text" name="dyn" size="50"><br>
        [must be verified in SES if SES Production Access is not
enabled]

        <br><br>

        <input type="Submit" value="Send">
```

```
</form>

<br><br>

</center>

</body>
</html>
```

Performs the email database insert as requested in email.php

[aws/development/website/htdocs/admin/email2.php]

```
<?php require "init.php";?>

<html>
<head>
        <link href="admstyle.css" type="text/css" rel="stylesheet">
</head>
<body>

<center>

<br><h2>Sending Email...</h2>

<?php

        // send test email
        $to=$_GET['predef'];
        if (isset($_GET['dyn'])) {
                if (!($_GET['dyn']==""))
                        $to=$_GET['dyn'];
        }
        $result=doSQL("insert into sendemails (userID, sendto,
sendfrom, sendsubject, sendmessage) values (?, ?, ?, ?, ?)", 1,
$to, $global_sendemailfrom, "Admin Email Test", "Testing 123...")
or die("Error");
?>

Sent to <?php echo $to;?>

<br><br>

Check the sendemails database table.

<br><br>

</center>


</body>
</html>
```

Sets up the Admin Website frameset.

[aws/development/website/htdocs/admin/index.php]

```
<?php require "init.php";?>

<HTML>
<head>
        <title>Admin Interface</title>
        <frameset cols="200,*" frameborder=1>
                <frame src="menu.php" name="bar" id="bar"
frameborder="1" scrolling="Auto" marginwidth="0" marginheight="0">
                <frame name="page" src="ataglance.php"
frameborder="1" marginwidth="0" marginheight="0" scrolling="Auto">
        </frameset>
</HEAD>
<body></body>
</HTML>
```

Contains the Admin Site global variables and database functions. Also performs security by checking for the existence of a cookie. Included at the beginning of all files in the site. You can allow pages to run without signing in by setting $signin=1 before including init.php - this is needed, for example, by scheduled files.

[aws/development/website/htdocs/admin/init.php]

```
<?php

        // when we upload to Production Environment, this is
replaced with 0
        $global_is_dev="SEDis_devSED";

        // when we upload to Production Environment,
        // this is replaced with emailsendfrom from
aws/master/vars.sh
        // which must be verified SES email
        $global_sendemailfrom="SEDsendemailfromSED";

        // sort the webaddress (/ on AWS, /admin/ for dev)
        $global_webprefix="/";
        if (strlen($global_is_dev)>1)
                $global_webprefix="/admin/";

        date_default_timezone_set('UTC');

        $db=null;

        // connect to the database with selected user
        // determines if in-house or aws
        function dbconnect($npriv) {

                global $global_is_dev, $db;

                $dbhost="";
                $dbname="";
```

```php
                $dbuser="";
                $dbpass="";

                if (strlen($global_is_dev)>1) {
                        // development
                        $dbhost="127.0.0.1";
                        $dbname="SEDdbnameSED";
                        if ($npriv==0) {
                                $dbuser="adminrw";
                                $dbpass="SEDDBPASS_adminrwSED";
                                }
                        else if ($npriv==1) {
                                $dbuser="a different user";
                                $dbpass="a different password";
                                }

                        }
                else {
                        // aws
                        $dbhost=$_SERVER['DBHOST'];
                        $dbname=$_SERVER['DBNAME'];
                        if ($npriv==0) {
                                $dbuser=$_SERVER['DBUSER_adminrw'];
                                $dbpass=$_SERVER['DBPASS_adminrw'];
                                }
                        }
                $db = new mysqli($dbhost, $dbuser, $dbpass,
$dbname);
                if (mysqli_connect_errno()) {
                        trigger_error("Unable to connect to
database.");
                        exit;
                        }
                $db->set_charset('UTF-8');
                }

        // runs a parametrised sql query
        // if query has no parameters:
        //  if query returns no data, return 1 (success) 0 (error)
        //  if query returns data, return data array (success) or 0
(error)
        // if query has parameters:
        //  if query returns no data, return 1 (success) 0 (error)
        //  if query returns data, return data array (success) or 0
(error)
        function doSQL($nquery) {
                global $db;
                $args = func_get_args();
                if (count($args) == 1) {
                        $result = $db->query($nquery);
                        if (is_bool($result)) {
                                if ($result==1)
                                        return 1;
                                return 0;
                                }
                        if ($result->num_rows) {
                                $out = array();
                                while (null != ($r = $result-
>fetch_array(MYSQLI_ASSOC)))
                                        $out [] = $r;
                                return $out;
```

```
                                        }
                                return 1;
                                }
                        else {
                                if (!$stmt = $db->prepare($nquery))
                                        //trigger_error("Unable to prepare
statement: {$nquery}, reason: " . $db->error . "");
                                        return 0;
                                array_shift($args); //remove $nquery from
args
                                //the following three lines are the only
way to copy an array values in PHP
                                $a = array();
                                foreach ($args as $k => &$v)
                                        $a[$k] = &$v;
                                $types = str_repeat("s", count($args));
//all params are strings, works well on MySQL and SQLite
                                array_unshift($a, $types);
                                call_user_func_array(array($stmt,
'bind_param'), $a);
                                $stmt->execute();
                                //fetching all results in a 2D array
                                $metadata = $stmt->result_metadata();
                                $out = array();
                                $fields = array();
                                if (!$metadata)
                                        return 1;
                                $length = 0;
                                while (null != ($field =
mysqli_fetch_field($metadata))) {
                                        $fields [] = &$out [$field->name];
                                        $length+=$field->length;
                                        }
                                call_user_func_array(array($stmt,
"bind_result"), $fields);
                                $output = array();
                                $count = 0;
                                while ($stmt->fetch()) {
                                        foreach ($out as $k => $v)
                                                $output [$count] [$k] = $v;
                                        $count++;
                                        }
                                $stmt->free_result();
                                return ($count == 0) ? 1 : $output;
                                }
                        }

        if (!isset($signin)) {

                if (!isset($_COOKIE['ADMIN'])) {
                        header("Location:
{$global_webprefix}signin.php");
                        exit;
                        }

                if (!($_COOKIE['ADMIN']=="ok")) {
                        header("Location:
{$global_webprefix}signin.php");
                        exit;
                        }
```

```
        }
    dbconnect(0);

?>
```

Menu access to the Admin Website pages. Note the link to Mmonit.

[aws/development/website/htdocs/admin/menu.php]

```
<?php require "init.php";?>

<html>
<head>
    <link href="admstyle.css" type="text/css" rel="stylesheet">
</head>
<body bgcolor="#EBEDFF" style="padding:5px 5px 5px 5px;">

<h1>ADMIN</h1>

<br><a href="ataglance.php" target="page">At A Glance</a><br>

<br><a href="alllogs.php" target="page">All Logs</a><br>

<br><a href="email.php" target="page">Test Email</a><br>

<br><a href="slowqueries.php" target="page">Slow Queries</a><br>

<br><a href="phpinfo.php" target="page">PHP Info</a><br>

<br><a href="https://<?php echo $_SERVER['SERVER_NAME'];?>:8443/"
target="page">M/Monit</a>
<br><a href="/loganalyzer/" target="page">LogAnalyzer</a>
<br><a href="/phpmyadmin/" target="page">PHPMyAdmin</a>

</body>
</html>
```

Shows Admin Server PHP Info.

[aws/development/website/htdocs/admin/phpinfo.php]

```
<?php require "init.php";?>
<?php phpinfo();?>
```

Sign In form for the Admin Website.

[aws/development/website/htdocs/admin/signin.php]

```
<html>
```

AWS Scripted   132

```
<head>
        <link href="admstyle.css" type="text/css" rel="stylesheet">
</head>
<body>

<center>

<br><h2>Sign In</h2>

<form id="signinform" action="signin2.php" method="post">
        <b>Password:</b> <input value="" type="password"
name="password" onkeydown="if (event.keyCode == 13)
submit();"></td>
        <input id="submitbutton" value="SIGN IN" type="submit">
</form>

</center>

</body>
</html>
```

Checks the password and sets a cookie if correct.

[aws/development/website/htdocs/admin/signin2.php]

```
<?php
        $signin=1;
        require "init.php";
        if ($_POST['password']=="admin") {
                // set cookie (expiry on close browser)
                setcookie("ADMIN", "ok");
                }
        else
                header("Location: signin.php");
?>
<!DOCTYPE HTML>
<html>
<head>
        <script>window.onload=function(){
                location.href='<?php echo $global_webprefix;?>';
                };
        </script>
</head>
</html>
```

Shows slow query data. Note the useful printtable() function.

[aws/development/website/htdocs/admin/slowqueries.php]

```
<?php require "init.php";?>

<html>
<head>
        <link href="admstyle.css" type="text/css" rel="stylesheet">
</head>
```

```
<body>

<center>

<br><h2>Slow Queries</h2>

<?php

        // generic function to print a table (very handy)
        function printtable($nresult, $ntablename) {
                if (is_array($nresult)) {
                        echo "<table border=1 cellspacing=0
cellpadding=5>";
                        $keys=array_keys($nresult[0]);
                        echo "<tr bgcolor='cccccc'>";
                        foreach ($keys as $key)
                                echo "<td>".$key."</td>";
                        echo "</tr>";
                        foreach ($nresult as $row) {
                                echo "<tr>";
                                foreach ($row as $value)
                                        echo "<td>".$value."</td>";
                                echo "</tr>";
                                }
                        echo "</table><br>";
                        }
                else
                        echo "<table border=1 cellspacing=0
cellpadding=5><tr bgcolor='cccccc'><td>{$ntablename} No
Data</td></tr></table><br>";
                }

        // read the slow queries table
        $result=doSQL("select * from mysql.slow_log order by
start_time asc;") or die("Query failed : " . mysql_error());
        printtable($result, "slow_log");
?>

</center>

</body>
</html>
```

An example scheduled file. Send an email with At A Glance log data. The page is run with cron and sends output to a logfile (see comments in the file below).

[aws/development/website/htdocs/admin/sched/ataglance.php]

```
<?php

        // an example of how to do a scheduled page
        // this page is 'cron'ed in
aws/ami/admin/install_admin_template.php
        // output is piped to a log file (/var/log/ataglance.log)
        // with /usr/bin/logger
```

```php
        // can be called without signing in
        $signin=1;
        require "../init.php";

        // these will be sent to the log file
        ini_set("show_errors", 1);

        // do a listing of log files
        $logdir="/var/log/";
        $logs=array("adminhttpderr.log", "webhttpderr.log",
"javamail.log", "adminhttpd.log", "webhttpd.log", "ataglance.log");
        foreach ($logs as $log) {
                $output = shell_exec('ls -lart '.$logdir.$log.'
2>&1');
                $msg.=$output."\n";
                $output = shell_exec('tail -n 3 '.$logdir.$log.'
2>&1');
                $msg.=$output."\n\n";
                }

        // send them in an email
        $result=doSQL("insert into sendemails (userID, sendto,
sendfrom, sendsubject, sendmessage) values (?, ?, ?, ?, ?)", 1,
$global_sendemailfrom, $global_sendemailfrom, "At A Glance", $msg)
or die("Error");

        // send a message to the logfile
        echo "At a glance done";
?>
```

To connect to the Admin Website, see **Chapter 14 - Connecting to Admin**.

Chapter 9 - LAP Server

The LAP Server is a Linux Apache PHP server, also referred to as a Webphp Server in this book. Multiple instances are run behind the ELB. They are completely interchangeable and replaceable, there being no sessions stored on any one machine. Log files are piped via rsyslog to the Admin Server, so there is nothing of permanent value on these servers. You can tear them down and build new ones as you wish.

The LAP (or Webphp) Servers are also Security Critical, given that they accept requests direct from the Internet (forwarded by the ELB). So they need to be ultra-hardened.

ModSecurity

ModSecurity is the single most effective security tool in your arsenal. It is free, installable from the AWS repositories and utterly hardcore. The default configuration could even be called excessively secure, and you will need to 'unsecure' a few things to get everything working.

Every HTTP request is run through a set of rules (hundreds of rules actually). If anything looks suspicious, the request is dropped with a 403 Denied response. Thanks to OWASP, the ruleset is phenomenal. Checks range from missing request headers to accessing via an IP address to common SQL-Injection patterns to requests that just have too many darn funny characters!

In my experience, there is very little in a web site that normal use via a normal browser will trigger. But try anything dodgy, and ModSecurity will kick in.

There is not much configuration you need to do for ModSecurity. However, a brief discussion of the workings of the file aws/ami/webphp/modsecurity_overrides is in order. What you will notice in your log files is that ModSecurity is overly restrictive for certain requests. The main example is, for instance, that the ELB, when calling your elb.htm file for a heartbeat check, uses the IP Address of your server and ModSecurity doesn't like this. Here is the http log entry showing a rejected elb.htm call:

[aws/snippets/snippet_modsecurityexample.txt]

```
[error] [client 10.0.10.76] ModSecurity: Access denied with code
403 (phase 2). Pattern match "^[\\\\d.:]+$" at
REQUEST_HEADERS:host. [file
"/etc/httpd/modsecurity.d/activated_rules/modsecurity_crs_21_protoc
ol_anomalies.conf"] [line "98"] [id "960017"] [rev "2"] [msg "Host
header is a numeric IP address"] [data "10.0.0.11"] [severity
"WARNING"] [ver "OWASP_CRS/2.2.8"] [maturity "9"] [accuracy "9"]
[tag "OWASP_CRS/PROTOCOL_VIOLATION/IP_HOST"] [tag "WASCTC/WASC-21"]
[tag "OWASP_TOP_10/A7"] [tag "PCI/6.5.10"] [tag
"http://technet.microsoft.com/en-
us/magazine/2005.01.hackerbasher.aspx"] [hostname "10.0.0.11"] [uri
"/elb.htm"] [unique_id "VEtG7QoAAAsAAAZsHnUAAAAB"]
```

OK, take a second. This is saying that 10.0.10.76 (the ELB) tried to call /elb.htm but was denied by rule 960017 because "Host header is a numeric IP address".

Now you can go two ways on this: either turn off ModSecurity entirely for this file; or selectively limit rules until the ELB can successfully call the page. For the first approach, you would need to add the following line to the modsecurity_overrides file (which needs to be included BEFORE other ModSecurity conf files):

```
SecRule REQUEST_FILENAME "^/elb.htm$"
"id:'99996',phase:1,nolog,allow,ctl:ruleEngine=Off"
```

To turn off rules one by one (more laborious but more secure) you will need to add the following to modsecurity_overrides instead:

[aws/snippets/snippet_modsecurityremoverule.txt]

```
<LocationMatch "/elb.htm">
SecRuleRemoveById 960017
</LocationMatch>
```

which turns off Rule 960017 only for the /elb.htm file. Now, you will notice that the ELB heartbeat call works. Note that in many situations, you will need to turn off several rules. In this case, go back to the logs, see which rule is doing the denying and add that in under the last SecRuleRemoveById.

PHP Suhosin

This is a standard install and forget package to shore up a few PHP buffer overflow bugs and the like. Easy and an absolute must. Free and available from the AWS repositories.

PHP Restrictions

PHP in a secure environment needs to be secured. This mainly involves turning off file uploads, fopen functions and several other functions which could be used for nefarious purposes.

Apache Chroot

Chrooting your Internet-facing web site is absolutely essential and since Apache 2.2 it's pretty easy. The directive 'ChrootDir /jail' in httpd.conf switches child Apache processes to the new root '/jail'. What this means is that Apache child process switch to a restricted file system with very little or no functionality. There isn't even a shell or bash command to be found. So even if someone were to successfully hijack an Apache process, they would find themselves in a proverbial jail, with no execute permissions and no commands to execute.

ModRpaf

ModRpaf is absolutely essential because the IP address that Apache and PHP receive is, by default, the IP of the ELB! ModRpaf automatically reads the X-Forwarded-For header and replaces the ELB IP so all logging and PHP scripts get the real request address.

File Permissions

Apache starts with root privileges and then switches to a new user for child processes which actually handle requests. This is vital because if someone somehow manages to hijack an Apache process, they will be running under this sub user and not as root. But, things like config files can still be secured as only root readable. Hence, a hacker would not only have to be able to run commands on your server, but also escalate his privileges to root. There are ways to do this, but it is not for the faint hearted - one exploit relies on crashing the system and using a poor choice of file permissions on a crash dump file...

So, for our config files we chown to root:root. We set permissions to 400 (root can read, nothing else), as there is no need to change these files under normal circumstances. Within our chroot jail, we chown everything to root:apache and change directory permissions to 550 (root and apache read execute or directory traverse) and file permissions to 440 (root and apache read only).

File Upload

Don't do it. Simple as that. It doesn't matter what people tell you - "this file upload system is safe"... You are basically allowing hackers to upload arbitrary files to your servers and who knows what weird way they will find to execute them.

If you really really need File Uploads, consider using an email alternative (ie people attach files to an email and send you this). It can be automated with an IMAP download script which saves files to a server.

Otherwise, use a completely different server just for File Uploads. You will need to consolidate files in any case with a multi LAP server setup, since you can't really store some files on one server and some on another.

SSL Certificate Validation with curl

Note that if you use curl with SLL or wish to use Certificate Validation (which you should), the Apache Chroot will cause you a whole host of problems. This can be fixed by copying a few .so libraries into the chroot. You also need to allow DNS from the chroot, or names won't resolve:

[aws/snippets/snippet_curlinjail.sh]

```
# allow dns to work in jail
mkdir -p /jail/etc
cp /etc/resolv.conf /jail/etc/resolv.conf
# allow curl ssl and verify to work
mkdir -p /jail/etc
cp /etc/nsswitch.conf /jail/etc/nsswitch.conf
cp -r /etc/pki /jail/etc
cp -r /etc/ssl /jail/etc
mkdir -p /jail/usr/lib64
cp /usr/lib64/libnsspem.so /jail/usr/lib64/libnsspem.so
cp /usr/lib64/libsoftokn3.so /jail/usr/lib64/libsoftokn3.so
cp /usr/lib64/libnsssysinit.so /jail/usr/lib64/libnsssysinit.so
cp /usr/lib64/libfreebl3.so /jail/usr/lib64/libfreebl3.so
cp /usr/lib64/libnssdbm3.so /jail/usr/lib64/libnssdbm3.so
# set the default certificate bundle
echo curl.cainfo=/etc/ssl/certs/ca-bundle.crt >>
/etc/php.d/curl.ini
```

You can find this bash code (in its proper context) in the aws/upload/website/install.sh script. The reason it is executed in the upload script is that when we upload a website update, we tear down the entire jail directory and recreate it from scratch.

What about iptables?

Iptables is an excellent firewall/nat service embedded in the Linux kernel. It is very efficient and fast. However, inbound traffic is automatically firewalled by the ELB and by AWS Security Groups. Iptables could be useful for limiting outbound access. When a hacker gets into your server, the first thing they try to do is download a hacker-pack to that server which allows privilege escalation or further intrusion. So if iptables were severely limiting outbound paths, this would prevent further downloads.

We need to differentiate between outbound packets that are a new connection (state=NEW) and outbound packets which are a reply to an inbound request (state=ESTABLISHED). We must allow outbound packets resulting from inbound requests on port 80, otherwise the web server won't work. If a hacker gets into a Webphp Server as root, all bets are off as iptables can just be turned off. If a hacker gets in as say the apache user (more likely but still very unlikely) these rules would apply.

The problem with iptables is that it cannot be used with domain style names. So, if you turn it on, you need to allow access out to everything (defeating the object) or limit access out to certain sites only. If the site you need access to has a domain name, eg secure.someserver.com, rather than an IP address, iptables is a bust. Because when you specify the name on the command line, it is resolved to an IP address. So if the IP address changes (substantially the point of having a DNS name), iptables will fail.

Installation scripts

Like the Admin Server, the creation scripts are quite complex.

This is the main installer script:

[aws/ami/webphp/make.sh]

```
#!/bin/bash

# makes a webphp linux box, from linux hardened image
# ssh on 38142
# webphpebsvolumesize GB EBS root volume

# parameters <N> where this is the Nth web box (1-5)

# check dir
where=$(pwd)
where="${where: -3}"
if test "$where" = "aws"; then
 echo "running from correct directory"
else
 echo "must be run from aws directory with ./ami/webphp/make.sh
<N>"
 exit
fi
```

```
# include global variables
. ./master/vars.sh

bdm=[{\"DeviceName\":\"/dev/sda1\",\"Ebs\":{\"VolumeSize\":
$webphpebsvolumesize}}]
echo bdm=$bdm

rm -f $sshknownhosts

cd $basedir

webid=$1
if test -z "$webid"; then
 webid=1
fi

echo "building web$webid"

echo "check web$webid does not exist"
exists=$(aws ec2 describe-key-pairs --key-names web$webid --output
text --query 'KeyPairs[*].KeyName' 2>/dev/null)

if test "$exists" = "web$webid"; then
 echo "key web$webid already exists = exiting"
 #exit
else
 echo "key web$webid not found - proceeding"
fi

cd $basedir

source credentials/passwords.sh

if test "$webid" = "1"; then
 rootpass=$password8
 ec2pass=$password9
elif test "$webid" = "2"; then
 rootpass=$password10
 ec2pass=$password11
elif test "$webid" = "3"; then
 rootpass=$password12
 ec2pass=$password13
elif test "$webid" = "4"; then
 rootpass=$password14
 ec2pass=$password15
elif test "$webid" = "5"; then
 rootpass=$password16
 ec2pass=$password17
elif test "$webid" = "6"; then
 rootpass=$password18
 ec2pass=$password19
else
 echo "password for web$webid not found - exiting"
 exit
fi

myip=$(curl http://checkip.amazonaws.com/)
echo myip=$myip

echo "making keypair"
```

AWS Scripted   143

```
rm credentials/web$webid.pem
aws ec2 delete-key-pair --key-name web$webid
aws ec2 create-key-pair --key-name web$webid --query 'KeyMaterial'
--output text > credentials/web$webid.pem
chmod 600 credentials/web$webid.pem
echo "keypair web$webid made"

echo "making sg"
websg=web$webid
websg+=sg
vpc_id=$(aws ec2 describe-vpcs --filters Name=tag-
key,Values=vpcname --filters Name=tag-value,Values=$vpcname
--output text --query 'Vpcs[*].VpcId')
echo vpc_id=$vpc_id
aws ec2 delete-security-group --group-name $websg
sg_id=$(aws ec2 create-security-group --group-name $websg
--description "web$webid security group" --vpc-id $vpc_id --output
text --query 'GroupId')
echo sg_id=$sg_id
aws ec2 create-tags --resources $sg_id --tags
Key=sgname,Value=$websg
vpcwebsg_id=$(aws ec2 describe-security-groups --filters Name=tag-
key,Values=sgname --filters Name=tag-value,Values=$websg --output
text --query 'SecurityGroups[*].GroupId')
echo vpcwebsg_id=$vpcwebsg_id
aws ec2 authorize-security-group-ingress --group-id $vpcwebsg_id
--protocol tcp --port 38142 --cidr $myip/32
echo "$websg made"

echo "getting subnet id"
subnet_id=$(aws ec2 describe-subnets --filters Name=vpc-
id,Values=$vpc_id --filters Name=tag-key,Values=subnet --filters
Name=tag-value,Values=1 --output text --query
'Subnets[*].SubnetId')
echo subnet_id=$subnet_id

echo "getting basic secure linux ami id"
bslami_id=$(aws ec2 describe-images --filters
'Name=name,Values=Basic Secure Linux' --output text --query
'Images[*].ImageId')
echo bslami_id=$bslami_id

echo "getting adminhost private ip"
adminhost=$(aws ec2 describe-instances --filters Name=key-
name,Values=admin --output text --query
'Reservations[*].Instances[*].PrivateIpAddress')
echo adminhost=$adminhost

echo "getting adminhost security group id"
vpcadminsg_id=$(aws ec2 describe-security-groups --filters
Name=tag-key,Values=sgname --filters Name=tag-value,Values=adminsg
--output text --query 'SecurityGroups[*].GroupId')
echo vpcadminsg_id=$vpcadminsg_id

echo "allowing access to admin server :514 for rsyslog"
aws ec2 authorize-security-group-ingress --group-id $vpcadminsg_id
--protocol tcp --port 514 --source-group $vpcwebsg_id

echo "allowing access to admin server :8080 for mmonit"
aws ec2 authorize-security-group-ingress --group-id $vpcadminsg_id
```

AWS Scripted   144

```
--protocol tcp --port 8080 --source-group $vpcwebsg_id

echo "allowing access to webphp from admin server :2812 for mmonit
callback"
aws ec2 authorize-security-group-ingress --group-id $vpcwebsg_id
--protocol tcp --port 2812 --source-group $vpcadminsg_id

echo "allowing access to rds database"
vpcdbsg_id=$(aws ec2 describe-security-groups --filters Name=tag-
key,Values=sgname --filters Name=tag-value,Values=dbsg --output
text --query 'SecurityGroups[*].GroupId')
echo vpcdbsg_id=$vpcdbsg_id
aws ec2 authorize-security-group-ingress --group-id $vpcdbsg_id
--source-group $vpcwebsg_id --protocol tcp --port 3306

dbendpoint=$(aws rds describe-db-instances --db-instance-identifier
$dbinstancename --output text --query
'DBInstances[*].Endpoint.Address')
echo dbendpoint=$dbendpoint

echo "making instance web$webid"
instance_id=$(aws ec2 run-instances --image $bslami_id --placement
AvailabilityZone=$deployzone --key web$webid --security-group-ids
$vpcwebsg_id --instance-type $webphpinstancetype --block-device-
mapping $bdm --region $deployregion --subnet-id $subnet_id
--private-ip-address 10.0.0.1$webid --associate-public-ip-address
--output text --query 'Instances[*].InstanceId')
echo instance_id=$instance_id

# build data

cd $basedir/ami/webphp

rm -f monit.conf
rm -f rsyslog.conf
rm -f httpd.conf
rm -f chp_ec2-user.sh
rm -f chp_root.sh

sed "s/SEDadminhostSED/$adminhost/g" monit_template.conf >
monit.conf

sed "s/SEDadminhostSED/$adminhost/g" rsyslog_template.conf >
rsyslog.conf

cd $basedir

# make the AES key for PHP sessions
# its a hex encoded version of $password20
aes1=$password20
# convert to hex
aes2=$(hexdump -e '"%X"' <<< "$aes1")
# lowercase
aes3=$(echo $aes2 | tr '[:upper:]' '[:lower:]')
# only the first 64 characters
aes4=${aes3:0:64}

# sed httpd.conf
source credentials/account.sh
source credentials/recaptcha.sh
```

```
sed -e "s/SEDdbhostSED/$dbendpoint/g" -e "s/SEDdbnameSED/$dbname/g"
-e "s/SEDdbpass_webphprwSED/$password5/g" -e "s/SEDaeskeySED/
$aes4/g" -e "s/SEDserveridSED/$webid/g" -e
"s/SEDaws_deployregionSED/$deployregion/g" -e "s/SEDaws_accountSED/
$aws_account/g" -e "s/SEDrecaptcha_privatekeySED/
$recaptcha_privatekey/g" -e "s/SEDrecaptcha_publickeySED/
$recaptcha_publickey/g" ami/webphp/httpd_template.conf >
ami/webphp/httpd.conf

sed "s/SED-EC2-USER-PASS-SED/$ec2pass/g" ami/shared/chp_ec2-user.sh
> ami/webphp/chp_ec2-user.sh
chmod +x ami/webphp/chp_ec2-user.sh

sed "s/SED-ROOT-PASS-SED/$rootpass/g" ami/shared/chp_root.sh >
ami/webphp/chp_root.sh
chmod +x ami/webphp/chp_root.sh

echo -n "waiting for instance"
while state=$(aws ec2 describe-instances --instance-ids
$instance_id --output text --query
'Reservations[*].Instances[*].State.Name'); test "$state" =
"pending"; do
 echo -n . ; sleep 3;
done; echo " $state"

priv_ip_address=$(aws ec2 describe-instances --instance-ids
$instance_id --output text --query
'Reservations[*].Instances[*].PrivateIpAddress')
echo priv_ip_address=$priv_ip_address

ip_address=$(aws ec2 describe-instances --instance-ids $instance_id
--output text --query
'Reservations[*].Instances[*].PublicIpAddress')
echo ip_address=$ip_address

echo -n "waiting for ssh"
while ! ssh -i credentials/web$webid.pem -p 38142 -o
ConnectTimeout=60 -o BatchMode=yes -o StrictHostKeyChecking=no ec2-
user@$ip_address > /dev/null 2>&1 true; do
 echo -n . ; sleep 3;
done; echo " ssh ok"

echo "transferring files"
scp -i credentials/web$webid.pem -P 38142 ami/webphp/rsyslog.conf
ec2-user@$ip_address:
scp -i credentials/web$webid.pem -P 38142 ami/webphp/monit.conf
ec2-user@$ip_address:
scp -i credentials/web$webid.pem -P 38142 ami/webphp/httpd.conf
ec2-user@$ip_address:
scp -i credentials/web$webid.pem -P 38142
ami/webphp/modsecurity_overrides ec2-user@$ip_address:
scp -i credentials/web$webid.pem -P 38142 ami/webphp/php.ini ec2-
user@$ip_address:
scp -i credentials/web$webid.pem -P 38142
ami/webphp/install_webphp.sh ec2-user@$ip_address:
scp -i credentials/web$webid.pem -P 38142 ami/webphp/chp_ec2-
user.sh ec2-user@$ip_address:
scp -i credentials/web$webid.pem -P 38142 ami/webphp/chp_root.sh
ec2-user@$ip_address:
scp -i credentials/web$webid.pem -P 38142 ami/webphp/mod_rpaf-0.6-
```

```
0.7.x86_64.rpm ec2-user@$ip_address:
echo "transferred files"

rm -f ami/webphp/monit.conf
rm -f ami/webphp/rsyslog.conf
rm -f ami/webphp/httpd.conf
rm -f ami/webphp/chp_ec2-user.sh
rm -f ami/webphp/chp_root.sh

echo "running install_webphp.sh"
ssh -i credentials/web$webid.pem -p 38142 -t -o ConnectTimeout=60
-o BatchMode=yes -o StrictHostKeyChecking=no ec2-user@$ip_address
sudo ./install_webphp.sh
echo "finished install_webphp.sh"

# register with elb
echo "registering with elb"
aws elb register-instances-with-load-balancer --load-balancer-name
$elbname --instances $instance_id

echo "add elb sg to instance sg"
vpcelbsg_id=$(aws ec2 describe-security-groups --filters Name=tag-
key,Values=sgname --filters Name=tag-value,Values=elbsg --output
text --query 'SecurityGroups[*].GroupId')
echo vpcelbsg_id=$vpcelbsg_id
aws ec2 authorize-security-group-ingress --group-id $vpcwebsg_id
--source-group $vpcelbsg_id --protocol tcp --port 80
aws ec2 authorize-security-group-ingress --group-id $vpcwebsg_id
--source-group $vpcelbsg_id --protocol tcp --port 443

echo "removing ssh access from sg"
aws ec2 revoke-security-group-ingress --group-id $vpcwebsg_id
--protocol tcp --port 38142 --cidr $myip/32

cd $basedir

echo "web php done - needs upload"
```

This is the main script which is run on the server once created:

[aws/ami/webphp/install_webphp.sh]

```
#!/bin/bash

# install packages
yum -y install php php-bcmath php-mysql php-mbstring php-mcrypt
openssl httpd
yum -y install mod_security mod_security_crs.noarch
yum --disablerepo="*" --enablerepo="epel" -y install php-suhosin

# install mod_rpaf
rpm -ivh mod_rpaf-0.6-0.7.x86_64.rpm

# copy conf files
cp -f httpd.conf /etc/httpd/conf/httpd.conf
cp -f php.ini /etc/php.ini
cp -f mod_evasive.conf /etc/httpd/conf.d/mod_evasive.conf
```

```
cp -f modsecurity_overrides
/etc/httpd/modsecurity.d/modsecurity_overrides

# set permissions on conf files
chown root:root /etc/httpd/conf/httpd.conf
chmod 400 /etc/httpd/conf/httpd.conf
chown root:root /etc/php.ini
chmod 400 /etc/php.ini
chown root:root /etc/httpd/modsecurity.d/modsecurity_overrides
chmod 400 /etc/httpd/modsecurity.d/modsecurity_overrides

# clear current webroot
rm -f -R /var/www/cgi-bin
rm -f -R /var/www/error
rm -f -R /var/www/icons
rm -f -R /var/www/html/*
rm -f -R /jail

# make the jailed webroot
mkdir -p /jail/var/www/html
mkdir -p /jail/var/www/phpinclude

# install monit
yum install -y monit
# configure monit
cd /home/ec2-user
cp -f monit.conf /etc/monit.conf
# start at boot
chkconfig --levels 2345 monit on

# turn off autostart services (monit handles them)
chkconfig --levels 2345 ntpd off
chkconfig --levels 2345 sshd off
chkconfig --levels 2345 httpd off

# configure rsyslog
cd /home/ec2-user
cp -f rsyslog.conf /etc/rsyslog.conf
chown root:root /etc/rsyslog.conf
chmod 400 /etc/rsyslog.conf

# remove ec2-user no password from sshed with key feature
echo "ec2-user ALL = ALL" > /etc/sudoers.d/cloud-init

# install expect
yum install -y expect

# update root and ec2-user passwords
cd /home/ec2-user
./chp_ec2-user.sh
./chp_root.sh

# remove expect
yum erase -y expect

# clear any files
rm -f -R /home/ec2-user/*

# further configuration is done in /aws/upload/website/uploadall.sh
reboot
```

AWS Scripted   148

This is the Apache configuration file (note SED***SED items are replaced with real values):

[aws/ami/webphp/httpd_template.conf]

```
ServerTokens Prod
ServerRoot "/etc/httpd"
PidFile run/httpd.pid
Timeout 30
LimitRequestBody 4096
LimitRequestFields 50
LimitRequestFieldSize 2048
KeepAlive On
MaxKeepAliveRequests 500
KeepAliveTimeout 30
<IfModule prefork.c>
StartServers          8
MinSpareServers       5
MaxSpareServers      20
ServerLimit         256
MaxClients          256
MaxRequestsPerChild  10000
</IfModule>
<IfModule worker.c>
StartServers          4
MaxClients          300
MinSpareThreads      25
MaxSpareThreads      75
ThreadsPerChild      25
MaxRequestsPerChild  10000
</IfModule>

Listen 80
ChrootDir /jail

LoadModule authz_host_module modules/mod_authz_host.so
LoadModule include_module modules/mod_include.so
LoadModule log_config_module modules/mod_log_config.so
LoadModule logio_module modules/mod_logio.so
LoadModule env_module modules/mod_env.so
LoadModule ext_filter_module modules/mod_ext_filter.so
LoadModule mime_magic_module modules/mod_mime_magic.so
LoadModule expires_module modules/mod_expires.so
LoadModule deflate_module modules/mod_deflate.so
LoadModule headers_module modules/mod_headers.so
LoadModule usertrack_module modules/mod_usertrack.so
LoadModule setenvif_module modules/mod_setenvif.so
LoadModule mime_module modules/mod_mime.so
LoadModule status_module modules/mod_status.so
LoadModule vhost_alias_module modules/mod_vhost_alias.so
LoadModule negotiation_module modules/mod_negotiation.so
LoadModule dir_module modules/mod_dir.so
LoadModule actions_module modules/mod_actions.so
LoadModule speling_module modules/mod_speling.so
LoadModule alias_module modules/mod_alias.so
LoadModule substitute_module modules/mod_substitute.so
LoadModule rewrite_module modules/mod_rewrite.so
```

```
LoadModule cache_module modules/mod_cache.so
LoadModule suexec_module modules/mod_suexec.so
LoadModule disk_cache_module modules/mod_disk_cache.so
LoadModule cgi_module modules/mod_cgi.so
LoadModule version_module modules/mod_version.so

Include modsecurity.d/modsecurity_overrides
Include conf.d/*.conf

User apache
Group apache

ServerAdmin youremail@yourcompany.com
ServerName www.yourcompany.com:80
UseCanonicalName Off
DocumentRoot "/var/www/html"

<Directory />
    Options None
    AllowOverride None
        Order Deny,Allow
        Deny from all
</Directory>
<Directory "/var/www/html">
    Options None
    AllowOverride None
    <Limit GET POST>
        Order allow,deny
        Allow from all
    </Limit>
    <LimitExcept GET POST>
        Order deny,allow
        Deny from all
    </LimitExcept>
</Directory>

<IfModule mod_userdir.c>
    UserDir disabled
</IfModule>

AccessFileName .htaccess
<Files ~ "^\.ht">
    Order allow,deny
    Deny from all
    Satisfy All
</Files>

TypesConfig /etc/mime.types

DefaultType text/plain

<IfModule mod_mime_magic.c>
    MIMEMagicFile conf/magic
</IfModule>

HostnameLookups Off

#ErrorLog logs/error_log
ErrorLog syslog:local4
```

```
LogLevel warn
LogFormat "%h %l %u %t \"%r\" %>s %b \"%{Referer}i\" \"%{User-
Agent}i\"" combined
LogFormat "%h %l %u %t \"%r\" %>s %b" common
LogFormat "%{Referer}i -> %U" referer
LogFormat "%{User-agent}i" agent

SetEnvIf Request_URI "^/elb\.htm$" dontlog
SetEnvIf Request_URI ".(js|css|jpg|ico|png|gif|ttf|woff|svg|eot|
pem|wav|txt)$" dontlog

#CustomLog logs/access_log combined
#CustomLog logs/access_log combined env=!dontlog
CustomLog "|/usr/bin/logger -t httpd -p local6.info" combined env=!
dontlog

ServerSignature Off

LanguagePriority en
ForceLanguagePriority Prefer Fallback
AddDefaultCharset UTF-8
AddType application/x-compress .Z
AddType application/x-gzip .gz .tgz

ErrorDocument 400 /public/error.php
ErrorDocument 401 /public/error.php
ErrorDocument 403 "Forbidden"
ErrorDocument 404 /public/error.php
ErrorDocument 405 /public/error.php
ErrorDocument 408 /public/error.php
ErrorDocument 410 /public/error.php
ErrorDocument 411 /public/error.php
ErrorDocument 412 /public/error.php
ErrorDocument 413 /public/error.php
ErrorDocument 414 /public/error.php
ErrorDocument 415 /public/error.php
ErrorDocument 500 /public/error.php
ErrorDocument 501 /public/error.php
ErrorDocument 502 /public/error.php
ErrorDocument 503 /public/error.php
ErrorDocument 506 /public/error.php

BrowserMatch "Mozilla/2" nokeepalive
BrowserMatch "MSIE 4\.0b2;" nokeepalive downgrade-1.0 force-
response-1.0
BrowserMatch "RealPlayer 4\.0" force-response-1.0
BrowserMatch "Java/1\.0" force-response-1.0
BrowserMatch "JDK/1\.0" force-response-1.0

BrowserMatch "Microsoft Data Access Internet Publishing Provider"
redirect-carefully
BrowserMatch "MS FrontPage" redirect-carefully
BrowserMatch "^WebDrive" redirect-carefully
BrowserMatch "^WebDAVFS/1.[0123]" redirect-carefully
BrowserMatch "^gnome-vfs/1.0" redirect-carefully
BrowserMatch "^XML Spy" redirect-carefully
BrowserMatch "^Dreamweaver-WebDAV-SCM1" redirect-carefully

SetEnv DBHOST SEDdbhostSED
SetEnv DBPORT 3306
```

```
SetEnv DBNAME SEDdbnameSED
SetEnv DBUSER_webphprw webphprw
SetEnv DBPASS_webphprw SEDdbpass_webphprwSED

SetEnv AWS_ACCOUNT SEDaws_accountSED
SetEnv AWS_DEPLOYREGION SEDaws_deployregionSED

SetEnv AESKEY SEDaeskeySED

SetEnv RECAPTCHA_PRIVATEKEY SEDrecaptcha_privatekeySED
SetEnv RECAPTCHA_PUBLICKEY SEDrecaptcha_publickeySED

SetEnv SERVERID SEDserveridSED
```

This is a file to override some ModSecurity rules:

[aws/ami/webphp/modsecurity_overrides]

```
# turn off modsecurity for some files
SecRule REQUEST_FILENAME "^/elb.htm$"
"id:'99996',phase:1,nolog,allow,ctl:ruleEngine=Off"
SecRule REQUEST_FILENAME "^/sns/bounce.php$"
"id:'99998',phase:1,nolog,allow,ctl:ruleEngine=Off"
SecRule REQUEST_FILENAME "^/sns/complaint.php$"
"id:'99999',phase:1,nolog,allow,ctl:ruleEngine=Off"
```

Note that this file needs to be included before the other ModSecurity includes in the httpd.conf file, hence in aws/ami/webphp/httpd_template.conf we use:

```
Include modsecurity.d/modsecurity_overrides
Include conf.d/*.conf
```

This is the Monit configuration file (note SED***SED items are replaced with real values):

[aws/ami/webphp/monit_template.conf]

```
# monit for webphp

set daemon  10
set logfile syslog facility log_daemon
set eventqueue
 basedir /var/monit

set mmonit http://monit:monit@SEDadminhostSED:8080/collector

set httpd port 2812
 allow monit:monit

# ntp
```

```
check process ntpd with pidfile /var/run/ntpd.pid
        start program = "/etc/init.d/ntpd start"
        stop  program = "/etc/init.d/ntpd stop"
        if failed host 127.0.0.1 port 123 type udp then alert
        if 5 restarts within 5 cycles then timeout

# ssh
check process sshd with pidfile /var/run/sshd.pid
        start program  "/etc/init.d/sshd start"
        stop program  "/etc/init.d/sshd stop"

# apache
check process apache with pidfile /var/run/httpd/httpd.pid
    start program = "/etc/init.d/httpd start" with timeout 60
seconds
    stop program = "/etc/init.d/httpd stop"
    if cpu > 95% for 10 cycles then alert
    if totalmem > 1000.0 MB for 5 cycles then alert
    if children > 50 then alert
    if loadavg(5min) greater than 10 for 8 cycles then alert

# general
check system localhost
    if loadavg (1min) > 4 then alert
    if loadavg (5min) > 2 then alert
    if memory usage > 90% then alert
    if swap usage > 25% then alert
    if cpu usage (user) > 70% then alert
    if cpu usage (system) > 30% then alert
    if cpu usage (wait) > 20% then alert

include /etc/monit.d/*
```

This is the PHP ini file:

[aws/ami/webphp/php.ini]

```
[PHP]

engine = On
short_open_tag = Off
asp_tags = Off
precision = 14
y2k_compliance = On
output_buffering = 4096
zlib.output_compression = Off
implicit_flush = Off
unserialize_callback_func =
serialize_precision = 100
allow_call_time_pass_reference = Off
safe_mode = Off
safe_mode_gid = Off
safe_mode_include_dir =
safe_mode_exec_dir =
safe_mode_allowed_env_vars = PHP_
safe_mode_protected_env_vars = LD_LIBRARY_PATH
```

```
disable_functions = php_uname, getmyuid, getmypid, passthru, leak,
listen, diskfreespace, tmpfile, link, ignore_user_abord,
shell_exec, dl, set_time_limit, exec, system, highlight_file,
source, show_source, fpaththru, virtual, posix_ctermid,
posix_getcwd, posix_getegid, posix_geteuid, posix_getgid,
posix_getgrgid, posix_getgrnam, posix_getgroups, posix_getlogin,
posix_getpgid, posix_getpgrp, posix_getpid, posix, _getppid,
posix_getpwnam, posix_getpwuid, posix_getrlimit, posix_getsid,
posix_getuid, posix_isatty, posix_kill, posix_mkfifo,
posix_setegid, posix_seteuid, posix_setgid, posix_setpgid,
posix_setsid, posix_setuid, posix_times, posix_ttyname,
posix_uname, proc_open, proc_close, proc_get_status, proc_nice,
proc_terminate, phpinfo, curl_multi_exec, parse_ini_file, ini_get,
ini_get_all, get_cfg_var, ini_set, get_loaded_extensions,
ini_restore, getINIEntries

disable_classes = ReflectionExtension

expose_php = Off

max_execution_time = 30
max_input_time = 60
max_input_vars = 1000
memory_limit = 64M

error_reporting = E_ALL & ~E_DEPRECATED
display_errors = Off
display_startup_errors = Off
log_errors = On
log_errors_max_len = 1024
ignore_repeated_errors = Off
ignore_repeated_source = Off
report_memleaks = On
track_errors = Off
html_errors = Off

variables_order = "GPCS"
request_order = "GP"
register_globals = Off
register_long_arrays = Off
register_argc_argv = Off
auto_globals_jit = On
post_max_size = 4K
magic_quotes_gpc = Off
magic_quotes_runtime = Off
magic_quotes_sybase = Off
auto_prepend_file =
auto_append_file =
default_mimetype = "text/html"

doc_root = /var/www/html
user_dir =
enable_dl = Off
cgi.force_redirect = 1

file_uploads = Off
upload_max_filesize = 2M
max_file_uploads = 20
```

AWS Scripted   154

```
allow_url_fopen = Off
allow_url_include = Off
default_socket_timeout = 60

date.timezone = UTC

define_syslog_variables  = Off

SMTP = localhost
smtp_port = 25
sendmail_path = /usr/sbin/sendmail -t -i
mail.add_x_header = On

sql.safe_mode = Off

mysql.allow_persistent = On
mysql.max_persistent = -1
mysql.max_links = -1
mysql.default_port =
mysql.default_socket =
mysql.default_host =
mysql.default_user =
mysql.default_password =
mysql.connect_timeout = 60
mysql.trace_mode = Off

mysqli.allow_persistent 1
mysqli.max_links = -1
mysqli.default_port = 3306
mysqli.default_socket =
mysqli.default_host =
mysqli.default_user =
mysqli.default_pw =
mysqli.reconnect = Off

pgsql.allow_persistent = On
pgsql.auto_reset_persistent = Off
pgsql.max_persistent = -1
pgsql.max_links = -1
pgsql.ignore_notice = 0
pgsql.log_notice = 0

bcmath.scale = 0

session.save_handler = files
session.save_path = "/var/lib/php/session"
session.use_cookies = 1
session.use_only_cookies = 1
session.name = PHPSESSID
session.auto_start = 0
session.cookie_lifetime = 0
session.cookie_path = /
session.cookie_domain =
session.cookie_httponly = 1
session.serialize_handler = php

session.gc_probability = 1
session.gc_divisor = 1000
session.gc_maxlifetime = 1440
```

AWS Scripted   155

```
session.bug_compat_42 = Off
session.bug_compat_warn = Off
session.referer_check =
session.entropy_length = 0
session.entropy_file =
session.cache_limiter = nocache
session.cache_expire = 180
session.use_trans_sid = 0
session.hash_function = 0
session.hash_bits_per_character = 5
url_rewriter.tags =
"a=href,area=href,frame=src,input=src,form=fakeentry"

tidy.clean_output = Off
soap.wsdl_cache_enabled=1
soap.wsdl_cache_dir="/tmp"
soap.wsdl_cache_ttl=86400
```

This is the rsyslog configuration file (note SED***SED items are replaced with real values):

[aws/ami/webphp/rsyslog_template.conf]

```
# rsyslog for webphp

$ModLoad imuxsock # provides support for local system logging (e.g.
via logger command)
$ModLoad imklog   # provides kernel logging support (previously
done by rklogd)
#$ModLoad immark  # provides --MARK-- message capability

$ActionFileDefaultTemplate RSYSLOG_TraditionalFileFormat

authpriv.*
/var/log/secure
mail.*
-/var/log/maillog
cron.*
/var/log/cron
*.emerg                                                          *
uucp,news.crit
/var/log/spooler
local7.*
/var/log/boot.log

# httpd error sends on local4

$WorkDirectory /var/lib/rsyslog # where to place spool files
$ActionQueueFileName fwdRule1 # unique name prefix for spool files
$ActionQueueMaxDiskSpace 1g   # 1gb space limit (use as much as
possible)
$ActionQueueSaveOnShutdown on # save messages to disk on shutdown
$ActionQueueType LinkedList   # run asynchronously
$ActionResumeRetryCount -1    # infinite retries if host is down
local4.* @@SEDadminhostSED:514

# httpd access sends on local6 (with tag)
```

```
$WorkDirectory /var/lib/rsyslog # where to place spool files
$ActionQueueFileName fwdRule2 # unique name prefix for spool files
$ActionQueueMaxDiskSpace 1g   # 1gb space limit (use as much as
possible)
$ActionQueueSaveOnShutdown on # save messages to disk on shutdown
$ActionQueueType LinkedList   # run asynchronously
$ActionResumeRetryCount -1    # infinite retries if host is down
local6.* @@SEDadminhostSED:514

$IncludeConfig /etc/rsyslog.d/*.conf
```

The last file is a package to install the mod_rpaf extension, mod_rpaf-0.6-0.7.x86_64.rpm. ModRpaf allows us to access the real IP address of incoming http requests, rather than the ELB's IP address.

You can find more details on uploading required files to the Webphp Servers and Remote Access in **Chapter 13 - Deploying Assets** and **Chapter 14 - Remote Access**.

Original Files

The configuration files above have been edited and most comments removed for clarity and succinctness. You can find the original unedited files in the aws/ami/webphp/original folder. The locations for these files are as follows:

1. httpd.conf (Apache)

   run: yum -y install httpd (on a new AWS box)

   /etc/httpd/conf/httpd.conf

2. php.ini (Apache)

   run: yum -y install php (on a new AWS box)

   /etc/php.ini

3. monit.conf (Monit)

run: yum -y install monit (on a new AWS box)

/etc/monit.conf

4. rsyslog.conf (Rsyslog)

on a new AWS box

/etc/rsyslog.conf

Chapter 10 - PHP Website

A full, working demonstration website is provided for you in the aws/development/website directory. It demonstrates all the points discussed below in working form.

Development vs Production

Typically, you will have an in-house development platform: a central server with Apache, PHP and MySQL running and developers accessing files via a source control system to build the Application. It is vital to automate the process of transferring from the Development System to the Production one. To demonstrate this, the package includes the aws/development/website directory with sample code. You can change this in aws/master/vars.sh to point to your development directory, or manually copy data when you need to do a deploy.

The full scripts for deployment are in **Chapter 13 - Deploying Assets**, but in essence we tweak the PHP code to tell the website it is now running on an AWS and/or Production environment. We also minify JS and CSS code.

Handling SSL

Because we terminate SSL on the ELB, everything which comes in the the PHP site is plain HTTP. However, we may want to enforce the use of SSL and if someone visits http://www.yourwebsite.com we would probably want to redirect them instead to https://www.yourwebsite.com (the SSL address).

The ELB will send through what the original protocol was in the HTTP_X_FORWARDED_PROTO _SERVER variable. You can accomplish the forwarding with the following PHP Code:

[aws/snippets/snippet_enforcessl.php]

```
if ($_SERVER['HTTP_X_FORWARDED_PROTO']!="https") {
        $redirect= "https://".$_SERVER['HTTP_HOST'].
$_SERVER['REQUEST_URI'];
        header("Location:$redirect");
        exit;
        }
```

Remember the PHP header() function needs to be called before any output is sent to the browser.

Sessions on a Multi-Server System

Sessions on a multi-server system are hardly more complex, but they are a little more expensive. Instead of storing Session Data in files on a web server (which cannot be shared), we need to do a database query every request. To mitigate this cost, we design our system to be as efficient as possible, which involves 2 things:

1. Fetching Session Data from the database is an indexed, fast query
2. We do as much validation as possible before resorting to the database

Bypassing the in-built PHP Session System is a good idea because we have full control. Another bonus is that we don't need to allow write access in our Apache Chroot jail for session storage.

The aws/development/website/phpinclude/sessions.php file contains the main code for session management. These session functions rely on a few global functions, found in the aws/development/website/phpinclude/globalfunctions.php file. See **PHP Source Code** at the end of this Chapter for listings.

One drawback to database-driven sessions is that sessions when a user is not signed in are harder. We need a valid user table record to store session data in. If a user has not signed in, either this record does not exist or we can't identify it. It is actually pretty rare to need sessions before a user has authenticated, but there are some cases, such as a multi-page Sign Up process. You can go two ways on this: either set up a temporary users table and a completely separate temporary sessions system (quite a headache but not impossible); or design your pre-authenticated forms so they don't need sessions. The latter is highly preferable and will lead to better form design in any case. Use AJAX to validate inputs before form submission. If you really need multiple pages for Sign Up, make the first page a username/password entry page, and then sign the user in. Then you can use sessions for subsequent pages.

Session Security

Session Security is perhaps the single biggest issue for PHP security. What it is is this: to recognise a client between requests, PHP sends a cookie (normally called PHPSESSID) which the client then sends back with every request; with this token, which stays the same between requests, the server knows who the client is and maintains a session. Now, say that a client has authenticated (ie signed in). The PHPSESSID cookie is now THE ONLY requirement for full access to that client's account. If a hacker were to get the value of the cookie, they would also have complete access to the client's account. This is because we don't send usernames and passwords with every request - this is done once and then the session state records that the user is signed in, what their user ID is and so on.

This attack is called Session Hijacking. PHP allows you to place the PHPSESSID variable in the URL (although this can be disabled) eg http://www.somewebsite.com/index.php? PHPSESSID=xxx. If you were to follow this link, and a hacker knew it, and then you were to sign in, the hacker would know that with 'xxx' they could impersonate you. You can stop PHPSESSID being recognised in the URL, but it's still pretty easy to construct an HTTP request with a faked cookie.

There is a huge amount of literature on this subject, which we won't go into because we use our own Session System. We make no use of PHP's built in Session Management. The reason is that as we are on a multi-server system, sessions need to be databased anyway, so given we will be interacting with the database, we may as well do it all ourselves.

So, for security, when you start a session for the user we send 2 cookies which encapsulate 2 secure random tokens, the user's ID, the remote IP address and the remote User Agent. We encrypt the cookie contents with AES-256. When we receive the cookies, we unpack all the data, check it against current HTTP values and check against the database.

To protect against stolen cookies, if the IP changes, we disallow access to that session. This means that a hacker trying to use your token from a different IP would fail. Now, it is possible to spoof IP addresses, however, replies to a spoofed IP address are not received (because they are sent to the spoofed ip!). And many routers and firewalls prevent IP Spoofing.

However, if you are not using SSL, you are open to Session Hijacking. If I were connected to the same wireless network as you, I could sniff your packets and, unencrypted, I could get your cookie token and impersonate you. Hence SSL is THE MOST VITAL protection against Session hacks. On a brighter note, the fact that we check IP and User Agent makes it a non-trivial task to perpetrate this attack.

Secure Database Access

This is discussed in **Chapter 11 - MySQL Database**, but in essence it involves using separate MySQL users for separate tasks and parametrised queries.

Screening Inputs

ALL _GET and _POST variables into your PHP application should be whitelist verified. This means you only allow certain characters for any input. Do not use blacklisting (how can you be sure you have listed all the 'bad' characters, especially with UTF-8?). If a user enters characters which are not on your whitelist, do not print those characters. Just say: 'this field may only contain letters, numbers and the following characters !@$*():;+-?'. The reason for this is that an attacker could craft a link to your website with malicious code in the URL. If you don't whitelist the URL variables, you might print out that code to the page and you legitimate users would get malicious code in their browsers!

Here is an example whitelist PHP function (you can find more, including number/integer verification and also ajax versions, in /aws/development/website/phpinclude/globalfunctions.php):

[aws/snippets/snippet_whitelist.php]

```
// checks a string only contains chars from the array within
// returns original string if legal, or "Illegal Input" if not
function check_legal_chars($ns) {
        $legal=array("q", "w", "e", "r", "t", "y", "u", "i", "o",
"p", "a", "s", "d", "f", "g", "h", "j", "k", "l", "z", "x", "c",
"v", "b", "n", "m",
                        "Q", "W", "E", "R", "T", "Y", "U", "I",
"O", "P", "A", "S", "D", "F", "G", "H", "J", "K", "L", "Z", "X",
"C", "V", "B", "N", "M",
                        " ", "1", "2", "3", "4", "5", "6", "7",
"8", "9", "0",
                        "!", "@", "$", "*", "(", ")", ":", ";",
"+", "-", "?" );
        $s=$ns;
        for ($i=0; $i<count($legal); $i++)
                $s=str_replace($legal[$i], "", $s);
        if ($s=="")
                return $ns;
        return "Illegal Input";
        }
```

Another good tip is to use the PHP isset() function as much as possible. So instead of passing a message into a page (which could be corrupted and used for Script Injection or Cross Site Scripting), pass a variable which equals one, then test if it is set and if it is, print the appropriate message. Even if someone alters an URL using this method, what's the worst that can happen? They see a safe message, and that's about it. A good example of this is in the main, secure Account page of the Public Website, shown after Sign Up and Sign In:

[aws/snippets/snippet_issetexample.php]

```php
if (isset($_GET['signup']))
        echo "<h2>Thankyou You Signed Up Successfully</h2>";
else if (isset($_GET['signin']))
        echo "<h2>Signed In Successfully</h2>";
else
        echo "<h2>Your Account</h2>";
```

Hashing Passwords

It is amazing that many people do not do this: remember the last time you heard of so-and-so Big Corporation losing 63 million passwords? This is especially true when you consider that the code for hashing is really pretty easy, just a few lines.

When storing a password, store a hash instead:

[aws/snippets/snippet_passwordhash.php]

```php
// extract from aws/development/website/htdocs/public/signup2.php

// hash password
// create a random salt
$salt = "$2y$10$".bin2hex(openssl_random_pseudo_bytes(22));
// Hash the password with the salt
$hash = crypt($password, $salt);
// now insert $hash in the database, not $password
```

When checking a password, check the hash instead:

[aws/snippets/snippet_passwordcheck.php]

```php
// extract from aws/development/website/htdocs/public/signin2.php

// check hash
$passwordok=0;
if (crypt($password, $row['password']) === $row['password'])
        $passwordok=1;
if ($passwordok==0) {
        // error, password wrong
        header("Location: /public/signin.php?err=1");
        exit;
        }
```

The above examples use pretty simple hashing. For most applications this will be a sufficient deterrent to any hacker (if they get a backup of your database or similar). However, password hashing is a complex business and if you want absolute security you should check out the excellent article by Defuse Security at **https://crackstation.net/hashing-security.htm** which provides full in-depth discussion of the issues and also full PHP source code.

Supplying Passwords Securely

The PHP Application will need access to various passwords and keys to function properly. Now, we could just put these into a PHP file. However, PHP files on the server have permissions to allow the apache user access and we can be more secure by putting these sensitive values in a root-accessible only file, such as the httpd.conf file. Look at it this way: if a hacker somehow manages to edit your PHP code and run it, all bets are off - it doesn't matter where you put passwords and keys. But if they only manage to download your PHP code, this technique will protect your sensitive data because it is stored *outside* the Apache Chroot and therefore inaccessible to Apache child processes.

Here is how we specify database passwords (or other keys) in httpd.conf (SED***SED are replaced):

```
SetEnv DBPASS_webphprw SEDdbpass_webphprwSED
```

Then from PHP we can use the following to retrieve the value from the httpd.conf file:

```
$dbpass=$_SERVER['DBPASS_webphprw'];
```

JS/CSS Minification

On a Production System, you need minified JavaScript and CSS, not only for the reduced download size, but also because the obfuscation is a good security practice. We use the YUI Compressor for this. See **Chapter 13 - Deploying Assets** for more information.

If you are using JQuery (highly likely) and associated Javacript libraries, it is recommended that you use the minified versions of these rather than minify them yourself - they take a while to minify.

Google Recaptcha

We use this excellent free service to stop automatons from creating accounts. The integration is slightly complex, but a full example is provided in the demo web site.

One recent problem: Google stopped issuing globally valid keys. This is a bit of a headache but you can get round it for the 3 environments we deal with as follows:

In-House Development

Set the domain name to the IP address of your Development Server, or the name you use to access it. The keys go into the aws/development/website/phpinclude/globalvariables.php file.

AWS Development Environment

You will probably access the test site from either your ELB name or your real domain name, so set the domain to "yourdomain.com,amazonaws.com". The keys go into the aws/credentials/recaptcha.sh file.

AWS Production Environment

You will access the test site from your real domain name, so set the domain to "yourdomain.com". The keys go into the aws/credentials/recaptcha.sh file.

PHP Source Code

A simple PHP website is provided which demonstrates Session Management, Sign Up and Sign In functionality, a secure section (/account/) and an overall page structure. Some testing pages for email and curl are also provided. JQuery is used for AJAX calls.

We use the separate folder 'phpinclude' for PHP include files which we don't want to be callable directly from the web. Pages are presented in directory listing order.

A secure page which can only be accessed if signed in. Users are brought here after Sign Up or Sign In, with a message. Security is enforce in 'secure.php' in the same folder.

[aws/development/website/htdocs/account/index.php]

```php
<?php include '../../phpinclude/init.php';?>
<?php include 'secure.php';?>
<?php include '../../phpinclude/begin.php';?>

<?php
        if (isset($_GET['signup']))
                echo "<h2>Thankyou You Signed Up
Successfully</h2>";
        else if (isset($_GET['signin']))
                echo "<h2>Signed In Successfully</h2>";
        else
                echo "<h2>Your Account</h2>";
?>

This page is secure and only accessible if Signed In.

<br><br><br><br><br><br><br><br>

<?php include '../../phpinclude/end.php';?>
```

This file enforces security by checking if a valid session exists. You could make additional checks here, depending on your requirements. This file can be in the webroot as even if it is called directly from the Internet, it doesn't do anything (except a redirect).

[aws/development/website/htdocs/account/secure.php]

```php
<?php
        if (!isset($S['userID'])) {
```

```
        header('Location: ../public/signin.php');
        exit;
        }
    if ($S['userID']==0) {
        header('Location: ../public/signin.php');
        exit;
        }
?>
```

The heartbeat file needed by ELB.

[aws/development/website/htdocs/elb.htm]

```
ok
```

Redirects to the index.php in /public/. We need to include init.php from the phpinclude folder to check SSL and redirect to an SSL version if required.

[aws/development/website/htdocs/index.php]

```
<?php
        include "../phpinclude/init.php";
        header("Location: /public/");
?>
```

Javascript code to handle AJAX and validation on the Sign Up page (signup.php). This code will be minified for production. It is included in /phpinclude/begin.php, and although this seems rather wasteful (ie that it is included on every page, even when not needed), remember that if you have several Javascript files, they will be minified and collated into one file. Hence the need to include that one file on every page. Once downloaded, it will be cached anyway, so it is not a huge resource drain.

[aws/development/website/htdocs/jscss/dev/js/site/signup.js]

```
function do_check_signup(is_submit) {
        $('#msg').html('Working...');
        $.ajax({
                type: 'POST',
                url: 'checkusername.php',
                data: { s: is_submit, u: $('#usernamesu').val() },
                success: function(ndata) {
                        data=ndata.trim();
                        if (data=='AVAIL') {
                                if (is_submit==0)
```

```
                                                        $('#msg').html('This
username is available');
                                        else
                                                $('#msg').html('');
                                }
                        else if (data=='TAKEN')
                                $('#msg').html('This username is
not available');
                        else if (data=='EMPTY')
                                $('#msg').html('Username is
empty');
                        else if (data=='LONG')
                                $('#msg').html('Username is too
long (max 16 chars)');
                        else if (data=='ILL')
                                $('#msg').html('Illegal
characters');
                        else if (data=='SUB') {
                                $('#msg').html('This username is
available');
                                do_check_rc();
                                }
                        else
                                $('#msg').html('Sorry, please try
again');
                        },
                error: function(ndata) {
                        $('#msg').html('Sorry, please try again');
                        }
                });
        }

function do_check_rc() {
        $('#msgrc').html('Working...');
        var rcc=$.base64.encode(Recaptcha.get_challenge());
        var rcr=$.base64.encode(Recaptcha.get_response());
        $.ajax({
                type: 'POST',
                url: 'checkrecaptcha.php',
                data: { recaptcha_challenge_field: rcc,
recaptcha_response_field: rcr },
                success: function(ndata) {
                        data=ndata.trim();
                        if (data=='ERR')
                                $('#msgrc').html('The reCAPTCHA was
wrong');
                        else {
                                $('#msgrc').html('reCAPTCHA
confirmed');
                                $('#rcc').val(rcc);
                                $('#rcr').val(rcr);
                                $('#rch').val(data);
                                $('#signupform').submit();
                                }
                        },
                error: function(ndata) {
                        $('#msgrc').html('The reCAPTCHA was
wrong');
                        }
                });
```

AWS Scripted   169

```
        }
function check_submit() {
        $('#msg1').html('');
        $('#msg2').html('');
        $('#msg3').html('');
        $('#msg4').html('');
        $('#msgrc').html('');
        p=$('#passwordsu').val();
        c=$('#passwordsu2').val();
        e=$('#emailsu').val();
        c2=$('#emailsu2').val();
        t=($('#terms').is(":checked"))?1:0;
        if (e=='')
                $('#msg3').html('Email cannot be blank');
        else if (!(e==c2)) {
                $('#msg3').html('Emails do not match');
                }
        else if (p=='')
                $('#msg2').html('Password cannot be blank');
        else if (p.length<6)
                $('#msg2').html('Password must be at least 6
characters');
        else if (!(p==c))
                $('#msg2').html('Passwords do not match');
        else if (!(t==1))
                $('#msg4').html('You must accept our Terms and
Conditions');
        else
                do_check_signup(1);
        }
```

The Google Recaptcha is checked via an AJAX call to this file, but then we need to tell our main php script (signup2.php) that the Recaptcha succeeded. Obviously, this can't just be a simple variable or it could be imitated by a script. So, we hash the client's IP Address and the Recaptcha data with some randomish numbers so the ensuing PHP page signup2.php can verify this information crytographically. As hashes are irreversible, a hacker cannot break this system.

[aws/development/website/htdocs/public/checkrecaptcha.php]

```php
<?php include '../../phpinclude/init.php'; ?>

<?php
        // called when checking recaptcha for signin
        $res=checkrecaptcha($_SERVER["REMOTE_ADDR"],
base64_decode($_POST["recaptcha_challenge_field"]),
base64_decode($_POST["recaptcha_response_field"]));
        if ($res=="") {
                $salt =
"$2y$10$".bin2hex(openssl_random_pseudo_bytes(22));
                $hash = crypt($_SERVER["REMOTE_ADDR"]."836429".
```

```
$_POST["recaptcha_challenge_field"]."7364528".
$_POST["recaptcha_response_field"], $salt);
            echo base64_encode($hash);
            exit;
            }
     echo "ERR";
?>
```

A file called via AJAX to determine if a username is valid and available. This can't be done in Javascript as we need access to the database.

[aws/development/website/htdocs/public/checkusername.php]

```
<?php include '../../phpinclude/init.php'; ?>

<?php

     // called via AJAX when checking new username available on
web

     $submit=0;
     if (isset($_POST['s'])) {
            if ($_POST['s']=="1")
                    $submit=1;
            }

     if (!isset($_POST['u'])) {
            echo "ERR";
            exit;
            }

     $username=$_POST['u'];
     if (strlen($username)==0) {
            echo "EMPTY";
            exit;
            }

     if (strlen($username)>16) {
            echo "LONG";
            exit;
            }

     $illegal=check_legal_chars($username);
     if ($illegal=="Illegal Input") {
            echo ("ILL");
            exit;
            }

     // check any reserved words
     if (in_array(strtolower($username),
$global_reserved_usernames)) {
            echo "TAKEN";
            exit;
            }
```

```
        // username exists?
        dbconnect(0);
        $result=doSQL("select * from users where username=?;",
$username) or die("ERR");
        if (is_array($result))
                // exists
                echo "TAKEN";
        else {
                // available
                if ($submit==1)
                        echo "SUB";
                else
                        echo "AVAIL";
                }
?>
```

Curl from a chroot is problematic. This page provides a few tests to check it is working. SSL Certificate Validation is important because it prevents Man-in-the-Middle attacks. Consider: a hacker intercepts your initial SSL request (which asks for an encryption key); the hacker sends you a fake key but passes your request on to the real server and gets the real key as well; then the hacker sits in the middle of your session receiving data from you encrypted with the fake key, decrypts it, re-encrypts it with the real key and passes it to the real server; and similarly for replies sent from the real server back to you. This dismisses the fallacy that Man-in-the-Middle attacks are difficult because you need to spoof an entire server or web site. Well, they are still difficult because doing the above is by no means trivial! But, with SSL Certificate Validation, this attack fails, because the fake key that is sent to you at the beginning does not pass the cryptographic tests which ensure that it is a valid key from a Certified Authority.

[aws/development/website/htdocs/public/curl.php]

```
<?php include '../../phpinclude/init.php';?>
<?php include '../../phpinclude/begin.php';?>

<div class="titletext">Test Curl</div>

<br><br>

<?php

// do a curl GET operation
// don't do ssl verification
function docurlgetnv($nrequest) {
        echo "do curl GET NOVERIFY(".$nrequest.")<br>";
        $curlOptions = array (
```

```php
                    CURLOPT_URL => $nrequest,
                    CURLOPT_VERBOSE => 1,
                    CURLOPT_RETURNTRANSFER => 1,
                    CURLOPT_SSL_VERIFYPEER => FALSE
                    );
        $ch = curl_init();
        curl_setopt_array($ch, $curlOptions);
        $response = curl_exec($ch);
        $err=curl_errno($ch);
        if ($err) {
                $errors = curl_error($ch);
                curl_close($ch);
                echo "error ".$err."<br>";
                echo $errors."<br><br>";
                }
        else  {
                curl_close($ch);
                echo "success [ ".$response." ]<br><br>";
                }
        }

// do a curl GET operation
// do ssl verification
function docurlgetv($nrequest) {
        echo "do curl GET VERIFY(".$nrequest.")<br>";
        $curlOptions = array (
                CURLOPT_URL => $nrequest,
                CURLOPT_VERBOSE => 1,
                CURLOPT_RETURNTRANSFER => 1,
                CURLOPT_SSL_VERIFYPEER => TRUE,
                CURLOPT_SSL_VERIFYHOST => 2
                );
        $ch = curl_init();
        curl_setopt_array($ch, $curlOptions);
        $response = curl_exec($ch);
        $err=curl_errno($ch);
        if ($err) {
                $errors = curl_error($ch);
                curl_close($ch);
                echo "error ".$err."<br>";
                echo $errors."<br><br>";
                }
        else  {
                curl_close($ch);
                echo "success [ ".$response." ]<br><br>";
                }
        }

// test some addresses
// should return 302 Document has moved
// if you get the dreaded 77 error, something is wrong
docurlgetnv("http://www.google.com");
docurlgetnv("https://www.google.com");
docurlgetv("https://www.google.com");

?>

<?php include '../../phpinclude/end.php';?>
```

A page to test email.

[aws/development/website/htdocs/public/email.php]

```php
<?php include '../../phpinclude/init.php';?>
<?php include '../../phpinclude/begin.php';?>

<div class="titletext">Test Email</div>

<?php if (!isset($S['userID'])) { ?>
        You must be Signed In to Test Email<br><br>
<?php } ?>

<form action="email2.php" method="get">

        Sending from <?php echo $global_sendemailfrom;?>

        <br><br>

        To:
        <select name="predef">
                <option
value="success@simulator.amazonses.com">success@simulator.amazonses
.com
                <option
value="bounce@simulator.amazonses.com">bounce@simulator.amazonses.c
om
                <option
value="complaint@simulator.amazonses.com">complaint@simulator.amazo
nses.com
                <option
value="suppressionlist@simulator.amazonses.com">suppressionlist@sim
ulator.amazonses.com
        </select>

        <br><br>

        or: <input type="text" name="dyn" size="50"><br>
        [must be verified in SES if SES Production Access is not
enabled]

        <br><br>

        <input type="Submit" value="Send">

</form>

<br><br>

<?php include '../../phpinclude/end.php';?>
```

A page which processes the email test request from email.php above.

[aws/development/website/htdocs/public/email2.php]

```php
<?php include '../../phpinclude/init.php';?>
<?php include '../../phpinclude/begin.php';?>

<div class="titletext">Test Email</div>

<h2>Sending Email...</h2>

<?php

        // send test email
        $to=$_GET['predef'];
        if (isset($_GET['dyn'])) {
                if (!($_GET['dyn']==""))
                        $to=$_GET['dyn'];
        }
        sendemail($S['userID'], $to, "Test Email", "Testing
123...");
?>

Sent to <?php echo $to;?>

<br><br>

Check the sendemails database table.

<br><br>

<?php include '../../phpinclude/end.php';?>
```

The general error page. Note how we check any message printed for illegal characters. This page is referenced in the configuration file aws/ami/webphp/httpd_template.conf via the ErrorDocument directives.

[aws/development/website/htdocs/public/error.php]

```php
<?php include '../../phpinclude/init.php';?>
<?php include '../../phpinclude/begin.php';?>

<?php
        $message="unspecified";
        if (isset($_GET['err']))

$message=check_legal_chars(urldecode($_GET['err']));
?>

<div class="titletext">An error occurred: <?php echo $message;?
></div>

<br><br><br><br><br><br><br><br><br><br><br><br>

<?php include '../../phpinclude/end.php';?>
```

A page to indicate an expired session.

[aws/development/website/htdocs/public/expired.php]

```php
<?php include '../../phpinclude/init.php';?>
<?php include '../../phpinclude/begin.php';?>

<div class="titletext">Your Session Has Expired or Was
Transferred</div>

<br><br><br><br><br><br><br>

<div align="center">

To protect your security, your session expires after a period of
inactivity.

<br><br>

In addition, we only allow you to be Signed In once for any
account.

<br><br>

So, if you Signed In with this account elsewhere, this session
would have been terminated.

</div>

<br><br><br><br><br><br><br>

<br><br>

<?php include '../../phpinclude/end.php';?>
```

The main, publicly-accessible Home Page

[aws/development/website/htdocs/public/index.php]

```php
<?php include '../../phpinclude/init.php';?>
<?php include '../../phpinclude/begin.php';?>

<div class="titletext">Home</div>

<br><br>

This is the Home Page

<br><br>

<a href="curl.php">Test Curl</a>

<br><br>

<a href="email.php">Test Email</a>

<br><br><br><br><br><br>
```

```php
<?php include '../../phpinclude/end.php';?>
```

The Sign In form.

[aws/development/website/htdocs/public/signin.php]

```php
<?php include '../../phpinclude/init.php';?>
<?php include '../../phpinclude/begin.php';?>

<?php
        if (!isset($S)) { ?>

        <form id="signinform" action="signin2.php" method="post"
enctype="application/x-www-form-urlencoded">
                <div class="titletext">Sign In to your
account</div>
                <table cellpadding="5">
                        <?php if (isset($_GET['err'])) { ?>
                                <tr><td colspan="2"
align="center"><div class="errmessage">Email/Password not
recognised</div></td></tr>
                        <?php } ?>
                        <tr>
                                <td><b>Email:</b></td>
                                <td><input value="" type="text"
name="email"></td>
                        </tr>
                        <tr>
                                <td><b>Password:</b></td>
                                <td><input value="" type="password"
name="password" onkeydown="if (event.keyCode == 13)
submit();"></td>
                        </tr>
                        <tr>
                                <td> </td>
                                <td><br><input value="SIGN IN"
type="submit"></td>
                        </tr>
                </table>

        </form>

<?php } else { ?>

        <div class="titletext">Signed In as <?php echo
$S['email'];?></div>
        <input value="SIGN OUT" type="button"
onclick="location.href='/public/signout.php';">

<?php } ?>

<br><br>

<?php include '../../phpinclude/end.php';?>
```

The page that processes the Sign In request. Validates inputs, checks the email address exists in the database, than compares password hashes and, if successful, creates a session.

[aws/development/website/htdocs/public/signin2.php]

```php
<?php
        require '../../phpinclude/init.php';

        // get, check and clean inputs
        $email=check_text_input($_POST['email'], 1, 255, "Email",
"/public/signin.php?err");
        $password=check_text_input($_POST['password'], 1, 32,
"Password", "/public/signin.php?err");

        dbconnect(0);

        // email exists?
        $result=doSQL("select userID, password from users where
email=?;", $email) or die("ERR");
        if (!is_array($result)) {
                // error, email inexistent
                header("Location: /public/signin.php?err=1");
                exit;
                }
        // get password
        $row=$result[0];

        // check hash
        $passwordok=0;
        if (crypt($password, $row['password']) ===
$row['password'])
                $passwordok=1;

        if ($passwordok==0) {
                // error, password wrong
                header("Location: /public/signin.php?err=1");
                exit;
                }

        // sign in
        sessionstart($row['userID']);
        header("Location: /account/index.php?signin=1");

?>
```

Called on Sign Out, destroys the session.

[aws/development/website/htdocs/public/signout.php]

```php
<?php include '../../phpinclude/init.php';?>

<?php
        // cancel session
        if (isset($S['userID']))
                $S=sessionend($S['userID']);
```

AWS Scripted   178

```
?>

<?php include '../../phpinclude/begin.php';?>

<div class="titletext">Signed Out</div>

<?php include '../../phpinclude/end.php';?>
```

The Sign Up page. Some complex AJAX (found in signup.js) allows this form not to use Session Variables (unavailable until authenticated). Google Recaptcha integration is particularly tricky...

[aws/development/website/htdocs/public/signup.php]

```
<?php include '../../phpinclude/init.php';?>
<?php include '../../phpinclude/begin.php';?>

<?php
        // jump if already signed in
        if (isset($S)) {
                echo
"<script>location.href='/account/profile.php';</script>";
                exit;
                }
?>

<script type="text/javascript"
src="https://www.google.com/recaptcha/api/js/recaptcha_ajax.js"></s
cript>

<?php
        $message1=" ";
        if (isset($_GET['msg1']))
                $message1=check_legal_chars($_GET['msg1']);
        $message2=" ";
        if (isset($_GET['msg2']))
                $message2=check_legal_chars($_GET['msg2']);
        $message3=" ";
        if (isset($_GET['msg3']))
                $message3=check_legal_chars($_GET['msg3']);
        $messagerc=" ";
        if (isset($_GET['msgrc']))
                $messagerc=check_legal_chars($_GET['msgrc']);
?>

<div class="titletext">Sign Up for an Account</div>

<table width="500">
<form name="signupform" id="signupform" action="signup2.php"
method="post" enctype="application/x-www-form-urlencoded">
        <tr><td colspan='3'> </td></tr>
        <tr>
                <td align="right"><b>Email:</b></td>
                <td align="left" valign="middle"><input type="Text"
name="emailsu" id="emailsu" value="" maxlength="255" onchange="$
```

```
('#msg3').html('');"></td>
                <td align="left"> </td>
        </tr>
        <tr>
                <td align="right"><b>Confirm:</b></td>
                <td align="left" valign="middle"><input type="Text"
name="emailsu2" id="emailsu2" value="" maxlength="255" onchange="$
('#msg3').html('');"></td>
                <td></td>
        </tr>
        <tr><td> </td><td colspan='2'><div id="msg3"
class="errmessage"><?php echo $message3;?></div></td></tr>
        <tr>
                <td align="right"><b>Password:</b></td>
                <td align="left"><input type="Password"
name="passwordsu" id="passwordsu" maxlength="32" onchange="$
('#msg2').html('');"></td>
                <td align="left">[at least 6 characters]</td>
        </tr>
        <tr>
                <td align="right"><b>Confirm:</b></td>
                <td colspan="2" align="left"><input type="Password"
name="passwordsu2" id="passwordsu2" maxlength="32" onchange="$
('#msg2').html('');"></td>
        </tr>
        <tr><td> </td><td colspan='2'><div id="msg2"
class="errmessage"><?php echo $message2;?></div></td></tr>
        <tr>
                <td align="right"><b>Username:</b></td>
                <td align="left" valign="middle"><input type="Text"
name="usernamesu" id="usernamesu" value="" maxlength="16"
onchange="$('#msg').html('');"></td>
                <td>
                        <input type="button" name="button_su1"
value="CHECK" onclick="do_check_signup(0);">
                </td>
        </tr>
        <tr><td> </td><td colspan='2'><div id="msg"
class="errmessage"><?php echo $message1;?></div></td></tr>

        <tr>
                <td align="right"><b>Terms:</b></td>
                <td colspan='2' align="left"><input type="checkbox"
id="terms" name="terms" value="1"> I accept the <a
href="/public/terms.php" target="external">Terms and
Conditions</a></td>
        </tr>
        <tr><td> </td><td colspan='2'><div id="msg4"
class="errmessage"> </div></td></tr>

        <tr><td align="right"
valign="top"><b>reCAPTCHA:</b></td><td colspan='2'>
                <div id="recaptchadiv"></div>
                <input type="hidden" name="rcc" id="rcc" value="">
                <input type="hidden" name="rcr" id="rcr" value="">
                <input type="hidden" name="rch" id="rch" value="">
        </td></tr>
        <tr><td> </td><td colspan='2'><div id="msgrc"
class="errmessage"><?php echo $messagerc;?></div></td></tr>
        <tr>
```

```
              <td colspan='3' align="center"><br><input
type="button" value="SIGN UP NOW" onclick="check_submit();"></td>
        </tr>

</form>
</table>

<br><br>

<script type="text/javascript">
        Recaptcha.create("<?php echo $global_recaptcha_publickey;?
>", "recaptchadiv", {theme: "white", callback:
Recaptcha.focus_response_field});
</script>

<?php include '../../phpinclude/end.php';?>
```

This page processes the Sign Up request. Inputs are validated; then we check email and username are available in the database; then we check the Recaptcha hash generated by the actual Recaptcha AJAX call (generated in phpinclude/checkrecaptcha.php); then we create the password hash, insert everything into the database and sign the user in by creating a session. Lastly, we jump to the secure Account homepage.

[aws/development/website/htdocs/public/signup2.php]

```
<?php include '../../phpinclude/init.php'; ?>

<?php
        if (isset($S)) {
                echo "<script>location.href='/account/profile.php?
signin=1';</script>";
                exit;
                }
?>

<?php
        // called for new sign in

        $erraddr1='signup.php?msg1';
        $erraddr2='signup.php?msg2';
        $erraddr3='signup.php?msg3';
        $erraddrrc='signup.php?msgrc';

        // check and clean inputs
        $username=check_text_input($_POST['usernamesu'], 1, 16,
'Username', $erraddr1);
        $password=check_text_input($_POST['passwordsu'], 6, 32,
'First Password', $erraddr2);
        $password2=check_text_input($_POST['passwordsu2'], 6, 32,
'Confirm Password', $erraddr2);
        $email=check_text_input($_POST['emailsu'], 1, 255, 'First
Email', $erraddr3);
```

```
                $email2=check_text_input($_POST['emailsu2'], 1, 255,
'Confirm Email', $erraddr3);

            if (!(check_legal_chars($username)==$username))
                    do_err($erraddr1, 'Illegal characters in
Username');
            if (!($password==$password2))
                    do_err($erraddr2, 'Passwords do not match');
            if (!($email==$email2))
                    do_err($erraddr3, 'Emails do not match');

            dbconnect(0);

            // check email still available
            $result=doSQL("select * from users where email=?;", $email)
or do_err($erraddr3, "Database Error");
            if (is_array($result))
                    // no, exists, quit
                    do_err($erraddr3, "Email in use");

            // check username still available
            $result=doSQL("select * from users where username=?;",
$username) or do_err($erraddr1, "Database Error");
            if (is_array($result))
                    // no, exists, quit
                    do_err($erraddr1, "Username in use");

            // check recaptcha
            $rcc=$_POST["rcc"];
            $rcr=$_POST["rcr"];
            $rch=base64_decode($_POST["rch"]);
            $rcstr=$_SERVER["REMOTE_ADDR"]."836429".$rcc."7364528".
$rcr;
            if (!(crypt($rcstr, $rch) === $rch))
                    do_err($erraddrrc, "The reCAPTCHA was wrong ".
$rcerr);

            // hash password
            // create a random salt
            $salt = "$2y$10$".bin2hex(openssl_random_pseudo_bytes(22));

            // Hash the password with the salt
            $hash = crypt($password, $salt);

            // insert user
            $result=doSQL("insert into users (username, password,
email) values (?, ?, ?);", $username, $hash, $email) or
do_err($erraddr3, "Database Error");
            $nid=$db->insert_id;

            // signin
            sessionstart($nid);

            // jump
            header('Location: ../account/index.php?signup=1');

    ?>
```

An example publicly-accessible page (here for Terms and

Conditions).

[aws/development/website/htdocs/public/terms.php]

```php
<?php require '../../phpinclude/init.php';?>
<?php require '../../phpinclude/begin.php';?>

<div class="titletext">Terms and Conditions</div>

<table width="600" cellpadding="5" cellspacing="0" border="0">
        <tr>
                <td align="justify">

<b>Terms of Website Use</b><br><br>

Please read these terms of use carefully before you start to use
the site. By using our site, you indicate that you accept these
terms of use and that you agree to abide by them. If you do not
agree to these terms of use, please refrain from using our
site.<br><br>

etc...<br><br>

Thank you for visiting our site.<br><br>

                </td>
        </tr>
</table>

<br><br>

<?php require '../../phpinclude/end.php';?>
```

The page called by AWS SNS to subscribe and notify of events for email bounces.

[aws/development/website/htdocs/sns/bounce.php]

```php
<?php

        // called by aws sns with json payload for subscribe sns or
bounced email
        // can't be called on the dev environment

        if($_SERVER['REQUEST_METHOD'] != 'POST')
                exit;

        $post = file_get_contents('php://input');

        require_once('../../phpinclude/snsverify.php');
        if(!verify_sns($post, $_SERVER['AWS_DEPLOYREGION'],
$_SERVER['AWS_ACCOUNT'], array('EmailBounce')))
                exit;
```

```php
            $msg = json_decode($post, true);

        if ($msg['Type'] == 'SubscriptionConfirmation') {
                // need to visit SubscribeURL
                $surl=$msg['SubscribeURL'];
                $curlOptions = array (
                        CURLOPT_URL => $surl,
                        CURLOPT_VERBOSE => 1,
                        CURLOPT_RETURNTRANSFER => 1,
                        CURLOPT_SSL_VERIFYPEER => TRUE,
                        CURLOPT_SSL_VERIFYHOST => 2
                        );
                $ch = curl_init();
                curl_setopt_array($ch, $curlOptions);
                $response = curl_exec($ch);
                if (curl_errno($ch)) {
                        $errors = curl_error($ch);
                        curl_close($ch);
                        echo $errors;
                        }
                else  {
                        curl_close($ch);
                        echo $response;
                        }
                exit;
                }

        elseif ($msg['Type'] == 'Notification') {
                // init db
                $global_is_dev="0";
                include '../../phpinclude/db.php';
                // check if resend and data already stored
                dbconnect(0);
                $messageid=$msg['MessageId'];
                $sql=doSQL("select count(*) as tot from
snsnotifications where messageid=?", $messageid) or die ("error1");
                $tot=0;
                if (!is_array($sql))
                        $tot=0;
                else {
                        $tot=$sql[0]['tot'];
                        $tot=($tot=="")?0:$tot;
                        }
                if ($tot>0)
                        exit;
                // new message
                $subject="";
                if (isset($msg['Subject']))
                        $subject=$msg['Subject'];
                $message="";
                if (isset($msg['Message']))
                        $message=$msg['Message'];

                $result = json_decode($message, true);
                if ($result['notificationType']=="Bounce") {
                        if ($result['bounce']
['bounceType']=="Permanent") {
                                $emailaddr=$result['bounce']
['bouncedRecipients'][0]['emailAddress'];
                                doSQL("insert into snsnotifications
```

```
(messageid, subject, message, email) values (?, ?, ?, ?);",
$messageid, $subject, $message, $emailaddr) or die ("error2");
                              $nid=$db->insert_id;
                              doSQL("update users set
emailbounce=? where email=?;", $nid, $emailaddr) or die ("error3");
                              exit;
                              }
                    }

            // if we get here nothing has been inserted to
snsnotifications, insert for posterity
            doSQL("insert into snsnotifications (messageid,
subject, message, email) values (?, ?, ?, ?);", $messageid,
$subject, $message, "") or die ("error4");

            }
?>
```

The page called by AWS SNS to subscribe and notify of events for email complaints (ie 'Marked as Spam').

[aws/development/website/htdocs/sns/complaint.php]

```php
<?php

        // called by aws sns with json payload for subscribe sns or
complaint email
        // can't be called on the dev environment

        if($_SERVER['REQUEST_METHOD'] != 'POST')
                exit;

        $post = file_get_contents('php://input');

        require_once('../../phpinclude/snsverify.php');
        if(!verify_sns($post, $_SERVER['AWS_DEPLOYREGION'],
$_SERVER['AWS_ACCOUNT'], array('EmailComplaint')))
                exit;

        $msg = json_decode($post, true);

        if ($msg['Type'] == 'SubscriptionConfirmation') {
                // need to visit SubscribeURL
                $surl=$msg['SubscribeURL'];
                $curlOptions = array (
                        CURLOPT_URL => $surl,
                        CURLOPT_VERBOSE => 1,
                        CURLOPT_RETURNTRANSFER => 1,
                        CURLOPT_SSL_VERIFYPEER => TRUE,
                        CURLOPT_SSL_VERIFYHOST => 2
                        );
                $ch = curl_init();
                curl_setopt_array($ch, $curlOptions);
                $response = curl_exec($ch);
                if (curl_errno($ch)) {
                        $errors = curl_error($ch);
                        curl_close($ch);
```

```php
                echo $errors;
                }
        else    {
                curl_close($ch);
                echo $response;
                }
        exit;
        }

    elseif ($msg['Type'] == 'Notification') {
        // init db
        $global_is_dev="0";
        include '../../phpinclude/db.php';
        // check if resend and data already stored
        dbconnect(0);
        $messageid=$msg['MessageId'];
        $sql=doSQL("select count(*) as tot from
snsnotifications where messageid=?", $messageid) or die ("error1");
        $tot=0;
        if (!is_array($sql))
                $tot=0;
        else    {
                $tot=$sql[0]['tot'];
                $tot=($tot=="")?0:$tot;
                }
        if ($tot>0)
                exit;
        // new message
        $subject="";
        if (isset($msg['Subject']))
                $subject=$msg['Subject'];
        $message="";
        if (isset($msg['Message']))
                $message=$msg['Message'];

        $result = json_decode($message, true);
        if ($result['notificationType']=="Complaint") {
                $emailaddr=$result['complaint']
['complainedRecipients'][0]['emailAddress'];
                doSQL("insert into snsnotifications
(messageid, subject, message, email) values (?, ?, ?, ?);",
$messageid, $subject, $message, $emailaddr) or die ("error2");
                $nid=$db->insert_id;
                doSQL("update users set emailcomplaint=?
where email=?;", $nid, $emailaddr) or die ("error3");
                exit;
                }

        // if we get here nothing has been inserted to
snsnotifications, insert for posterity
        doSQL("insert into snsnotifications (messageid,
subject, message, email) values (?, ?, ?, ?);", $messageid,
$subject, $message, "") or die ("error4");

        }
?>
```

The website header page included on all displayed pages. Includes conditional code to use development or minified Javascript and conditional code to display a different nav bar for public or authenticated users. See phpinclude/end.php for the footer.

[aws/development/website/phpinclude/begin.php]

```html
<!DOCTYPE HTML>

<html>
<head>
        <meta charset="utf-8">
        <title>Secure PHP Site Demo</title>
        <meta name="description" content="Secure PHP Site Demo" />
        <meta name="keywords" content="Secure PHP Site Demo" />
        <meta name="viewport" content="width=device-height" />
        <link rel="shortcut icon" href="/favicon.ico">

        <?php if ($global_minifyjscss==0) { ?>

                <link rel="stylesheet" type="text/css"
href="/jscss/dev/css/style.css" />

                <script type="text/javascript"
src="/jscss/dev/js/jq/jquery.js"></script>
                <script type="text/javascript"
src="/jscss/dev/js/jq/jquery.base64.min.js"></script>
                <script type="text/javascript"
src="/jscss/dev/js/site/signup.js"></script>

        <?php } else { ?>

                <link rel="stylesheet" type="text/css"
href="/jscss/prod/style.css" />

                <script type="text/javascript"
src="/jscss/prod/jquery.min.js"></script>
                <script type="text/javascript"
src="/jscss/prod/general.min.js"></script>

        <?php } ?>

</head>
<body>

<!--- If using Google Analytics, paste code here --->

<div align="center"><br>

<?php if (!isset($S['email'])) { ?>

        <map name="navbar">
                <area shape="rect" coords="140,0,250,40"
href="/public/" alt="Home">
                <area shape="rect" coords="251,0,380,40"
href="/public/signin.php" alt="Sign In">
                <area shape="rect" coords="381,0,500,40"
href="/public/signup.php" alt="Sign Up">
```

```
        </map>
        <img src="/img/navbar.png" height="40" width="640"
border="0" usemap="#navbar"/>

<?php } else { ?>

        <map name="navbar2">
                <area shape="rect" coords="140,0,250,40"
href="/public/" alt="Home">
                <area shape="rect" coords="251,0,380,40"
href="/account/" alt="Account">
                <area shape="rect" coords="381,0,500,40"
href="/public/signout.php" alt="Sign Out">
        </map>
        <img src="/img/navbar2.png" height="40" width="640"
border="0" usemap="#navbar2"/>

<?php } ?>

<br><br>
```

Provides the code to connect to a database (for in-house or aws and for different mysql users) and the function to perform parametrised queries.

[aws/development/website/phpinclude/db.php]

```php
<?php

        $db=null;

        // open a connection to the database
        // $npriv determines which mysql user to use
        function dbconnect($npriv) {

                global $global_is_dev, $db;

                $dbhost="";
                $dbname="";
                $dbuser="";
                $dbpass="";

                if (strlen($global_is_dev)>1) {
                        // development
                        $dbhost="127.0.0.1";
                        $dbname="SEDdbnameSED";
                        if ($npriv==0) {
                                $dbuser="webphprw";
                                $dbpass="SEDDBPASS_webphprwSED";
                        }
                        else if ($npriv==1) {
                                $dbuser="a different user";
                                $dbpass="a different password";
                        }
                }
                else {
```

```
                    // aws
                    $dbhost=$_SERVER['DBHOST'];
                    $dbname=$_SERVER['DBNAME'];
                    if ($npriv==0) {

$dbuser=$_SERVER['DBUSER_webphprw'];

$dbpass=$_SERVER['DBPASS_webphprw'];
                    }
            }
            $db = new mysqli($dbhost, $dbuser, $dbpass,
$dbname);
            if (mysqli_connect_errno()) {
                    trigger_error("Unable to connect to
database.");
                    exit;
            }
            $db->set_charset('UTF-8');
            }

    //  runs a parametrised sql query
    // if query has no parameters:
    //   if query returns no data, return 1 (success) 0 (error)
    //   if query returns data, return data array (success) or 0
(error)
    // if query has parameters:
    //   if query returns no data, return 1 (success) 0 (error)
    //   if query returns data, return data array (success) or 0
(error)
    function doSQL($nquery) {
            global $db;
            $args = func_get_args();
            if (count($args) == 1) {
                    $result = $db->query($nquery);
                    if (is_bool($result)) {
                            if ($result==1)
                                    return 1;
                            return 0;
                    }
                    if ($result->num_rows) {
                            $out = array();
                            while (null != ($r = $result-
>fetch_array(MYSQLI_ASSOC)))
                                    $out [] = $r;
                            return $out;
                    }
                    return 1;
            }
            else {
                    if (!$stmt = $db->prepare($nquery))
                            //trigger_error("Unable to prepare
statement: {$nquery}, reason: " . $db->error . "");
                            return 0;
                    array_shift($args); //remove $nquery from
args
                    //the following three lines are the only
way to copy an array values in PHP
                    $a = array();
                    foreach ($args as $k => &$v)
                            $a[$k] = &$v;
```

```
                        $types = str_repeat("s", count($args));
//all params are strings, works well on MySQL and SQLite
                        array_unshift($a, $types);
                        call_user_func_array(array($stmt,
'bind_param'), $a);
                        $stmt->execute();
                        //fetching all results in a 2D array
                        $metadata = $stmt->result_metadata();
                        $out = array();
                        $fields = array();
                        if (!$metadata)
                                return 1;
                        $length = 0;
                        while (null != ($field =
mysqli_fetch_field($metadata))) {
                                $fields [] = &$out [$field->name];
                                $length+=$field->length;
                        }
                        call_user_func_array(array($stmt,
"bind_result"), $fields);
                        $output = array();
                        $count = 0;
                        while ($stmt->fetch()) {
                                foreach ($out as $k => $v)
                                        $output [$count] [$k] = $v;
                                $count++;
                        }
                        $stmt->free_result();
                        return ($count == 0) ? 1 : $output;
                }
        }

?>
```

The footer included on every displayed page which closes up constructs created in the phpinclude/begin.php header. Of interest is the line 'Server: <?php echo $global_serverid;?> which can identify which server you are on. Normally, I unobtrusively print this invisibly with colour matching background, but if I drag it with the cursor I can see the value. Quite handy for debugging.

[aws/development/website/phpinclude/end.php]

```
<br><br>

<?php if (!isset($S['userID'])) { ?>
        Not signed in
           
        <a href="/public/signin.php">Sign In</a>
           
        <a href="/public/signup.php">Sign Up</a>
<?php } else { ?>
        Signed in as <?php echo $S['email'];?>   <a
href="/public/signout.php">Sign Out</a>
<?php } ?>
```

```
   
&copy; 2014 C S Cerri
   
<a href="/public/terms.php">Terms</a>
   
Server: <?php echo $global_serverid;?>
   
<?php echo date('D jS M Y H:i:s e');?>

</div>

</body>
</html>
```

Global PHP functions used by all pages including: variable validation; password generation; AES encryption/decryption; sending email; and checking Google Recaptcha.

[aws/development/website/phpinclude/globalfunctions.php]

```php
<?php
        // an error occurred
        function do_err($naddr, $nmsg) {
                if ($naddr=="")
                        exit();
                header('Location: '.$naddr.'='.$nmsg);
                exit();
                }

        // a standard error occurred
        function do_std_err($nmsg) {
                header('Location: /public/error.php?err='.$nmsg);
                exit();
                }

        // check a text input is the correct length
        // min, max -1 to ignore
        function check_text_input($var, $min, $max, $errname,
$erraddr) {
                $ret=$var;
                if ( (!($min==-1)) && (strlen($ret)<$min) )
                        do_err($erraddr, $errname." too short");
                if ( (!($max==-1)) && (strlen($ret)>$max) )
                        do_err($erraddr, $errname." too long");
                return $ret;
                }

        // check a numeric value lies within a range
        // min, max -1 to ignore
        function check_num_input($var, $min, $max, $errname,
$erraddr) {
                $ret=$var;
                if (!is_numeric($ret))
                        do_err($erraddr, $errname." not a number");
```

```
                if ( (!($min==-1)) && ($ret<$min) )
                        do_err($erraddr, $errname." min is ".$min);
                if ( (!($max==-1)) && ($ret>$max) )
                        do_err($erraddr, $errname." max is ".$max);
                return $ret;
                }

        // ajax version of text size checker
        // min, max -1 to ignore
        function check_text_input_ajax($var, $min, $max, $errname,
$erraddr) {
                $ret=$var;
                if ( (!($min==-1)) && (strlen($ret)<$min) )
                        return false;
                if ( (!($max==-1)) && (strlen($ret)>$max) )
                        return false;
                return $ret;
                }

        // ajax version of numeric range checker
        // min, max -1 to ignore
        function check_num_input_ajax($var, $min, $max) {
                $ret=$var;
                if (!is_numeric($ret))
                        return false;
                if ( (!($min==-1)) && ($ret<$min) )
                        return false;
                if ( (!($max==-1)) && ($ret>$max) )
                        return false;
                return $ret;
                }

        // check a string exists in a string array
        function check_text_input_in_array($var, $arr, $errname,
$erraddr) {
                $ret=$var;
                if (!(in_array($ret, $arr)))
                        do_err($erraddr, $errname." not found");
                return $ret;
                }

        // checks a string only contains chars from the array
within
        // returns original string if legal, or "Illegal Input" if
not
        function check_legal_chars($ns) {
                $legal=array("q", "w", "e", "r", "t", "y", "u",
"i", "o", "p", "a", "s", "d", "f", "g", "h", "j", "k", "l", "z",
"x", "c", "v", "b", "n", "m",
                                        "Q", "W", "E", "R", "T",
"Y", "U", "I", "O", "P", "A", "S", "D", "F", "G", "H", "J", "K",
"L", "Z", "X", "C", "V", "B", "N", "M",
                                        " ", "1", "2", "3", "4",
"5", "6", "7", "8", "9", "0",
                                        "!", "@", "$", "*", "(",
")", ":", ";", "+", "-", "?" );
                $s=$ns;
                for ($i=0; $i<count($legal); $i++)
                        $s=str_replace($legal[$i], "", $s);
                if ($s=="")
```

```php
                return $ns;
            return "Illegal Input";
            }

    // seed the generator
    function makerandseed() {
            list($usec, $sec) = explode(' ', microtime());
            return (float) $sec + ((float) $usec * 100000);
            }

    // return a password of length $nlength from the $legal
array
    function makepassword($nlength) {
            $legal=array("q", "w", "e", "r", "t", "y", "u",
"i", "o", "p", "a", "s", "d", "f", "g", "h", "j", "k", "l", "z",
"x", "c", "v", "b", "n", "m",
                                            "Q", "W", "E", "R", "T",
"Y", "U", "I", "O", "P", "A", "S", "D", "F", "G", "H", "J", "K",
"L", "Z", "X", "C", "V", "B", "N", "M",
                                            "1", "2", "3", "4", "5",
"6", "7", "8", "9", "0");
            $ret="";
            srand(makerandseed());
            for ($i=0; $i<$nlength; $i++) {
                    $rnd=rand(0, 61);
                    $ret.=$legal[$rnd];
                    }
            return $ret;
            }

    // encrypt a string with aes
    function aes_encrypt($ntext) {
            global $global_aeskey;
            $key = pack('H*', $global_aeskey);
            $iv_size = mcrypt_get_iv_size(MCRYPT_RIJNDAEL_128,
MCRYPT_MODE_CBC);
            $iv = mcrypt_create_iv($iv_size, MCRYPT_RAND);
            $ciphertext = mcrypt_encrypt(MCRYPT_RIJNDAEL_128,
$key, $ntext, MCRYPT_MODE_CBC, $iv);
            $ciphertext = $iv . $ciphertext;
            $ciphertext_base64 = base64_encode($ciphertext);
            return $ciphertext_base64;
            }

    // decrypt an aes encrypted string
    function aes_decrypt($ntext) {
            global $global_aeskey;
            $key = pack('H*', $global_aeskey);
            $iv_size = mcrypt_get_iv_size(MCRYPT_RIJNDAEL_128,
MCRYPT_MODE_CBC);
            $ciphertext_dec = base64_decode($ntext);
            $iv_dec = substr($ciphertext_dec, 0, $iv_size);
            $ciphertext_dec = substr($ciphertext_dec,
$iv_size);
            $plaintext = mcrypt_decrypt(MCRYPT_RIJNDAEL_128,
$key, $ciphertext_dec, MCRYPT_MODE_CBC, $iv_dec);
            return $plaintext;
            }

    // example function to send mail
```

```php
        // by inserting into the sendemails table
        function sendemail($nuserID, $nto, $nsubject, $nmessage) {
                global $global_sendemailfrom;
                // check not bouncer or complainer
                $result=doSQL("select emailbounce, emailcomplaint
from users where userID=?;", $nuserID) or do_std_err("Error getting
mail details");
                if (!is_array($result))
                        do_std_err("Error getting mail details");
                if ($result[0]['emailbounce']>0)
                        do_std_err("Email has Bounced previous
emails");
                if ($result[0]['emailcomplaint']>0)
                        do_std_err("Email has Complained about
previous emails");
                // send
                $emsg=$nmessage."\n\nThanks\n";
                $result=doSQL("insert into sendemails (userID,
sendto, sendfrom, sendsubject, sendmessage) values
(?, ?, ?, ?, ?)", $nuserID, $nto, $global_sendemailfrom, $nsubject,
$emsg) or do_std_err("Error sending mail");
                }

        // use the Google lib to check a recaptcha
        function checkrecaptcha($naddr, $nchallenge, $nresponse) {
                global $global_recaptcha_privatekey;
                require_once('recaptchalib.php');
                $privatekey = $global_recaptcha_privatekey;
                $resp = recaptcha_check_answer ($privatekey,
$naddr, $nchallenge, $nresponse);
                if (!$resp->is_valid)
                        // What happens when the CAPTCHA was
entered incorrectly
                        return $resp->error;
                return "";
                }

?>
```

Global PHP variables used by all pages. This page is edited by the deployment scripts to tell the website it is running on AWS. For in-house development, you will need to enter your Google Recaptcha keys.

[aws/development/website/phpinclude/globalvariables.php]

```php
<?php

        // when we upload to Production Environment, this is
replaced with 0
        $global_is_dev="SEDis_devSED";

        // when we upload to Production Environment,
        // this is replaced with emailsendfrom from
aws/master/vars.sh
        // which must be a verified SES email
```

```php
        $global_sendemailfrom="SEDsendemailfromSED";

        // whether to use development or minified js and css
        $global_minifyjscss=0;
        if (strlen($global_is_dev)==1)
                // minify if in an AWS environment
                $global_minifyjscss=1;
        // you can override $global_minifyjscss (set to 1)
        // to test minified code on the dev system

        // set UTC as the default time zone
        date_default_timezone_set('UTC');

        // the address of the standard error page
        $stderr="/public/error.php?err";

        // these usernames are denied for signing up
        $global_reserved_usernames=array("administrator",
"support", "admin", "security", "website", "site", "company",
"error", "warning", "moderator", "moderate", "staff", "employee");

        // 0=don't require ssl 1=require ssl
        // if required, non-ssl requests will be redirected to ssl
in init.php
        $global_require_ssl=1;

        // session times out after x seconds, eg 30 minutes = 1800
seconds
        $global_sessionexpiry=1800;

        // session can at most last x seconds, eg 1 week = 604800
seconds
        $global_sessionmaxtime=604800;

        // set variables based on environment
        if (strlen($global_is_dev)==1) {
                // we are on aws, get from httpd.conf
                // the id of this server
                $global_serverid=$_SERVER['SERVERID'];
                // the aeskey for session cookie encryption
                $global_aeskey=$_SERVER['AESKEY'];
                // the recaptcha private key (from
aws/credentials/recaptcha.sh)

$global_recaptcha_privatekey=$_SERVER['RECAPTCHA_PRIVATEKEY'];
                // the recaptcha public key (from
aws/credentials/recaptcha.sh)

$global_recaptcha_publickey=$_SERVER['RECAPTCHA_PUBLICKEY'];
                }
        else {
                // we are on our in-house development environment
                // we assume only one server
                $global_serverid=1;
                // a dummy key

$global_aeskey="bcb04b7e103a0cd8b54763051cef08bc55abe029fdebae5e1d4
17e2ffb2a00a3";
                // a recaptcha private key (see Chapter 10 - Google
Recaptcha)
```

```
                $global_recaptcha_privatekey="<your development
recaptcha private key>";
                // a recaptcha public key (see Chapter 10 - Google
Recaptcha)
                $global_recaptcha_publickey="<your development
recaptcha public key>";
        }

?>
```

The include file used by all pages to get access to global functions, variables and the database. Also enforces SSL if set. Tries to set up a session if available.

[aws/development/website/phpinclude/init.php]

```
<?php

        // global variables
        include 'globalvariables.php';

        // redirect to ssl if:
        // global_require_ssl is set
        // we are on an aws environment
        if
(    (strlen($global_is_dev)==1)&&($global_require_ssl==1)) {
                if ($_SERVER['HTTP_X_FORWARDED_PROTO']!="https") {
                        $redirect= "https://".
$_SERVER['HTTP_HOST'].$_SERVER['REQUEST_URI'];
                        header("Location:$redirect");
                        exit;
                        }
                }

        // include database functionality
        include 'db.php';

        // include shared functions
        include 'globalfunctions.php';

        // include session functions
        include 'sessions.php';

        // connect to the database
        // this can be called again with a different user as
required
        // eg dbconnect(1)
        dbconnect(0);

        // set up the session (if it exists)
        $S=sessionuse();

?>
```

A slightly modified version of the Google Recaptcha PHP Lib - we

replace fsockopen() with a curl rewrite.

[aws/development/website/phpinclude/recaptchalib.php]

```php
<?php
/*
 * This is a PHP library that handles calling reCAPTCHA.
 *       - Documentation and latest version
 *                 http://recaptcha.net/plugins/php/
 *       - Get a reCAPTCHA API Key
 *                 https://www.google.com/recaptcha/admin/create
 *       - Discussion group
 *                 http://groups.google.com/group/recaptcha
 *
 * Copyright (c) 2007 reCAPTCHA -- http://recaptcha.net
 * AUTHORS:
 *   Mike Crawford
 *   Ben Maurer
 *
 * Permission is hereby granted, free of charge, to any person
obtaining a copy
 * of this software and associated documentation files (the
"Software"), to deal
 * in the Software without restriction, including without
limitation the rights
 * to use, copy, modify, merge, publish, distribute, sublicense,
and/or sell
 * copies of the Software, and to permit persons to whom the
Software is
 * furnished to do so, subject to the following conditions:
 *
 * The above copyright notice and this permission notice shall be
included in
 * all copies or substantial portions of the Software.
 *
 * THE SOFTWARE IS PROVIDED "AS IS", WITHOUT WARRANTY OF ANY KIND,
EXPRESS OR
 * IMPLIED, INCLUDING BUT NOT LIMITED TO THE WARRANTIES OF
MERCHANTABILITY,
 * FITNESS FOR A PARTICULAR PURPOSE AND NONINFRINGEMENT. IN NO
EVENT SHALL THE
 * AUTHORS OR COPYRIGHT HOLDERS BE LIABLE FOR ANY CLAIM, DAMAGES OR
OTHER
 * LIABILITY, WHETHER IN AN ACTION OF CONTRACT, TORT OR OTHERWISE,
ARISING FROM,
 * OUT OF OR IN CONNECTION WITH THE SOFTWARE OR THE USE OR OTHER
DEALINGS IN
 * THE SOFTWARE.
 */

// this file is substantially the same as the Google distributed
one
// EXCEPT: _recaptcha_http_post() where we rewrite the fsockopen()
function
//               with curl() because we deny use of fsockopen() in
our php.ini
/**
 * The reCAPTCHA server URL's
```

```php
*/
define("RECAPTCHA_API_SERVER",
gethostbyname("http://www.google.com/recaptcha/api"));
define("RECAPTCHA_API_SECURE_SERVER",
gethostbyname("https://www.google.com/recaptcha/api"));
define("RECAPTCHA_VERIFY_SERVER", gethostbyname("www.google.com"));

/**
 * Encodes the given data into a query string format
 * @param $data - array of string elements to be encoded
 * @return string - encoded request
 */
function _recaptcha_qsencode ($data) {
        $req = "";
        foreach ( $data as $key => $value )
                $req .= $key . '=' .
urlencode( stripslashes($value) ) . '&';
        // Cut the last '&'
        $req=substr($req,0,strlen($req)-1);
        return $req;
        }

/**
 * Submits an HTTP POST to a reCAPTCHA server
 * @param string $host
 * @param string $path
 * @param array $data
 * @param int port
 * @return array response
 */
function _recaptcha_http_post($host, $path, $data, $port = 80) {

/*
        $req = _recaptcha_qsencode ($data);

        $http_request  = "POST $path HTTP/1.0\r\n";
        $http_request .= "Host: $host\r\n";
        $http_request .= "Content-Type: application/x-www-form-
urlencoded;\r\n";
        $http_request .= "Content-Length: " . strlen($req) .
"\r\n";
        $http_request .= "User-Agent: reCAPTCHA/PHP\r\n";
        $http_request .= "\r\n";
        $http_request .= $req;

        $response = '';
        if( false == ( $fs = @fsockopen($host, $port, $errno,
$errstr, 10) ) ) {
                die ('Could not open socket');
                }

        fwrite($fs, $http_request);

        while ( !feof($fs) )
                $response .= fgets($fs, 1160); // One TCP-IP packet
        fclose($fs);
        $response = explode("\r\n\r\n", $response, 2);

        return $response;
*/
```

AWS Scripted   198

```
        // curl rewrite

        $add_headers = array("Host: $host",);

        $curl = curl_init( 'http://' . $host . ':' . $port .
$path );
        curl_setopt( $curl, CURLOPT_POST, true );
        curl_setopt( $curl, CURLOPT_RETURNTRANSFER, true );
        curl_setopt( $curl, CURLOPT_CONNECTTIMEOUT, 10 );
        curl_setopt( $curl, CURLOPT_HTTP_VERSION,
CURL_HTTP_VERSION_1_0 );
        curl_setopt( $curl, CURLOPT_USERAGENT, 'reCAPTCHA/PHP' );
        curl_setopt( $curl, CURLOPT_POSTFIELDS, $data );
        curl_setopt( $curl, CURLOPT_HEADER, true );
        curl_setopt( $curl, CURLOPT_HTTPHEADER, $add_headers );
        if ( isset( $_ENV['http_proxy'] ) && !empty
( $_ENV['http_proxy'] ) ) {
                curl_setopt( $curl, CURLOPT_HTTPPROXYTUNNEL,
true );
                curl_setopt( $curl, CURLOPT_PROXYTYPE,
CURLPROXY_HTTP );
                curl_setopt( $curl, CURLOPT_PROXY,
$_ENV['http_proxy'] );
                }

        $response = curl_exec( $curl );
        if ( $response === false ) die('Error connecting to ' .
$host . '.');

        $response = explode("\r\n\r\n", $response, 2);

        return $response;

        }


/**
 * Gets the challenge HTML (javascript and non-javascript version).
 * This is called from the browser, and the resulting reCAPTCHA
HTML widget
 * is embedded within the HTML form it was called from.
 * @param string $pubkey A public key for reCAPTCHA
 * @param string $error The error given by reCAPTCHA (optional,
default is null)
 * @param boolean $use_ssl Should the request be made over ssl?
(optional, default is false)

 * @return string - The HTML to be embedded in the user's form.
 */
function recaptcha_get_html ($pubkey, $error = null, $use_ssl =
false) {
        if ($pubkey == null || $pubkey == '')
                die ("To use reCAPTCHA you must get an API key from
<a
href='https://www.google.com/recaptcha/admin/create'>https://www.go
ogle.com/recaptcha/admin/create</a>");

        if ($use_ssl)
```

```
                $server = RECAPTCHA_API_SECURE_SERVER;
        else
                $server = RECAPTCHA_API_SERVER;

        $errorpart = "";
        if ($error)
            $errorpart = "&amp;error=" . $error;
        return '<script type="text/javascript" src="'. $server .
'/challenge?k=' . $pubkey . $errorpart . '"></script>

        <noscript>
                <iframe src="'. $server . '/noscript?k=' .
$pubkey . $errorpart . '" height="300" width="500"
frameborder="0"></iframe><br/>
                <textarea name="recaptcha_challenge_field" rows="3"
cols="40"></textarea>
                <input type="hidden"
name="recaptcha_response_field" value="manual_challenge"/>
        </noscript>';
        }




/**
 * A ReCaptchaResponse is returned from recaptcha_check_answer()
 */
class ReCaptchaResponse {
        var $is_valid;
        var $error;
        }


/**
 * Calls an HTTP POST function to verify if the user's guess was
correct
 * @param string $privkey
 * @param string $remoteip
 * @param string $challenge
 * @param string $response
 * @param array $extra_params an array of extra variables to post
to the server
 * @return ReCaptchaResponse
 */
function recaptcha_check_answer ($privkey, $remoteip, $challenge,
$response, $extra_params = array()) {
        if ($privkey == null || $privkey == '')
                die ("To use reCAPTCHA you must get an API key from
<a
href='https://www.google.com/recaptcha/admin/create'>https://www.go
ogle.com/recaptcha/admin/create</a>");

        if ($remoteip == null || $remoteip == '')
                die ("For security reasons, you must pass the
remote ip to reCAPTCHA");

        //discard spam submissions
        if ($challenge == null || strlen($challenge) == 0 ||
$response == null || strlen($response) == 0) {
                $recaptcha_response = new ReCaptchaResponse();
```

```php
                $recaptcha_response->is_valid = false;
                $recaptcha_response->error = 'incorrect-captcha-
sol';
                return $recaptcha_response;
                }

        $response = _recaptcha_http_post (RECAPTCHA_VERIFY_SERVER,
"/recaptcha/api/verify",
                array (
                        'privatekey' => $privkey,
                        'remoteip' => $remoteip,
                        'challenge' => $challenge,
                        'response' => $response
                        ) + $extra_params
                        );

        $answers = explode ("\n", $response [1]);
        $recaptcha_response = new ReCaptchaResponse();

        if (trim ($answers [0]) == 'true')
                $recaptcha_response->is_valid = true;
        else {
                $recaptcha_response->is_valid = false;
                $recaptcha_response->error = $answers [1];
                }
        return $recaptcha_response;

        }

/**
 * gets a URL where the user can sign up for reCAPTCHA. If your
application
 * has a configuration page where you enter a key, you should
provide a link
 * using this function.
 * @param string $domain The domain where the page is hosted
 * @param string $appname The name of your application
 */
function recaptcha_get_signup_url ($domain = null, $appname = null)
{
        return "https://www.google.com/recaptcha/admin/create?" .
_recaptcha_qsencode (array ('domains' => $domain, 'app' =>
$appname));
        }

function _recaptcha_aes_pad($val) {
        $block_size = 16;
        $numpad = $block_size - (strlen ($val) % $block_size);
        return str_pad($val, strlen ($val) + $numpad,
chr($numpad));
        }

/* Mailhide related code */

function _recaptcha_aes_encrypt($val,$ky) {
        if (! function_exists ("mcrypt_encrypt"))
                die ("To use reCAPTCHA Mailhide, you need to have
the mcrypt php module installed.");
        $mode=MCRYPT_MODE_CBC;
        $enc=MCRYPT_RIJNDAEL_128;
```

```php
        $val=_recaptcha_aes_pad($val);
        return mcrypt_encrypt($enc, $ky, $val, $mode,
"\0\0\0\0\0\0\0\0\0\0\0\0\0\0\0\0");
        }


function _recaptcha_mailhide_urlbase64 ($x) {
        return strtr(base64_encode ($x), '+/', '-_');
        }

/* gets the reCAPTCHA Mailhide url for a given email, public key
and private key */
function recaptcha_mailhide_url($pubkey, $privkey, $email) {
        if ($pubkey == '' || $pubkey == null || $privkey == "" ||
$privkey == null) {
                die ("To use reCAPTCHA Mailhide, you have to sign
up for a public and private key, " .
                        "you can do so at <a
href='http://www.google.com/recaptcha/mailhide/apikey'>http://www.g
oogle.com/recaptcha/mailhide/apikey</a>");
        }

        $ky = pack('H*', $privkey);
        $cryptmail = _recaptcha_aes_encrypt ($email, $ky);

        return "http://www.google.com/recaptcha/mailhide/d?k=" .
$pubkey . "&c=" . _recaptcha_mailhide_urlbase64 ($cryptmail);
        }

/**
 * gets the parts of the email to expose to the user.
 * eg, given johndoe@example,com return ["john", "example.com"].
 * the email is then displayed as john...@example.com
 */
function _recaptcha_mailhide_email_parts ($email) {
        $arr = preg_split("/@/", $email );

        if (strlen ($arr[0]) <= 4)
                $arr[0] = substr ($arr[0], 0, 1);
        else if (strlen ($arr[0]) <= 6) {
                $arr[0] = substr ($arr[0], 0, 3);
        else
                $arr[0] = substr ($arr[0], 0, 4);
        return $arr;
        }

/**
 * Gets html to display an email address given a public an private
key.
 * to get a key, go to:
 *
 * http://www.google.com/recaptcha/mailhide/apikey
 */
function recaptcha_mailhide_html($pubkey, $privkey, $email) {
        $emailparts = _recaptcha_mailhide_email_parts ($email);
        $url = recaptcha_mailhide_url ($pubkey, $privkey, $email);

        return htmlentities($emailparts[0]) . "<a href='" .
htmlentities ($url) .
                "' onclick=\"window.open('" . htmlentities ($url) .
```

AWS Scripted   202

```
"', '',
'toolbar=0,scrollbars=0,location=0,statusbar=0,menubar=0,resizable=
0,width=500,height=300'); return false;\" title=\"Reveal this e-
mail address\">...</a>@" . htmlentities ($emailparts [1]);

        }

?>
```

The main session functions to start, use, update and destroy a
session are here. We use our own cookie-based session
management and completely bypass PHP's own session system.

[aws/development/website/phpinclude/sessions.php]

```php
<?php
        // to get mcrypt to work on osx installations of apache,
look at:
        // http://topicdesk.com/downloads/mcrypt/mcrypt-download
        // or use macports

        // setup a session just after signin
        // we use our own session system, not php sessions
        // you can call this function to reset the session
credentials if necessary
        // eg if you get a security context change
        function sessionstart($nuserID) {

                // session times out after x seconds, eg 30 minutes
= 1800 seconds
                global $global_sessionexpiry;
                // session can at most last x seconds, eg 1 week =
604800 seconds
                global $global_sessionmaxtime;

                // create 2 16 digit random tokens
                $sessiontoken1=makepassword(16);
                $sessiontoken2=makepassword(16);

                // get ip address and user agent
                $ipaddress=$_SERVER['REMOTE_ADDR'];
                $useragent=substr($_SERVER['HTTP_USER_AGENT'], 0,
64);

                // cookie 1 holds ipaddress, sessiontoken1 and
userid
                $cookie1=$ipaddress."|||".$sessiontoken1."|||".
$nuserID;

                // cookie 2 holds sessiontoken2 and useragent
                $cookie2=$sessiontoken2."&&&".$useragent;

                // encrypt the cookies
                $cookie1=aes_encrypt($cookie1);
                $cookie2=aes_encrypt($cookie2);
```

```php
                // send 2 cookies
                setcookie("TOKEN1", $cookie1, time()+
$global_sessionmaxtime, "/");
                setcookie("TOKEN2", $cookie2, time()+
$global_sessionmaxtime, "/");

                // update COOKIE globals
                $_COOKIE['TOKEN1']=$cookie1;
                $_COOKIE['TOKEN2']=$cookie2;

                // save data to the database
                $result=doSQL("update users set sessiontoken1=?,
sessiontoken2=?, sessionipaddress=?, sessionuseragent=?,
sessionlastdateSQL=now() where userID=?;", $sessiontoken1,
$sessiontoken2, $ipaddress, $useragent, $nuserID) or die("ERR");


        }

        // call on any page which needs to access session data
        // returns the $S session array, call with $S=sessionuse();
        // for demonstration, the $S array holds userID and email
        // you should add whatever session variables you need
        function sessionuse() {

                global $global_sessionexpiry;

                // check cookies exist and are not void
                if (!isset($_COOKIE['TOKEN1']))
                        return;
                if (!isset($_COOKIE['TOKEN2']))
                        return;
                if ($_COOKIE['TOKEN1']=="0")
                        return;
                if ($_COOKIE['TOKEN2']=="0")
                        return;

                // decrypt the cookies
                $cookie1=aes_decrypt($_COOKIE['TOKEN1']);
                $cookie2=aes_decrypt($_COOKIE['TOKEN2']);

                // break up the cookies
                $bits=explode("|||", $cookie1);
                $ipaddress=$bits[0];
                $sessiontoken1=$bits[1];
                $userID=$bits[2];
                $bits=explode("&&&", $cookie2);
                $sessiontoken2=$bits[0];
                $useragent=$bits[1];

                // check cookie values match current http values
                if (!($ipaddress==$_SERVER['REMOTE_ADDR'])) {
                        header("Location: /public/expired.php");
                        return;
                        }
                if (!
($useragent=substr($_SERVER['HTTP_USER_AGENT'], 0, 64))) {
                        header("Location: /public/expired.php");
                        return;
                        }
```

```
                // get database values and check they match
                $result=doSQL("select userID, email, sessiontoken1,
sessiontoken2, sessionipaddress, sessionuseragent,
timestampdiff(second, sessionlastdateSQL, now()) as inactivetime
from users where userID=?;", $userID) or die("ERR");

                // userID found?
                if (!is_array($result)) {
                        header("Location: /public/expired.php");
                        return;
                        }

                // check fields are populated
                if (($result[0]['sessionipaddress']=='')||
($result[0]['sessionuseragent']=='')||($result[0]
['sessiontoken1']=='')||($result[0]['sessiontoken2']=='')) {
                        header("Location: /public/expired.php");
                        return;
                        }


                // has session expired?
                if ($result[0]
['inactivetime']>$global_sessionexpiry) {
                        header("Location: /public/expired.php");
                        return;
                        }

                // values match?
                if (!($ipaddress==$result[0]['sessionipaddress']))
{
                        header("Location: /public/expired.php");
                        return;
                        }
                if (!($useragent==$result[0]['sessionuseragent']))
{
                        header("Location: /public/expired.php");
                        return;
                        }
                if (!($sessiontoken1==$result[0]['sessiontoken1']))
{
                        header("Location: /public/expired.php");
                        return;
                        }
                if (!($sessiontoken2==$result[0]['sessiontoken2']))
{
                        header("Location: /public/expired.php");
                        return;
                        }

                // all ok, set '$S' session array
                $S=array();
                $S['userID']=$result[0]['userID'];
                $S['email']=$result[0]['email'];
                // to add more session variables:
                //   add a column to the users table
                //   select that column in the query above
                //   add it to the $S array
                //   also update the sessionsave() and sessionend()
```

```
functions

            return $S;

        }

    // if session values change, call this to save the data to
the database
    // update the $S variable and pass it to this function
    // we assume the index field (userID) does not change
    function sessionsave($S) {

        // save data to the database
        // if you add new fields, update this query
        $result=doSQL("update users set email=? where
userID=?;", $S['email'], $S['userID']) or die("ERR");

    }

    // call to end a session
    // sends dud cookies to the client
    // and wipes the database
    function sessionend($nuserID) {

        // session can at most last x seconds, eg 1 week =
604800 seconds
        global $global_sessionmaxtime;

        // send 2 dud cookies
        setcookie("TOKEN1", "0", time()+
$global_sessionmaxtime, "/");
        setcookie("TOKEN2", "0", time()+
$global_sessionmaxtime, "/");

        // wipe data in the database
        $result=doSQL("update users set sessiontoken1='',
sessiontoken2='', sessionipaddress='', sessionuseragent='',
sessionlastdateSQL=now() where userID=?;", $nuserID) or die("ERR");

        return array();
    }

?>
```

These functions are needed by the SNS callback scripts found in
the /sns/bounce.php and /sns/complaint.php pages.

[aws/development/website/phpinclude/snsverify.php]

```
<?php

/* Adapted from:

    http://sns-public-
resources.s3.amazonaws.com/Verifying_Message_Signatures_4_26_10.pdf
    https://forums.aws.amazon.com/thread.jspa?threadID=45518
```

```
    Verify SNS JSON message against Amazon certificate. Following
message types can be verified:
        * SubscriptionConfirmation
        * Notification

    Region, account and one of topics[] must match the contents of
the "TopicArn" included
    in the message. Also, SigningCertURL's domain must end in
".amazonaws.com".

    Joni /2011
*/

function verify_sns($message, $region, $account, $topics) {
        $msg = json_decode($message);
        // Check that region, account and topic match
        $topicarn = explode(':', $msg->TopicArn);
        if ($topicarn[3] != $region || $topicarn[4] != $account
|| !in_array($topicarn[5], $topics))
                return false;
        $_region = $topicarn[3];
        $_account = $topicarn[4];
        $_topic = $topicarn[5];

        // Check that the domain in message ends with
'.amazonaws.com'
        if(!endswith(get_domain_from_url($msg->SigningCertURL),
'.amazonaws.com'))
                return false;

        // Load certificate and extract public key from it
        $surl=$msg->SigningCertURL;
        $curlOptions = array (
                CURLOPT_URL => $surl,
                CURLOPT_VERBOSE => 1,
                CURLOPT_RETURNTRANSFER => 1,
                CURLOPT_SSL_VERIFYPEER => TRUE,
                CURLOPT_SSL_VERIFYHOST => 2
                );
        $ch = curl_init();
        curl_setopt_array($ch, $curlOptions);
        $cert = curl_exec($ch);
        $pubkey = openssl_get_publickey($cert);
        if(!$pubkey)
                return false;

        // Generate a message string for comparison in Amazon-
specified format
        $text = "";
        if($msg->Type == 'Notification') {
                $text .= "Message\n";
                $text .= $msg->Message . "\n";
                $text .= "MessageId\n";
                $text .= $msg->MessageId . "\n";
                if (isset($msg->Subject)) {
                        if ($msg->Subject != "") {
                                $text .= "Subject\n";
                                $text .= $msg->Subject . "\n";
                                }
                        }
                }
```

```php
                    $text .= "Timestamp\n";
                    $text .= $msg->Timestamp . "\n";
                    $text .= "TopicArn\n";
                    $text .= $msg->TopicArn . "\n";
                    $text .= "Type\n";
                    $text .= $msg->Type . "\n";
                    }
            elseif($msg->Type == 'SubscriptionConfirmation') {
                    $text .= "Message\n";
                    $text .= $msg->Message . "\n";
                    $text .= "MessageId\n";
                    $text .= $msg->MessageId . "\n";
                    $text .= "SubscribeURL\n";
                    $text .= $msg->SubscribeURL . "\n";
                    $text .= "Timestamp\n";
                    $text .= $msg->Timestamp . "\n";
                    $text .= "Token\n";
                    $text .= $msg->Token . "\n";
                    $text .= "TopicArn\n";
                    $text .= $msg->TopicArn . "\n";
                    $text .= "Type\n";
                    $text .= $msg->Type . "\n";
                    }
            else
                    return false;

            // Get a raw binary message signature
            $signature = base64_decode($msg->Signature);

            // ..and finally, verify the message
            if(openssl_verify($text, $signature, $pubkey,
OPENSSL_ALGO_SHA1))
                    return true;

            return false;
            }

// http://stackoverflow.com/questions/619610/whats-the-most-
efficient-test-of-whether-a-php-string-ends-with-another-string
function endswith($string, $test) {
        $strlen = strlen($string);
        $testlen = strlen($test);
        if ($testlen > $strlen) return false;
        return substr_compare($string, $test, -$testlen) === 0;
        }

// http://codepad.org/NGlABcAC
function get_domain_from_url( $url, $max_node_count = 0 ) {
        $return_value='';
        $max_node_count=(int)$max_node_count;
        $url_parts=parse_url((string)$url);

if(is_array($url_parts)&&isset($url_parts['host'])&&strlen((string)
$url_parts['host'])>0) {
                $return_value=(string)$url_parts['host'];
                if($max_node_count>0) {
                        $host_parts=explode('.',$return_value);
                        $return_parts=array();
                        for($i=$max_node_count;$i>0;$i--) {
```

```php
$current_node=array_pop($host_parts);

if(is_string($current_node)&&$current_node!=='')

$return_parts[]=$current_node;
                                else
                                        break;
                                }
                        if(count($return_parts)>0)

$return_value=implode('.',array_reverse($return_parts));
                        else
                                $return_value='';
                        }
                }
        return $return_value;
        }

?>
```

Chapter 11 - MySQL Database

Database Security is vital. There are 3 ways this security is implemented:

1. Database Users

   Each part of the application connects with a different database user. Each database user has very limited permissions. So, for example, the JavaMail server can only select and update the sendemails table. If the JavaMail server were to be compromised, data could not be downloaded from the database (except a list of emails sent and to be sent).

2. Parametrised Queries

   ModSecurity provides excellent protection against SQL-Injection attacks. But to improve security further, we only issue parametrised queries. This means we bind data to a query, rather than build a string.

3. Hashed Passwords

   We never store passwords in the database. We store a hashed version (with salt). See **Chapter 10 - Hashing Passwords**.

Refer to **Chapter 13 - Deploying Assets** for how to upload the database and database users.

Database Creation Script

This is the script used to generate the database:

[aws/development/database/dbs.sql]

```
DROP DATABASE IF EXISTS `SEDdbnameSED`;
CREATE DATABASE `SEDdbnameSED`;

DROP TABLE IF EXISTS `SEDdbnameSED`.`users`;
CREATE TABLE  `SEDdbnameSED`.`users` (
  `userID` int(11) unsigned NOT NULL auto_increment,
  `dateSQL` timestamp(3) NOT NULL default CURRENT_TIMESTAMP(3),
  `username` varchar(16) NOT NULL UNIQUE,
  `password` varchar(128) NOT NULL,
  `email` varchar(255) default NULL UNIQUE,
  `emailbounce` int(11) unsigned NOT NULL default 0 comment '0=ok
>0=bounced holds snsnotifiationID',
  `emailcomplaint` int(11) unsigned NOT NULL default 0 comment
'0=ok >0=complained holds snsnotifiationID',
  `sessiontoken1` varchar(16) default NULL,
  `sessiontoken2` varchar(16) default NULL,
  `sessionipaddress` varchar(64) default NULL,
  `sessionuseragent` varchar(64) default NULL,
  `sessionlastdateSQL` datetime,
  PRIMARY KEY (`userID`)
) ENGINE=InnoDB AUTO_INCREMENT=12973 DEFAULT CHARSET=utf8;

DROP TABLE IF EXISTS `SEDdbnameSED`.`sendemails`;
CREATE TABLE  `SEDdbnameSED`.`sendemails` (
  `sendemailID` int(11) unsigned NOT NULL AUTO_INCREMENT,
  `dateSQL` timestamp(3) NOT NULL DEFAULT CURRENT_TIMESTAMP(3),
  `userID` int(11) unsigned NOT NULL,
  `sendto` varchar(255) NOT NULL DEFAULT '',
  `sendfrom` varchar(255) NOT NULL DEFAULT '',
  `sendsubject` varchar(255) NOT NULL DEFAULT '',
  `sendmessage` varchar(8192) NOT NULL DEFAULT '',
  `sendfailures` tinyint unsigned NOT NULL DEFAULT '0',
  `sent` tinyint unsigned NOT NULL DEFAULT '0',
  PRIMARY KEY (`sendemailID`)
) ENGINE=InnoDB AUTO_INCREMENT=1 DEFAULT CHARSET=utf8;

DROP TABLE IF EXISTS `SEDdbnameSED`.`snsnotifications`;
CREATE TABLE `SEDdbnameSED`.`snsnotifications` (
  `snsnotificationID` int(11) unsigned NOT NULL AUTO_INCREMENT,
  `dateSQL` timestamp(3) NOT NULL DEFAULT CURRENT_TIMESTAMP(3),
  `messageid` varchar(255) DEFAULT '',
  `subject` varchar(255) DEFAULT '',
  `message` varchar(2048) DEFAULT '',
  `email` varchar(255) DEFAULT '',
  PRIMARY KEY (`snsnotificationID`)
) ENGINE=InnoDB AUTO_INCREMENT=1 DEFAULT CHARSET=utf8;
```

OK, so on your in-house Development Environment, your database will be called 'SEDdbnameSED' - slightly annoying but not a deal-breaker!

User Generation Script

This is the script used to create database users and allocate their permissions:

[aws/development/database/dbusers.sql]

```
/*
        this file creates the required database users for MYDB
        these are:

        adminrw
                full access with grant

        webphprw
                can read, update, insert required tables for
website

        javamail
                can read, update required tables for sending mail


        useful SQL commands
        GRANT ALL PRIVILEGES  ON MYDB.* TO 'adminrw'@'%' WITH GRANT
OPTION;
        GRANT SELECT, INSERT ON MYDB.* TO 'someuser'@'somehost';
        GRANT SELECT (col1), INSERT (col1,col2) ON MYDB.mytable TO
'someuser'@'somehost';

*/

/* do admin first so that if there are any errors at least we can
connect to admin server */
DROP PROCEDURE IF EXISTS SEDdbnameSED.drop_user_if_exists ;
DELIMITER $$
CREATE PROCEDURE SEDdbnameSED.drop_user_if_exists()
BEGIN
  DECLARE foo BIGINT DEFAULT 0 ;
  SELECT COUNT(*)
  INTO foo
    FROM mysql.user
      WHERE User = 'adminrw' and  Host = '%';
   IF foo > 0 THEN
          DROP USER 'adminrw'@'%' ;
   END IF;
END ;$$
DELIMITER ;
CALL SEDdbnameSED.drop_user_if_exists() ;
DROP PROCEDURE IF EXISTS SEDdbnameSED.drop_users_if_exists ;

CREATE USER 'adminrw'@'%' IDENTIFIED BY 'SEDDBPASS_adminrwSED';
GRANT ALL PRIVILEGES  ON SEDdbnameSED.* TO 'adminrw'@'%' WITH GRANT
OPTION;
GRANT SELECT ON mysql.slow_log TO 'adminrw'@'%';


DROP PROCEDURE IF EXISTS SEDdbnameSED.drop_user_if_exists ;
DELIMITER $$
CREATE PROCEDURE SEDdbnameSED.drop_user_if_exists()
BEGIN
  DECLARE foo BIGINT DEFAULT 0 ;
```

```
SELECT COUNT(*)
INTO foo
  FROM mysql.user
    WHERE User = 'webphprw' and  Host = '%';
  IF foo > 0 THEN
        DROP USER 'webphprw'@'%' ;
  END IF;
END ;$$
DELIMITER ;
CALL SEDdbnameSED.drop_user_if_exists() ;
DROP PROCEDURE IF EXISTS SEDdbnameSED.drop_users_if_exists ;

CREATE USER 'webphprw'@'%' IDENTIFIED BY 'SEDDBPASS_webphprwSED';
GRANT SELECT, INSERT, UPDATE             ON SEDdbnameSED.users TO
'webphprw'@'%';
GRANT SELECT, INSERT                              ON
SEDdbnameSED.sendemails TO 'webphprw'@'%';
GRANT SELECT, INSERT                              ON
SEDdbnameSED.snsnotifications TO 'webphprw'@'%';


DROP PROCEDURE IF EXISTS SEDdbnameSED.drop_user_if_exists ;
DELIMITER $$
CREATE PROCEDURE SEDdbnameSED.drop_user_if_exists()
BEGIN
  DECLARE foo BIGINT DEFAULT 0 ;
  SELECT COUNT(*)
  INTO foo
    FROM mysql.user
      WHERE User = 'javamail' and  Host = '%';
  IF foo > 0 THEN
        DROP USER 'javamail'@'%' ;
  END IF;
END ;$$
DELIMITER ;
CALL SEDdbnameSED.drop_user_if_exists() ;
DROP PROCEDURE IF EXISTS SEDdbnameSED.drop_users_if_exists ;

CREATE USER 'javamail'@'%' IDENTIFIED BY 'SEDDBPASS_javamailSED';
GRANT SELECT,              UPDATE         ON
SEDdbnameSED.sendemails TO 'javamail'@'%';
```

Connecting from PHP

We use a function to set up the connection from PHP to MySQL:

[aws/snippets/snippet_phpdbconnect.php]

```
// excerpt from aws/development/website/phpinclude/db.sql

    $db=null;

    function dbconnect($npriv) {

        global $global_is_dev, $db;
```

```
$dbhost="";
$dbname="";
$dbuser="";
$dbpass="";

if (strlen($global_is_dev)>1) {
        // development
        $dbhost="127.0.0.1";
        $dbname="SEDdbnameSED";
        if ($npriv==0) {
                $dbuser="webphprw";
                $dbpass="SEDDBPASS_webphprwSED";
                }
        else if ($npriv==1) {
                $dbuser="a different user";
                $dbpass="a different password";
                }
        }
else {
        // aws
        $dbhost=$_SERVER['DBHOST'];
        $dbname=$_SERVER['DBNAME'];
        if ($npriv==0) {

$dbuser=$_SERVER['DBUSER_webphprw'];

$dbpass=$_SERVER['DBPASS_webphprw'];
                }
        }
$db = new mysqli($dbhost, $dbuser, $dbpass,
$dbname);
if (mysqli_connect_errno()) {
        trigger_error("Unable to connect to
database.");
        exit;
        }
$db->set_charset('UTF-8');
}
```

The function dbconnect() serves two purposes: it uses different credentials for an in-house or an AWS environment (based on the $global_is_dev variable); and it uses different credentials based on the $npriv parameter.

You can edit this function to provide more users. Using several users with restricted permissions is key to database security. So, if you have a section of your website which only reads data from one or two tables, set a user up (in the **User Generation Script** earlier in this Chapter) who can only read from those tables - no other permissions. Then, even if a SQL Injection attack should get past ModSecurity (unlikely), the rest of the database is still secure, and an attacker won't be able to change any data or read other tables in the database.

Before calling any queries, simply use:

```
dbconnect(0);
```

or change the '0' to whichever user is required.

Querying from PHP

Thanks to OWASP for this technique for parametrised queries. Instead of building a query as a string (which is inherently vulnerable to SQL Injection), we bind values to a query instead.

How NOT to do it:

[aws/snippets/snippet_querywong.php]

```
// simple wrong way to do a query
dbconnect(0);
$somevar="data from a GET or POST variable - potential sql
injection";
$query="select * from users where email='".$somevar."';";
$result=$db->query($query);

// what if $somevar="' or '1'='1"?
// then your query becomes:
// select * from users where email='' or '1'='1';
// and all records will be returned
```

The right way:

[aws/snippets/snippet_queryright.php]

```
// runs a parametrised sql query
// if query has no parameters:
//  if query returns no data, return 1 (success) 0 (error)
//  if query returns data, return data array (success) or 0 (error)
// if query has parameters:
//  if query returns no data, return 1 (success) 0 (error)
//  if query returns data, return data array (success) or 0 (error)
function doSQL($nquery) {
        global $db;
        $args = func_get_args();
        if (count($args) == 1) {
                $result = $db->query($nquery);
                if (is_bool($result)) {
```

```php
                        if ($result==1)
                                return 1;
                        return 0;
                        }
                if ($result->num_rows) {
                        $out = array();
                        while (null != ($r = $result-
>fetch_array(MYSQLI_ASSOC)))
                                $out [] = $r;
                        return $out;
                        }
                return 1;
                }
        else {
                if (!$stmt = $db->prepare($nquery))
                        //trigger_error("Unable to prepare
statement: {$nquery}, reason: " . $db->error . "");
                        return 0;
                array_shift($args); //remove $nquery from args
                //the following three lines are the only way to
copy an array values in PHP
                $a = array();
                foreach ($args as $k => &$v)
                        $a[$k] = &$v;
                $types = str_repeat("s", count($args)); //all
params are strings, works well on MySQL and SQLite
                array_unshift($a, $types);
                call_user_func_array(array($stmt, 'bind_param'),
$a);
                $stmt->execute();
                //fetching all results in a 2D array
                $metadata = $stmt->result_metadata();
                $out = array();
                $fields = array();
                if (!$metadata)
                        return 1;
                $length = 0;
                while (null != ($field =
mysqli_fetch_field($metadata))) {
                        $fields [] = &$out [$field->name];
                        $length+=$field->length;
                        }
                call_user_func_array(array($stmt, "bind_result"),
$fields);
                $output = array();
                $count = 0;
                while ($stmt->fetch()) {
                        foreach ($out as $k => $v)
                                $output [$count] [$k] = $v;
                        $count++;
                        }
                $stmt->free_result();
                return ($count == 0) ? 1 : $output;
                }
        }

// now the actual query, safely
dbconnect(0);
$somevar="data from a GET or POST variable - potential sql
injection";
```

```
// you should also whitelist sanitise $somevar first
$result=$doSQL("select * from users where email=?;", $somevar);
// note that for multiple variables, you just list them in order,
eg
// $result=$doSQL("select * from users where email=? and
verified=?;", $email, $verified);
```

So now, not only do you have more readable queries, they are also injection proof. And linked with ModSecurity and restrictive database users, this makes for a powerful defence against any hacker.

Backups, Replication and Failover

AWS RDS handles Backups for you. If you go with a Multi-AZ (AZ stands for Availability Zone), it will also handle Failover by creating a Synchronous Slave Replica in a different availability zone, which will kick in should the master go down.

Bear in mind that Multi-AZ servers are slightly less than twice the price of non replicated servers. Unless you really need high availability, I don't recommend it. First, a quick check of AWS incidents show NO outages since 2012, so it is very unlikely that your RDS server will go down. And the outages that happened in 2012 show that ALL zones went down, so the Multi-AZ feature was useless anyway. Also, the switchover if a failure occurs is not instantaneous, so there will be some outage, a few minutes it seems, even with Multi-AZ.

Read Replicas are very easy to set up and look like a great option for shifting database load away from the main read/write database. Just bear in mind that replication times are reported to be anything between 10 seconds and 5 minutes! So Read Replicas are only really viable for very static data.

One thing RDS is not very good at is allowing you to actually download a dump of your database. You can't do this via the AWS CLI or the AWS Console. If your database is small, you can use PHPMyAdmin to create a dump and download it. But I have had problems with this approach for databases whose size exceeds about one GB. For those, you'll want to use a mysqldump command on the Admin Server which can be generated from the following script:

[aws/ami/rds/dump.sh]

```
#!/bin/bash

# makes a mysql dump command to dump your database
# you can copy and paste it to the admin server
# after ./credentials/connectssh.sh admin

# check dir
where=$(pwd)
where="${where: -3}"
if test "$where" = "aws"; then
 echo "running from correct directory"
else
 echo "must be run from aws directory with ./ami/rds/dump.sh"
 exit
fi

# include global variables
. ./master/vars.sh

cd $basedir

# include passwords
source credentials/passwords.sh

# this is the address, or endpoint, for the db
dbendpoint=$(aws rds describe-db-instances --db-instance-identifier
$dbinstancename --output text --query
'DBInstances[*].Endpoint.Address')
echo dbendpoint=$dbendpoint

echo $'\nthis is the dump command:\n'
echo "mysqldump --host=$dbendpoint --user=mainuser
--password=$password1 $dbname > dump.sql"
echo $'\nrun it on the admin server'
```

Then, you'll need to download the dump file from the remote Admin Server, see **Appendix A - Copying Files to and from a Remote Server**.

Chapter 12 - Java Servers

When to Use Java

There are lots of things PHP is no good at. One of them is fast-repeating scheduled files. As an example, we send mail by inserting a record into a database. Now, we could have a cron running a PHP page on the Admin Server every minute to check for unsent emails and then send them. But this is unacceptable for 2 reasons: running cron jobs with very short cycles could result in a page being called when the page is already running (which could cause data inconsistencies); and even 1 minute is really too long for an email to be sent, given users will be expecting their 'password reset' email within a few seconds.

In these sorts of situations, a Java server is the perfect solution. By server here we mean server application and not a server instance. The AWS Linux distribution comes with Java as standard, and these very simple servers are very hardy, almost never crash and take up minimal resources.

Java Mail Server

A fully functioning Java mail forwarder is provided as an Eclipse Kepler project in aws/development/java/javamail. If you use a different Java IDE, you will need to copy the .java files, the jars and the config script and create a new project. Also required are the javax.mail.jar and mysql-connector-java-5.0.8-bin.jar files.

In Eclipse (Kepler), to create the final jar javaMail.jar, we do File → Export.., select Runnable JAR File, choose the 'mailServer - javaMail' launch configuration, set the Export Destination to be javaMail/javaMail.jar and select 'Extract required libraries into generated JAR'. This means we get a single jar file, and don't have to worry about linking javax.mail and the mysql jars at runtime.

The java source files follow.

The mainServer class is the main Java entry point. It creates the objects which read the configuration file and connect to the database, then makes the server workhorse, the pollMail object. For a different server, just change the last two lines (which deal with pollMail) and replace with your new objects.

[aws/development/java/javaMail/src/com/aws/mail/mailServer.java]

```
package com.aws.mail;

public class mailServer {

                // no args
                public static void main(String[] args) {

                        System.out.println("Started");

                        config c=new config();
                        c.getconfig();

                        dbManager dbm=new
dbManager(c.prop.getProperty("dbhost"),
c.prop.getProperty("dbport"), c.prop.getProperty("dbname"),
c.prop.getProperty("dbuser"), c.prop.getProperty("dbpassword"));

                        pollMail pm=new pollMail(dbm,
c.prop.getProperty("smtphost"), c.prop.getProperty("smtpport"),
c.prop.getProperty("smtpuser"), c.prop.getProperty("smtppass"));
                        pm.start();

                }

        }
```

The pollMail class is where the main action is. It's Runnable, so this is where the thread runs. It uses dbManager to get emails from the database that need to be sent, sends them to AWS SES with the sendMailSES class and then updates the database regarding what it has done. Forever. You could use this class as a template to create any number of servers, eg grab some data from the Internet and save it to the database, or handle transactions for a bitcoin trading exchange.

[aws/development/java/javaMail/src/com/aws/mail/pollMail.java]

```
package com.aws.mail;
```

```java
import java.sql.Connection;
import java.sql.PreparedStatement;
import java.sql.ResultSet;
import java.sql.Statement;
import java.text.SimpleDateFormat;
import java.util.Date;
import java.util.regex.Matcher;
import java.util.regex.Pattern;

public class pollMail implements Runnable {

        private static dbManager dbm;
        private Thread runner;
        private sendMailSES sm;

        private int maxattempts=3;

        SimpleDateFormat sdf = new SimpleDateFormat("dd MMM yyyy
HH:mm:ss");

        public pollMail(dbManager ndbm, String nsmtphost, String
nsmtpport, String nsmtpuser, String nsmtppass) {
                dbm=ndbm;
                runner = new Thread(this, "pollMail");
                System.out.println(getdate()+" Created Thread
"+runner.getName());
                sm=new sendMailSES(nsmtphost, nsmtpport, nsmtpuser,
nsmtppass);
                }

        public void start() {
                runner.start();
                System.out.println(getdate()+" Started Thread
"+runner.getName());
                }

        public void run() {

                Runtime.getRuntime().addShutdownHook(new Thread() {
                    public void run() {
                            System.out.println(getdate()+"
STOPPED");
                            }
                    });

                while (true) {

                        Connection c=dbm.getConnection();

                        try {
                                Statement statement =
c.createStatement();
                                ResultSet res =
statement.executeQuery("select sendemailID, sendto, sendfrom,
sendsubject, sendmessage, sendfailures from sendemails where sent=0
and sendfailures<"+maxattempts+" order by sendemailID asc limit
1;");
```

```
                                long sendemailID;
                                String sendto;
                                String sendfrom;
                                String sendsubject;
                                String sendmessage;
                                int sendfailures;
                                if (res.next()) {

sendemailID=res.getLong("sendemailID");

sendto=res.getString("sendto");

sendfrom=res.getString("sendfrom");

sendsubject=res.getString("sendsubject");

sendmessage=res.getString("sendmessage");

sendfailures=res.getInt("sendfailures");
                                                boolean
isvalid=isValidEmailAddress(sendto);
                                                boolean result=false;
                                                if (isvalid)

result=sm.send(sendto, sendfrom, sendsubject, sendmessage);
                                                if (result==true) {
                                                        PreparedStatement
pstatement=c.prepareStatement("update sendemails set sent=1 where
sendemailID="+sendemailID+";");

pstatement.executeUpdate();
                                                        pstatement.close();

System.out.println(getdate()+" sent email ok "+sendto+" ID:
"+sendemailID);
                                                }
                                                else {
                                                        PreparedStatement
pstatement=c.prepareStatement("update sendemails set
sendfailures=sendfailures+1 where sendemailID="+sendemailID+";");

pstatement.executeUpdate();
                                                        pstatement.close();

System.out.println(getdate()+" sent email err '"+sendto+"'
"+sendemailID+" failures "+(sendfailures+1)+" EMAIL"+((isvalid)?"
VALID":" INVALID"));
                                                }
                                        res.close();
                                        statement.close();
                                        }
                                else {
                                        res.close();
                                        statement.close();
                                        Thread.sleep(1000L);
                                        System.gc();
                                        }
                                }
                        catch (Exception e) {
                                e.printStackTrace();
```

```
                                      System.out.println(getdate()+"
Error getting next email");
                                      try {Thread.sleep(2000L);} catch
(Exception e2) {}
                                      }

                         }
                  }

        public boolean isValidEmailAddress(String email) {
                  Pattern p = Pattern.compile("^.+@.+\\..+$");
                  Matcher m = p.matcher(email);
                  return m.matches();
                  }

        private String getdate() {
                  return sdf.format(new Date());
                  }

        }
```

The sendMailSES class is where we talk to SES. We format up a message, connect to SES and send the message.

[aws/development/java/javaMail/src/com/aws/mail/sendMailSES.java]

```java
package com.aws.mail;

import java.util.Properties;

import javax.mail.*;
import javax.mail.internet.*;

public class sendMailSES {

        private String host;
        private String port;
        private String username;
        private String password;

        public sendMailSES(String nhost, String nport, String
nusername, String npassword) {
                  host=nhost;
                  port=nport;
                  username=nusername;
                  password=npassword;
                  }

        public boolean send(String nto, String nfrom, String
nsubject, String nbody) {

                  // Create a Properties object to contain connection
configuration information.
                  Properties props = System.getProperties();
                  props.put("mail.transport.protocol", "smtp");
                  props.put("mail.smtp.port", port);
```

```
                // Set properties indicating that we want to use
STARTTLS to encrypt the connection.
                // The SMTP session will begin on an unencrypted
connection, and then the client
                // will issue a STARTTLS command to upgrade to an
encrypted connection.
                props.put("mail.smtp.auth", "true");
                props.put("mail.smtp.starttls.enable", "true");
                props.put("mail.smtp.starttls.required", "true");

                // Create a Session object to represent a mail
session with the specified properties.
                Session session =
Session.getDefaultInstance(props);

                // Create a message with the specified information.
                MimeMessage msg = new MimeMessage(session);
                try {
                        msg.setFrom(new InternetAddress(nfrom));
                        msg.setRecipient(Message.RecipientType.TO,
new InternetAddress(nto));
                        msg.setSubject(nsubject);
                        msg.setContent(nbody,"text/plain");
                        }
                catch (Exception e) {
                        System.out.println("Error creating
message");
                        e.printStackTrace();
                        return false;
                        }

                // Create a transport.
                Transport transport=null;

                // Send the message.
                boolean success=false;
                try {
                        transport = session.getTransport();
                        System.out.println("Attempting to send an
email through the Amazon SES SMTP interface...");

                        // Connect to Amazon SES using the SMTP
username and password you specified above.
                        transport.connect(host, username,
password);

                        // Send the email.
                        transport.sendMessage(msg,
msg.getAllRecipients());
                        System.out.println("Email sent!");
                        success=true;
                        }
                catch (Exception ex) {
                        System.out.println("The email was not
sent.");
                        System.out.println("Error message: " +
ex.getMessage());
                        }

                try {
```

```
                            // Close and terminate the connection.
                            transport.close();
                            }
                catch (Exception e) {
                            System.out.println("Could not close
transport");
                            e.printStackTrace();
                            }

                return success;
                }

        }
```

The dbManager class is a simple implementation of a database connection. Nothing fancy, but it works. You could improve it with transactions and rollbacks.

[aws/development/java/javaMail/src/com/aws/mail/dbManager.java]

```
package com.aws.mail;

import java.sql.Connection;
import java.sql.DriverManager;

public class dbManager {

        private Connection c;

        public dbManager(String nipaddress, String nport, String
ndb, String nuser, String npassword) {
                try {
                        Class.forName("com.mysql.jdbc.Driver");
                        String url
="jdbc:mysql://"+nipaddress+":"+nport+"/"+ndb;
                        System.out.println("Connect url  "+url);
                        c = DriverManager.getConnection(url, nuser,
npassword);
                        System.out.println("Connected to "+ndb);
                        }
                catch (Exception e) {
                        System.out.println("Could Not Connect to
"+ndb);
                        e.printStackTrace();
                        }
                }

        public Connection getConnection() {
                return c;
                }

        public void closeConnection() {
                try {
                        c.close();
                        }
                catch(Exception e) {
```

```
                            System.out.println("Close Connection
Error");
                            e.printStackTrace();
                            }
                }

        }
```

A reusable class to read configuration values from the config.properties file. I prefer this approach to putting arguments on the command line.

[aws/development/java/javaMail/src/com/aws/mail/config.java]

```
package com.aws.mail;
import java.io.FileInputStream;
import java.io.InputStream;
import java.util.Properties;

public class config {

        public Properties prop;

        public void getconfig() {

                prop = new Properties();
                InputStream input = null;

                try {

                        input = new
FileInputStream("config.properties");

                        // load a properties file
                        prop.load(input);

                        // get the property value and print it out
//
System.out.println(prop.getProperty("dbhost"));

                        input.close();

                        }
                catch (Exception e) {
                        e.printStackTrace();
                        }
                }

        }
```

The properties file to configure the server. SED***SED values are replaced.

[aws/development/java/javaMail/config_template.properties]

```
# java mail server secure properties file
dbhost=SEDdbhostSED
dbport=3306
dbname=SEDdbnameSED
dbuser=javamail
dbpassword=SEDDBPASS_javamailSED
smtphost=SEDSMTPHOSTSED
smtpport=SEDSMTPPORTSED
smtpuser=SEDSMTPUSERSED
smtppass=SEDSMTPPASSSED
```

Installation, Starting and Monit

In order to have our java server monitored and started correctly, we need to link it into Monit. This requires a start stop script for the java server, as follows:

[aws/ami/admin/launch_javaMail.sh]

```
#!/bin/bash

case $1 in
 start)
  cd /java/javamail
  echo $$ > javaMail.pid;
  exec 2>&1 java -jar javaMail.jar |/usr/bin/logger -t javamail -p
local3.info
  ;;
 stop)
  pid1=$(ps axf | grep "java -jar javaMail.jar" | grep -v grep |
awk '{print $1}')
  pid2=$(ps axf | grep "/usr/bin/logger -t javamail -p local3.info"
| grep -v grep | awk '{print $1}')
  pid3=$(ps axf | grep "/bin/bash /java/javamail/launch_javaMail.sh
start" | grep -v grep | awk '{print $1}')
  kill $pid1
  sleep 2
  kill $pid2
  kill $pid3
  ;;
 *)
  echo "usage: launch_javaMail.sh {start|stop}" ;;
esac
exit 0
```

You can use this script to start and stop JavaMail manually with:

```
./launch_javaMail.sh start
```

and

```
./launch_javaMail.sh stop
```

Now we can use this launch script to tell Monit how to monitor JavaMail. In the monit.conf file on the Admin Server we use:

[aws/snippets/snippet_monitjava.conf]

```
# javaMail
check process javaMail with pidfile /java/javamail/javaMail.pid
        start = "/java/javamail/launch_javaMail.sh start"
        stop = "/java/javamail/launch_javaMail.sh stop"
```

Note that

```
  echo $$ > javaMail.pid;
```

in our launch script creates the file javaMail.pid which Monit uses to verify that JavaMail is running.

We also want to log the output of our java server so we can monitor it with LogAnalyzer. For this we use /usr/bin/logger to send output to rsyslog with the tag 'javamail'. This is then picked up in the rsyslog.conf file with:

```
:syslogtag, isequal, "javamail:" /var/log/javamail.log
:syslogtag, isequal, "javamail:" ~
```

which sends the output to the /var/log/javamail.log file. The second line drops the message so no further logging is done.

For the full deployment script, see **Chapter 13 - Uploading a Java Server.**

Chapter 13 - Deploying Assets

Preparing Assets

All assets are deployed from the aws/data directory. We use the following command to build the assets as needed:

```
./data/makedata.sh
```

The makedata.sh script copies data from the aws/development folder and performs other tasks such as separating the admin and public websites, minifying JS and CSS, and doing some sed search and replace to enable production functionality.

Remember, the aws/development folder is merely a proxy for your real development environment. You should change the variables webdir, admindir, javadir and databasedir in aws/master/vars.sh to point to your actual development folders. You may need to share drives etc if you are using a stand-alone development server. Check **Chapter 2 - Installing on your Development Environment** and **Chapter 2 - Global Variables** for more information.

This is the script:

[aws/data/makedata.sh]

```bash
#!/bin/bash

# copies web, admin, database and java data files to data/website/
data/admin/ data/database/ data/java/ respectively

# check dir
where=$(pwd)
where="${where: -3}"
if test "$where" = "aws"; then
 echo "running from correct directory"
else
 echo "must be run from aws directory with ./data/makedata.sh"
 exit
fi
```

```
# include global variables
. ./master/vars.sh

cd $basedir

# minify js and css in the development directory
# this is so you can test minified code by overriding
$global_minifyjscss in globalvariables.php
. ./minify/make.sh

# clear any existing data
rm -f -r data/website
rm -f -r data/admin
rm -f -r data/database
rm -f -r data/java

# remake the data directories
mkdir -p data/website
mkdir -p data/admin
mkdir -p data/database
mkdir -p data/java
mkdir -p data/java/javaMail

# prepare the website
cp -R $webdir/htdocs data/website/htdocs
rm -f -r data/website/htdocs/admin
rm -f -r data/website/htdocs/jscss/dev

# prepare php include files
cp -R $webdir/phpinclude data/website/phpinclude

# tell the website it's running on aws
# insert the email to send from
sed -e "s/SEDis_devSED/0/g" -e "s/SEDsendemailfromSED/
$emailsendfrom/g" data/website/phpinclude/globalvariables.php >
data/website/phpinclude/globalvariables2.php
rm -f data/website/phpinclude/globalvariables.php
mv data/website/phpinclude/globalvariables2.php
data/website/phpinclude/globalvariables.php

# prepare database files
cp -R $databasedir/* data/database

# prepare admin files
cp -R $admindir/* data/admin

# tell the admin website it's running on aws
# insert the email to send from
sed -e "s/SEDis_devSED/0/g" -e "s/SEDsendemailfromSED/
$emailsendfrom/g" data/admin/init.php > data/admin/init2.php
rm -f data/admin/init.php
mv data/admin/init2.php data/admin/init.php

# prepare javaMail files
cp $javadir/javaMail/javaMail.jar data/java/javaMail
cp $javadir/javaMail/config_template.properties data/java/javaMail

cd $basedir

echo "done"
```

This is the minification script called from the above script:

[aws/minify/make.sh]

```bash
#!/bin/bash

# make everything in /jscss/prod folder

# check dir
where=$(pwd)
where="${where: -3}"
if test "$where" = "aws"; then
 echo "running from correct directory"
else
 echo "must be run from aws directory with ./minify/make.sh"
 exit
fi

# include global variables
. ./master/vars.sh

minifydir=$basedir
minifydir+=/minify
jscssdir=$webdir
jscssdir+=/htdocs/jscss

echo "minifying js and css"

cd $minifydir

# clear current files
rm -f -R $jscssdir/prod/*

# copy the style sheet
cp $jscssdir/dev/css/style.css $jscssdir/prod/style.css

# copy minified jquery
cp $jscssdir/dev/js/jq/jquery.min.js $jscssdir/prod/jquery.min.js

# create a concatenation of all other javascript files
cat $jscssdir/dev/js/site/signup.js > $jscssdir/prod/general.js
cat $jscssdir/dev/js/jq/jquery.base64.min.js >>
$jscssdir/prod/general.js

# minify this file
java -jar yuicompressor-2.4.8.jar $jscssdir/prod/general.js -o
$jscssdir/prod/general.min.js

# remove the unminified file
rm -f $jscssdir/prod/general.js

cd $basedir
```

Note that we minify in the development directory (so you can test minified code by overriding $global_minifyjscss in globalvariables.php). However, when we copy to the data directory, we remove the unminified development files.

Uploading a New Admin Website

The Admin Website is installed with the command:

```
./upload/admin/upload.sh
```

We take the following steps:

1. Open up access to the Admin Sever
2. Build a zip of the Admin Website
3. Upload the zip and an install script
4. Use expect to sudo su and run the uploaded script
5. close SSH ports

Here is the script:

[aws/upload/admin/upload.sh]

```
#!/bin/bash

# uploads the admin website to admin server
# then runs the install script on the server
# data comes from from aws/data/admin dir, run ./data/makedata.sh
first

# check dir
where=$(pwd)
where="${where: -3}"
if test "$where" = "aws"; then
 echo "running from correct directory"
else
 echo "must be run from aws directory with
./upload/admin/upload.sh"
 exit
fi

# include global variables
. ./master/vars.sh

rm -f $sshknownhosts

cd $basedir

echo building zip

rm -f -R data/admin/admin.zip
```

```
cd data/admin
# only zip php and css files (leave out the annoying DSStore
files...)
zip -R admin '*.php' '*.css'

echo "uploading admin"

cd $basedir/credentials

source passwords.sh

echo connecting to admin

myip=$(curl http://checkip.amazonaws.com/)
echo myip=$myip

# get ip of server
ip_address=$(aws ec2 describe-instances --filters Name=key-
name,Values=admin --output text --query
'Reservations[*].Instances[*].PublicIpAddress')
echo ip_address=$ip_address

# allow ssh in sg
vpcadminsg_id=$(aws ec2 describe-security-groups --filters
Name=tag-key,Values=sgname --filters Name=tag-value,Values=adminsg
--output text --query 'SecurityGroups[*].GroupId')
echo vpcadminsg_id=$vpcadminsg_id
aws ec2 authorize-security-group-ingress --group-id $vpcadminsg_id
--protocol tcp --port 38142 --cidr $myip/32

cd $basedir

# wait for ssh
echo -n "waiting for ssh"
while ! ssh -i credentials/admin.pem -p 38142 -o ConnectTimeout=60
-o BatchMode=yes -o StrictHostKeyChecking=no ec2-user@$ip_address >
/dev/null 2>&1 true; do
 echo -n . ; sleep 3;
done; echo " ssh ok"

# upload files
ssh -i credentials/admin.pem -p 38142 -o ConnectTimeout=60 -o
BatchMode=yes -o StrictHostKeyChecking=no ec2-user@$ip_address exit
echo "transferring files"
scp -i credentials/admin.pem -P 38142 data/admin/admin.zip ec2-
user@$ip_address:
scp -i credentials/admin.pem -P 38142 upload/admin/install.sh ec2-
user@$ip_address:
echo "transferred files"

rm -f -R data/admin/admin.zip

cd $basedir/credentials

# make and run expect script
echo "#!/usr/bin/expect -f" > expect.sh
echo "set timeout -1" >> expect.sh
echo "spawn ssh -i admin.pem -p 38142 -o ConnectTimeout=60 -o
BatchMode=yes -o StrictHostKeyChecking=no ec2-user@$ip_address" >>
expect.sh
```

```
echo "sleep 3" >> expect.sh
echo "send \"sudo su\n\"" >> expect.sh
echo "expect \"password for ec2-user:\"" >> expect.sh
echo "send \"$password3\n\"" >> expect.sh
echo "expect \"]\"" >> expect.sh
echo "send \"./install.sh\n\"" >> expect.sh
echo "expect \"install.sh finished\"" >> expect.sh
echo "exit" >> expect.sh
echo "exit" >> expect.sh
echo "interact" >> expect.sh
chmod +x expect.sh
./expect.sh
rm expect.sh

# remove ssh in sg
aws ec2 revoke-security-group-ingress --group-id $vpcadminsg_id
--protocol tcp --port 38142 --cidr $myip/32
echo "revoked sg access"

cd $basedir
```

The install script which is uploaded and run on the server takes the following steps:

1. remove the current Admin Website
2. /phpmyadmin and /loganalyzer are not touched
3. copy the admin zip, unpack and delete it
4. set permissions on the webroot
5. clean up any uploaded files
6. tell expect we have finished

Here is the listing:

[aws/upload/admin/install.sh]

```
#!/bin/bash

# remove admin website, but not phpmyadmin or loganalyzer
rm -f /var/www/html/*.php
rm -f /var/www/html/*.css
rm -f -r /var/www/html/sched

# copy the admin zip, unpack and delete it
cp admin.zip /var/www/html/admin.zip
cd /var/www/html
unzip admin.zip
rm -f admin.zip

# set permissions on the webroot
find /var/www/html -type d -exec chown root:apache {} +
find /var/www/html -type d -exec chmod 550 {} +
find /var/www/html -type f -exec chown root:apache {} +
```

```
find /var/www/html -type f -exec chmod 440 {} +

# cleanup any uploaded files
rm -f -R /home/ec2-user/*
echo "deleted files from /home/ec2-user"

# needed for expect to finish
echo "install.sh finished"
```

Uploading a New Public Website

The Public Website has a slightly different upload system because it resides on several servers. Clearly, because requests might be piped to any server by the ELB, all the Webphp Servers need to be synchronised. So we use a top level script to prepare assets and then call a subscript repeatedly to upload to each server.

If your website is under heavy load and you want to avoid synchronisation discrepancies (because you have 20 servers and it takes a little time to upload them all), you will need to script something to set a maintenance page on all your servers. And do the update at the least busy time for your site. An exercise left to the reader.

The Public Website is installed with the command:

```
./upload/website/uploadall.sh
```

This script does the following:

1. prepare assets
2. call the individual server upload script
3. cleanup

Here is the listing:

[aws/upload/website/uploadall.sh]

```
#!/bin/bash

# uploads the website to all web instances
# then runs the install script on each server
# data from aws/data/website dir, run ./data/makedata.sh first
```

```
# check dir
where=$(pwd)
where="${where: -3}"
if test "$where" = "aws"; then
 echo "running from correct directory"
else
 echo "must be run from aws directory with
./upload/website/uploadall.sh"
 exit
fi

# include global variables
. ./master/vars.sh

cd $basedir

echo "uploading to all webs"

# build data

cd $basedir/data/website

rm -f htdocs/htdocs.zip
rm -f phpinclude/phpinclude.zip

cd $basedir/data/website/phpinclude
# only zip php files (leave out the annoying DSStore files...)
zip -R phpinclude '*.php'

cd $basedir/data/website/htdocs
# only zip recognised file types (leave out the annoying DSStore
files...)
# if you use different file types add them below
zip -R htdocs '*.php' '*.js' '*.css' '*.jpg' '*.ico' '*.png'
'*.gif' '*.htm' '*.txt'
#zip -R htdocs '*.*'

# upload to each existing webN

cd $basedir

exists=$(aws ec2 describe-key-pairs --key-names web1 --output text
--query 'KeyPairs[*].KeyName' 2>/dev/null)
if test "$exists" = "web1"; then
 echo "web1 exists"
 . ./upload/website/upload.sh 1
else
 echo "web1 not found"
fi

exists=$(aws ec2 describe-key-pairs --key-names web2 --output text
--query 'KeyPairs[*].KeyName' 2>/dev/null)
if test "$exists" = "web2"; then
 echo "web2 exists"
 . ./upload/website/upload.sh 2
else
 echo "web2 not found"
fi
```

```
exists=$(aws ec2 describe-key-pairs --key-names web3 --output text
--query 'KeyPairs[*].KeyName' 2>/dev/null)
if test "$exists" = "web3"; then
 echo "web3 exists"
 . ./upload/website/upload.sh 3
else
 echo "web3 not found"
fi

exists=$(aws ec2 describe-key-pairs --key-names web4 --output text
--query 'KeyPairs[*].KeyName' 2>/dev/null)
if test "$exists" = "web4"; then
 echo "web4 exists"
 . ./upload/website/upload.sh 4
else
 echo "web4 not found"
fi

exists=$(aws ec2 describe-key-pairs --key-names web5 --output text
--query 'KeyPairs[*].KeyName' 2>/dev/null)
if test "$exists" = "web5"; then
 echo "web5 exists"
 . ./upload/website/upload.sh 5
else
 echo "web5 not found"
fi

exists=$(aws ec2 describe-key-pairs --key-names web6 --output text
--query 'KeyPairs[*].KeyName' 2>/dev/null)
if test "$exists" = "web6"; then
 echo "web6 exists"
 . ./upload/website/upload.sh 6
else
 echo "web6 not found"
fi

# cleanup
cd $basedir/data/website/phpinclude
rm -f phpinclude.zip
cd $basedir/data/website/htdocs
rm -f htdocs.zip

cd $basedir
```

The individual server upload script does the following:

1. get the password for the server
2. open up SSH for the server
3. upload assets and install script
4. use expect to sudo su and run the install script on the server
5. close the SSH port

Here is the listing:

[aws/upload/website/upload.sh]

```
#!/bin/bash

# uploads the website to a webN instance
# parameters <N> where this is the Nth web box

# check dir
where=$(pwd)
where="${where: -3}"
if test "$where" = "aws"; then
 echo "running from correct directory"
else
 echo "must be run from aws directory with
./upload/website/upload.sh ..."
 exit
fi

# include global variables
. ./master/vars.sh

rm -f $sshknownhosts

cd $basedir

webid=$1
if test -z "$webid"; then
 exit
fi

echo "uploading web$webid"

cd $basedir/credentials

source passwords.sh

echo connecting to web$webid

# set the password for the server in question
if test "$webid" = "1"; then
 pass=$password9
 echo "set password for web1"
elif test "$webid" = "2"; then
 pass=$password11
 echo "set password for web2"
elif test "$webid" = "3"; then
 pass=$password13
 echo "set password for web3"
elif test "$webid" = "4"; then
 pass=$password15
 echo "set password for web4"
elif test "$webid" = "5"; then
 pass=$password17
 echo "set password for web5"
elif test "$webid" = "6"; then
 pass=$password19
 echo "set password for web6"
else
 echo "password for $1 not found - exiting"
```

```
  exit
fi

myip=$(curl http://checkip.amazonaws.com/)
echo myip=$myip

# get ip of server
ip_address=$(aws ec2 describe-instances --filters Name=key-
name,Values=web$webid --output text --query
'Reservations[*].Instances[*].PublicIpAddress')
echo ip_address=$ip_address

# get sg of server
serversg=web$webid
serversg+=sg
echo serversg=$serversg

# allow ssh in sg
vpcwebsg_id=$(aws ec2 describe-security-groups --filters Name=tag-
key,Values=sgname --filters Name=tag-value,Values=$serversg
--output text --query 'SecurityGroups[*].GroupId')
echo vpcwebsg_id=$vpcwebsg_id
aws ec2 authorize-security-group-ingress --group-id $vpcwebsg_id
--protocol tcp --port 38142 --cidr $myip/32

cd $basedir

# wait for ssh
echo -n "waiting for ssh"
while ! ssh -i credentials/web$webid.pem -p 38142 -o
ConnectTimeout=60 -o BatchMode=yes -o StrictHostKeyChecking=no ec2-
user@$ip_address > /dev/null 2>&1 true; do
 echo -n . ; sleep 3;
done; echo " ssh ok"

# upload files
ssh -i credentials/web$webid.pem -p 38142 -o ConnectTimeout=60 -o
BatchMode=yes -o StrictHostKeyChecking=no ec2-user@$ip_address exit
echo "transferring files"
scp -i credentials/web$webid.pem -P 38142
data/website/phpinclude/phpinclude.zip ec2-user@$ip_address:
scp -i credentials/web$webid.pem -P 38142
data/website/htdocs/htdocs.zip ec2-user@$ip_address:
scp -i credentials/web$webid.pem -P 38142 upload/website/install.sh
ec2-user@$ip_address:
echo "transferred files"

cd $basedir/credentials

# make and run expect script
echo "#!/usr/bin/expect -f" > expect.sh
echo "set timeout -1" >> expect.sh
echo "spawn ssh -i web$webid.pem -p 38142 -o ConnectTimeout=60 -o
BatchMode=yes -o StrictHostKeyChecking=no ec2-user@$ip_address" >>
expect.sh
echo "sleep 3" >> expect.sh
echo "send \"sudo su\n\"" >> expect.sh
echo "expect \"password for ec2-user:\"" >> expect.sh
echo "send \"$pass\n\"" >> expect.sh
echo "expect \"]\"" >> expect.sh
```

```
echo "send \"./install.sh\n\"" >> expect.sh
echo "expect \"install.sh finished\"" >> expect.sh
echo "exit" >> expect.sh
echo "exit" >> expect.sh
echo "interact" >> expect.sh
chmod +x expect.sh
./expect.sh
rm expect.sh

# remove ssh in sg
aws ec2 revoke-security-group-ingress --group-id $vpcwebsg_id
--protocol tcp --port 38142 --cidr $myip/32
echo "revoked sg access"

cd $basedir
```

The install script which is uploaded and run does the following:

1. stop Apache
2. delete and remake the webroot jail
3. unpack assets
4. put various things into the jail to make UTC time, DNS and curl work
5. set permissions on the jail
6. cleanup
7. tell expect in calling script we have finished

Here is the listing:

[aws/upload/website/install.sh]

```
#!/bin/bash

# stop apache
service httpd stop

# delete and recreate the jail
rm -f -R /jail
mkdir -p /jail/var/www/html
mkdir -p /jail/var/www/phpinclude

# copy and unpack assets
cp phpinclude.zip /jail/var/www/phpinclude/phpinclude.zip
cp htdocs.zip /jail/var/www/html/htdocs.zip
cd /jail/var/www/phpinclude
unzip phpinclude.zip
rm -f phpinclude.zip
cd /jail/var/www/html
unzip htdocs.zip
rm -f htdocs.zip
```

```
# if you were to use php sessions, you would need this
#mkdir -p /jail/var/lib/php/session

# this is so UTC can work
mkdir -p /jail/usr/share/zoneinfo
cp /usr/share/zoneinfo/UTC /jail/usr/share/zoneinfo

# modsecurity needs a writable folder
mkdir -p /jail/var/lib/mod_security

# allow dns to work
mkdir -p /jail/etc
cp /etc/resolv.conf /jail/etc/resolv.conf

# allow curl ssl and verify to work
mkdir -p /jail/etc
cp /etc/nsswitch.conf /jail/etc/nsswitch.conf
cp -r /etc/pki /jail/etc
cp -r /etc/ssl /jail/etc
mkdir -p /jail/usr/lib64
cp /usr/lib64/libnsspem.so /jail/usr/lib64/libnsspem.so
cp /usr/lib64/libsoftokn3.so /jail/usr/lib64/libsoftokn3.so
cp /usr/lib64/libnsssysinit.so /jail/usr/lib64/libnsssysinit.so
cp /usr/lib64/libfreebl3.so /jail/usr/lib64/libfreebl3.so
cp /usr/lib64/libnssdbm3.so /jail/usr/lib64/libnssdbm3.so

# set the default certificate bundle
echo curl.cainfo=/etc/ssl/certs/ca-bundle.crt >>
/etc/php.d/curl.ini

# set permissions on the jail
find /jail -type d -exec chown root:apache {} +
find /jail -type d -exec chmod 550 {} +
find /jail -type f -exec chown root:apache {} +
find /jail -type f -exec chmod 440 {} +

# for php sessions, apache needs write access
#chmod 660 /jail/var/lib/php/session

# mod_security needs write/traverse access
chown root:apache /jail/var/lib/mod_security
chmod 770 /jail/var/lib/mod_security

# cleanup
rm -f -R /home/ec2-user/*
echo "deleted files from /home/ec2-user"

# start apache
service httpd start

# needed for expect in calling script
echo "install.sh finished"
```

Uploading a New Database

The Database and Database Users are installed with the command:

```
./upload/database/upload.sh
```

The database and database users are installed via the Admin Server. We take the following steps:

1. prepare variables, eg own IP address, database endpoint, passwords
2. build database scripts with sed
3. open up the SSH port to the Admin Server
4. upload assets and install script
5. use expect to sudo su and run the install script
6. close the SSH port
7. cleanup

Here is the upload script:

[aws/upload/database/upload.sh]

```
#!/bin/bash

# uploads database files to the admin server
# then runs the install script on the server
# data comes from from aws/data/database dir, run
./data/makedata.sh first

# check dir
where=$(pwd)
where="${where: -3}"
if test "$where" = "aws"; then
 echo "running from correct directory"
else
 echo "must be run from aws directory with
./upload/database/upload.sh"
 exit
fi

# include global variables
. ./master/vars.sh

rm -f $sshknownhosts

cd $basedir

source credentials/passwords.sh

myip=$(curl http://checkip.amazonaws.com/)
echo myip=$myip

# get ip of server
ip_address=$(aws ec2 describe-instances --filters Name=key-
name,Values=admin --output text --query
```

```
'Reservations[*].Instances[*].PublicIpAddress')
echo ip_address=$ip_address

# get database endpoint
dbendpoint=$(aws rds describe-db-instances --db-instance-identifier
$dbinstancename --output text --query
'DBInstances[*].Endpoint.Address')

# build database scripts

cd $basedir

rm -f upload/database/dbs.sql
rm -f upload/database/dbusers.sql
rm -f upload/database/install.sh

sed "s/SEDdbnameSED/$dbname/g" data/database/dbs.sql >
upload/database/dbs.sql

sed -e "s/SEDdbnameSED/$dbname/g" -e "s/SEDDBPASS_adminrwSED/
$password4/g" -e "s/SEDDBPASS_webphprwSED/$password5/g" -e
"s/SEDDBPASS_javamailSED/$password6/g" data/database/dbusers.sql >
upload/database/dbusers.sql

sed -e "s/SEDdbhostSED/$dbendpoint/g" -e
"s/SEDdbmainuserpasswordSED/$password1/g" -e "s/SEDdbnameSED/
$dbname/g" upload/database/install_template.sh >
upload/database/install.sh
chmod +x upload/database/install.sh

# allow ssh in sg
vpcadminsg_id=$(aws ec2 describe-security-groups --filters
Name=tag-key,Values=sgname --filters Name=tag-value,Values=adminsg
--output text --query 'SecurityGroups[*].GroupId')
echo vpcadminsg_id=$vpcadminsg_id
aws ec2 authorize-security-group-ingress --group-id $vpcadminsg_id
--protocol tcp --port 38142 --cidr $myip/32

# wait for ssh
echo -n "waiting for ssh"
while ! ssh -i credentials/admin.pem -p 38142 -o ConnectTimeout=60
-o BatchMode=yes -o StrictHostKeyChecking=no ec2-user@$ip_address >
/dev/null 2>&1 true; do
 echo -n . ; sleep 3;
done; echo " ssh ok"

# upload files
ssh -i credentials/admin.pem -p 38142 -o ConnectTimeout=60 -o
BatchMode=yes -o StrictHostKeyChecking=no ec2-user@$ip_address exit
echo "transferring files"
scp -i credentials/admin.pem -P 38142 upload/database/dbs.sql ec2-
user@$ip_address:
scp -i credentials/admin.pem -P 38142 upload/database/dbusers.sql
ec2-user@$ip_address:
scp -i credentials/admin.pem -P 38142 upload/database/install.sh
ec2-user@$ip_address:
echo "transferred files"

rm -f upload/database/dbs.sql
rm -f upload/database/dbusers.sql
```

```
rm -f upload/database/install.sh

cd $basedir/credentials

# make and run expect script
echo "#!/usr/bin/expect -f" > expect.sh
echo "set timeout -1" >> expect.sh
echo "spawn ssh -i admin.pem -p 38142 -o ConnectTimeout=60 -o
BatchMode=yes -o StrictHostKeyChecking=no ec2-user@$ip_address" >>
expect.sh
echo "sleep 3" >> expect.sh
echo "send \"sudo su\n\"" >> expect.sh
echo "expect \"password for ec2-user:\"" >> expect.sh
echo "send \"$password3\n\"" >> expect.sh
echo "expect \"]\"" >> expect.sh
echo "send \"./install.sh\n\"" >> expect.sh
echo "expect \"install.sh finished\"" >> expect.sh
echo "exit" >> expect.sh
echo "exit" >> expect.sh
echo "interact" >> expect.sh
chmod +x expect.sh
#echo "start expect.sh"
#cat expect.sh
#echo "end expect.sh"
./expect.sh
rm expect.sh

# remove ssh in sg
aws ec2 revoke-security-group-ingress --group-id $vpcadminsg_id
--protocol tcp --port 38142 --cidr $myip/32
echo "revoked sg access"

cd $basedir
```

Here is the install script (note SED***SED items are replaced with
real values):

[aws/upload/database/install_template.sh]

```
#!/bin/bash

# install database from admin server

echo "installing db"
mysql --host=SEDdbhostSED --user=mainuser
--password=SEDdbmainuserpasswordSED --database=SEDdbnameSED
--execute="SOURCE dbs.sql"
echo "db installed"

echo "installing users"
mysql --host=SEDdbhostSED --user=mainuser
--password=SEDdbmainuserpasswordSED --database=SEDdbnameSED
--execute="SOURCE dbusers.sql"
echo "users installed"

echo "testing db"
mysql --host=SEDdbhostSED --user=mainuser
```

```
--password=SEDdbmainuserpasswordSED --database=SEDdbnameSED
--execute="show tables;"
echo "db tested"

rm -f -R /home/ec2-user/*
echo "deleted files from /home/ec2-user"

echo install.sh finished
```

We run the sql scripts with the mysql command, cleanup and tell expect in the calling script we have finished.

Uploading a Java Server

The JavaMail jar which sends email via SES is installed with the command:

```
./upload/java/upload.sh
```

The upload script does the following:

1. prepare variables such as passwords, SMTP details, database endpoint
2. prepare the JavaMail config file with sed
3. open up SSH to the Admin Server
4. upload assets and the install script
5. use expect to sudo su and run the install script
6. close the SSH port

Here is the script:

[aws/upload/java/upload.sh]

```
#!/bin/bash

# uploads javaMail to admin server
# then runs the install script on the server
# data comes from from aws/data/java dir, run ./data/makedata.sh
first

# check dir
where=$(pwd)
where="${where: -3}"
if test "$where" = "aws"; then
 echo "running from correct directory"
else
```

```
echo "must be run from aws directory with ./upload/java/upload.sh"
exit
fi

# include global variables
. ./master/vars.sh

rm -f $sshknownhosts

echo "uploading javamail to admin server"

cd $basedir/credentials

# include passwords
source passwords.sh

# include smtp details
source smtp.sh

echo "connecting to admin"

myip=$(curl http://checkip.amazonaws.com/)
echo myip=$myip

# get ip of server
ip_address=$(aws ec2 describe-instances --filters Name=key-
name,Values=admin --output text --query
'Reservations[*].Instances[*].PublicIpAddress')
echo ip_address=$ip_address

echo "getting db endpoint"
dbendpoint=$(aws rds describe-db-instances --db-instance-identifier
$dbinstancename --output text --query
'DBInstances[*].Endpoint.Address')
echo dbendpoint=$dbendpoint

cd $basedir/data/java/javaMail

rm -f config_javaMail.properties

sed -e "s/SEDdbhostSED/$dbendpoint/g" -e "s/SEDdbnameSED/$dbname/g"
-e "s/SEDDBPASS_javamailSED/$password6/g" -e "s/SEDSMTPHOSTSED/
$smtp_server/g" -e "s/SEDSMTPPORTSED/$smtp_port/g" -e
"s#SEDSMTPUSERSED#$smtp_user#g" -e "s#SEDSMTPPASSSED#$smtp_pass#g"
config_template.properties > config_javaMail.properties

cd $basedir

# allow ssh in sg
vpcadminsg_id=$(aws ec2 describe-security-groups --filters
Name=tag-key,Values=sgname --filters Name=tag-value,Values=adminsg
--output text --query 'SecurityGroups[*].GroupId')
echo vpcadminsg_id=$vpcadminsg_id
aws ec2 authorize-security-group-ingress --group-id $vpcadminsg_id
--protocol tcp --port 38142 --cidr $myip/32

# wait for ssh
echo -n "waiting for ssh"
while ! ssh -i credentials/admin.pem -p 38142 -o ConnectTimeout=60
-o BatchMode=yes -o StrictHostKeyChecking=no ec2-user@$ip_address >
```

AWS Scripted   248

```
/dev/null 2>&1 true; do
 echo -n . ; sleep 3;
done; echo " ssh ok"

# upload files
ssh -i credentials/admin.pem -p 38142 -o ConnectTimeout=60 -o
BatchMode=yes -o StrictHostKeyChecking=no ec2-user@$ip_address exit
echo "transferring files"
scp -i credentials/admin.pem -P 38142
data/java/javaMail/javaMail.jar ec2-user@$ip_address:
scp -i credentials/admin.pem -P 38142
data/java/javaMail/config_javaMail.properties ec2-user@$ip_address:
scp -i credentials/admin.pem -P 38142 upload/java/install.sh ec2-
user@$ip_address:
echo "transferred files"

rm -f data/java/javaMail/config_javaMail.properties

cd $basedir/credentials

# make and run expect script
echo "#!/usr/bin/expect -f" > expect.sh
echo "set timeout -1" >> expect.sh
echo "spawn ssh -i admin.pem -p 38142 -o ConnectTimeout=60 -o
BatchMode=yes -o StrictHostKeyChecking=no ec2-user@$ip_address" >>
expect.sh
echo "sleep 3" >> expect.sh
echo "send \"sudo su\n\"" >> expect.sh
echo "expect \"password for ec2-user:\"" >> expect.sh
echo "send \"$password3\n\"" >> expect.sh
echo "expect \"]\"" >> expect.sh
echo "send \"./install.sh\n\"" >> expect.sh
echo "expect \"install.sh finished\"" >> expect.sh
echo "exit" >> expect.sh
echo "exit" >> expect.sh
echo "interact" >> expect.sh
chmod +x expect.sh
./expect.sh
rm expect.sh

# remove ssh in sg
aws ec2 revoke-security-group-ingress --group-id $vpcadminsg_id
--protocol tcp --port 38142 --cidr $myip/32
echo "revoked sg access"

cd $basedir
```

See **Chapter 12 - Java Mail Server** for a listing of the java config file we rewrite with sed.

The uploaded install script does the following:

1. delete old java files
2. move in the new ones
3. set permissions on the java folder

4. cleanup
5. tell expect in the calling script we are finished

Here is the script:

[aws/upload/java/install.sh]

```
#!/bin/bash

# delete old java files
rm -f /java/javamail/javaMail.jar
rm -f /java/javamail/config.properties

# move new ones
mv /home/ec2-user/javaMail.jar /java/javamail/javaMail.jar
mv /home/ec2-user/config_javaMail.properties
/java/javamail/config.properties

# set permissions on the java folder
chown root:root /java
chmod 700 /java
find /java -type d -exec chown root:root {} +
find /java -type d -exec chmod 700 {} +
find /java -type f -exec chown root:root {} +
find /java -type f -exec chmod 700 {} +

# cleanup
rm -f -R /home/ec2-user/*
echo "deleted files from /home/ec2-user"

# tell expect in calling script we are finished
echo "install.sh finished"
```

Chapter 14 - Remote Access

SSHing to Boxes

We need a script to access SSH on any Webphp Server or Admin Server. By default, the ports in our AWS Security Group for SSH (now on 38142) are closed. So we need to open them, and only to our current IP address. And because we've disabled password-less 'sudo su' with a cloud key, we will need to sign in with a password. However, since the password is long and random, we really need to automate this, which we do with an expect script. Lastly, we want to close the SSH port in the security group when we are finished. You need to do a double 'exit' from your SSH session (once for the sudo su and once for the SSH). Then the script below continues and closes the port in question.

Here is the full script:

[aws/credentials/connectssh.sh]

```
#!/bin/bash

# open an ssh session to a server and auto sudo su with password
# can be admin, web1, web2 ... etc as long as ssh key exists
# do a double exit from ssh to exit, removes the sg ingress rule

# check dir
where=$(pwd)
where="${where: -3}"
if test "$where" = "aws"; then
 echo "running from correct directory"
else
 echo "must be run from aws directory with
./credentials/connectssh.sh ..."
 exit
fi

# include global variables
. ./master/vars.sh

cd $basedir/credentials

source passwords.sh

sshport=38142
sshuser=ec2-user
```

```
echo "connecting to $1 on $sshport with user $sshuser"

# get sg of server
serversg=$1
serversg+=sg
echo serversg=$serversg

if test "$1" = "web1"; then
 pass=$password9
 echo "set password for web1"
elif test "$1" = "web2"; then
 pass=$password11
 echo "set password for web2"
elif test "$1" = "web3"; then
 pass=$password13
 echo "set password for web3"
elif test "$1" = "web4"; then
 pass=$password15
 echo "set password for web4"
elif test "$1" = "web5"; then
 pass=$password17
 echo "set password for web5"
elif test "$1" = "web6"; then
 pass=$password19
 echo "set password for web6"
elif test "$1" = "admin"; then
 pass=$password3
 echo "set password for admin"
else
 echo "password for $1 not found - exiting"
 exit
fi

myip=$(curl http://checkip.amazonaws.com/)
echo myip=$myip

# get ip of server
ip_address=$(aws ec2 describe-instances --filters Name=key-
name,Values=$1 --output text --query
'Reservations[*].Instances[*].PublicIpAddress')
echo ip_address=$ip_address

# allow ssh in sg
vpcsg_id=$(aws ec2 describe-security-groups --filters Name=tag-
key,Values=sgname --filters Name=tag-value,Values=$serversg
--output text --query 'SecurityGroups[*].GroupId')
echo vpcsg_id=$vpcsg_id
aws ec2 authorize-security-group-ingress --group-id $vpcsg_id
--protocol tcp --port 38142 --cidr $myip/32

echo ssh -i $1.pem -p $sshport -o ConnectTimeout=60 -o
BatchMode=yes -o StrictHostKeyChecking=no $sshuser@$ip_address
# wait for ssh
echo -n "waiting for ssh"
while ! ssh -i $1.pem -p $sshport -o ConnectTimeout=60 -o
BatchMode=yes -o StrictHostKeyChecking=no $sshuser@$ip_address >
/dev/null 2>&1 true; do
 echo -n . ; sleep 3;
done; echo " ssh ok"
```

```
# make and run expect script
# use timeout -1 for no timeout
echo "#!/usr/bin/expect -f" > expect.sh
echo "set timeout -1" >> expect.sh
echo "spawn ssh -i $1.pem -p $sshport -o ConnectTimeout=60 -o
BatchMode=yes -o StrictHostKeyChecking=no $sshuser@$ip_address" >>
expect.sh
echo "send \"sudo su\n\"" >> expect.sh
echo "expect \"password for $sshuser:\"" >> expect.sh
echo "send \"$pass\n\"" >> expect.sh
echo "interact" >> expect.sh
chmod +x expect.sh
./expect.sh
rm expect.sh

# script now waits for double 'exit'

# remove ssh in sg
aws ec2 revoke-security-group-ingress --group-id $vpcsg_id
--protocol tcp --port $sshport --cidr $myip/32
echo "revoked sg access"

exit
```

You can call this from the aws folder with:

```
./credentials/connectssh.sh <web1|web2|web3|...|admin>
```

eg to connect to web1:

```
./credentials/connectssh.sh web1
```

Connecting to Admin

We use Chrome and a connect script to open up access to the Admin Server web interfaces (Admin Site, LogAnalyzer, PHPMyAdmin and Mmonit). The reason we use Chrome is that we use command-Q to quit from Chrome and run the port closing commands in the original script. If you are using Safari to browse other sites (such as AWS Console) it is a bit annoying to have to close Safari. The only problem with Chrome is that it loves to call lots of sites (presumably to log your activities, naughty Google). With your Parental Controls activated, these will be blocked, but you will get annoying popups. Live with it - don't allow these sites.

The script is as follows:

[aws/credentials/connectadmin.sh]

```bash
#!/bin/bash

# open up required sg inbounds and connect to admin server via
Chrome
# when Quit Chrome, close up security

# check dir
where=$(pwd)
where="${where: -3}"
if test "$where" = "aws"; then
 echo "running from correct directory"
else
 echo "must be run from aws directory with
./credentials/connectadmin.sh"
 exit
fi

# include global variables
. ./master/vars.sh

myip=$(curl -s http://checkip.amazonaws.com/)
echo myip=$myip

# get ip of server
ip_address=$(aws ec2 describe-instances --filters Name=key-
name,Values=admin --output text --query
'Reservations[*].Instances[*].PublicIpAddress')
echo admin_ip_address=$ip_address

echo "PRECONNECT: perhaps 38142 should be open to the world but
nothing else except security groups"
aws ec2 describe-security-groups --filters Name=tag-
key,Values=sgname --filters Name=tag-value,Values=adminsg --output
text

vpcadminsg_id=$(aws ec2 describe-security-groups --filters
Name=tag-key,Values=sgname --filters Name=tag-value,Values=adminsg
--output text --query 'SecurityGroups[*].GroupId')
echo vpcadminsg_id=$vpcadminsg_id

# allow 443 and 8443 in sg
echo -n authorising :443
result=$(aws ec2 authorize-security-group-ingress --group-id
$vpcadminsg_id --protocol tcp --port 443 --cidr $myip/32 --output
text)
if test "$result" = "true"; then
        echo " ok"
else
        echo " ERROR"
#       exit;
fi

echo -n authorising :8443
result=$(aws ec2 authorize-security-group-ingress --group-id
$vpcadminsg_id --protocol tcp --port 8443 --cidr $myip/32 --output
text)
if test "$result" = "true"; then
```

```
        echo " ok"
else
        echo " ERROR"
#       exit;
fi

echo "YOU MUST QUIT CHROME WITH command-Q"
echo connecting to https://$ip_address

open -a "Google Chrome" --args --homepage https://$ip_address
open -a "Google Chrome" https://$ip_address:8443
open -a "Google Chrome" https://$ip_address/phpmyadmin
open -a "Google Chrome" -W https://$ip_address/loganalyzer

# remove 443 and 8443 in sg
echo -n revoking :443
result=$(aws ec2 revoke-security-group-ingress --group-id
$vpcadminsg_id --protocol tcp --port 443 --cidr $myip/32 --output
text)
if test "$result" = "true"; then
        echo " ok"
else
        echo " ERROR"
fi

echo -n revoking :8443
result=$(aws ec2 revoke-security-group-ingress --group-id
$vpcadminsg_id --protocol tcp --port 8443 --cidr $myip/32 --output
text)
if test "$result" = "true"; then
        echo " ok"
else
        echo " ERROR"
fi

echo "POSTCONNECT: perhaps 38142 should be open to the world but
nothing else except security groups"
aws ec2 describe-security-groups --filters Name=tag-
key,Values=sgname --filters Name=tag-value,Values=adminsg --output
text

echo done
```

Note that if Chrome opens up with a blank first tab, it's because you didn't quit it with command-Q. Quit properly and try again.

Self-Signed SSL Certificates in OSX Chrome

The first time you open up the Admin Web Interfaces in Chrome, you will notice that all the pages give SSL errors because you are using a self-signed certificate. Unfortunately, fixing this is not as simple as clicking 'Always Trust this Certificate'. On OSX, you need to do the following to remove the warnings:

1. click the lock with the cross on it in the address bar
2. click 'Certificate Information' in the pop up
3. drag the certificate image to your desktop
4. double click the icon on the desktop, this opens KeyChain Access
5. click Always Trust
6. enter your Mac password
7. find the certificate in the login keychain and drag it to the System keychain
8. double click it in KeyChain Access and a window pops up
9. expand the trust section and select Always Trust
10. close the popup
11. close KeychainAccess
12. quit Chrome with command-Q
13. rerun the Admin connect script

Thanks to **Rob Peck** for this.

Appendix A - Bash Script Essentials

Bash is a tricky language, mainly because there seem to be a whole host of ways to do any one thing. Below are some of the essential methods you will need for automating AWS.

Getting Values from Commands

One of the most common things we need to do on the command line is get some output from a command and save it to a bash variable. Here's an example that gets our IP from Amazon and puts into the myip bash variable:

```
myip=$(curl http://checkip.amazonaws.com/)
echo myip=$myip
```

We use the $(...) notation to execute a command and put the output into a variable.

Waiting for Something to Complete

Many AWS commands do not complete immediately. Examples are creating new instances and RDS databases. In addition, even if an instance has been created, it may take a few seconds for something like SSH to come online (the box needs to boot after all).

Therefore, you will need to be able to run a wait loop as follows:

[aws/snippets/snippet_waitforinstance.sh]

```
# wait for instance
echo -n "waiting for instance"
while state=$(aws ec2 describe-instances --instance-ids
$instance_id --output text --query
'Reservations[*].Instances[*].State.Name'); test "$state" =
"pending"; do
 echo -n . ; sleep 3;
done; echo " $state"
```

What this does is execute the command "aws ec2 describe-instances --instance-ids $instance_id --output text --query 'Reservations[*].Instances[*].State.Name'" repeatedly until the output changes from 'pending'. We print a '.' (to know something is happening) and wait 3 seconds in between calls. This is an effective way to pause the script until our resources are ready to be used.

SSH is another important wait situation:

[aws/snippets/snippet_waitforssh.sh]

```
# wait for ssh
echo -n "waiting for ssh"
while ! ssh -i credentials/admin.pem -p 38142 -o ConnectTimeout=60
-o BatchMode=yes -o StrictHostKeyChecking=no ec2-user@$ip_address >
/dev/null 2>&1 true; do
 echo -n . ; sleep 3;
done; echo " ssh ok"
```

Here we are trying to connect to a server (the Admin Server) but SSH takes a few seconds to be ready. We are executing "ssh -i credentials/admin.pem -p 38142 -o ConnectTimeout=60 -o BatchMode=yes -o StrictHostKeyChecking=no ec2-user@$ip_address > /dev/null 2>&1" repeatedly. The " > /dev/null 2>&1" portion simply redirects stdout and stderr to /dev/null so we don't see any output. However, if the command succeeds, boolean true will be returned, and false if it fails. Hence "while ! XXX true" repeats if the XXX is unsuccessful.

Automating Search and Replace

The bash command for replacing text in a file is 'sed'. We use this extensively to build files on the fly in our scripts. Here is an example:

```
sed -e "s/SEDdbhostSED/$dbendpoint/g" -e "s/SEDdbnameSED/$dbname/g"
-e "s/SEDdbpass_adminrwSED/$password4/g"
ami/admin/httpd_template.conf  > ami/admin/httpd.conf
```

This excerpt takes the template file httpd_template.conf and runs it through 'sed' and pipes the output to httpd.conf (we don't want to overwrite or change our template files). The three '-e' options specify 3 search and replaces: SEDdbhostSED with $dbendpoint; SEDdbnameSED with $dbname; and SEDdbpass_adminrwSED with $password4. The variables $dbendpoint, $dbname and $password4 are all defined earlier in the script. We use the SEDxxxSED notation (in the file being searched and replaced) because this string won't occur in our template script for any other reasons.

Splitting Strings

You will sometimes receive data back from the aws command which is a space separated string. Chopping this string up can be achieved with this:

[aws/snippets/snippet_splitstring.sh]

```
# split a space delimited string
teststring="apple banana orange"
testarray=$(echo $teststring | tr " " "\n")
for i in $testarray
do
 echo found $i
done
```

If the delimiter is not a space, but something else, change the third line to reflect this, eg for comma separated:

```
testarray=$(echo $teststring | tr "," "\n")
```

Running a Script on a Remote Server

A variant of the ssh command involves setting the BatchMode=yes option and appending the command to be executed:

```
ssh -i credentials/admin.pem -p 38142 -t -o ConnectTimeout=60 -o
BatchMode=yes -o StrictHostKeyChecking=no ec2-user@$ip_address sudo
./install_admin.sh
```

In this case we would connect to our Admin Server and run

"sudo ./install_admin.sh". Note that if you have disabled password-less sudo su, you will need to use the more complex procedure involving expect, several examples can be found in the upload scripts in the /aws/upload folder and **Chapter 13 - Deploying Assets**.

Copying Files to and from a Remote Server

Once our instances have launched and SSH is available, we invariably need to send some files. Here's how with the scp command running on the box we are transferring from:

```
scp -i credentials/admin.pem -P 38142 ami/admin/httpd.conf ec2-
user@$ip_address:
```

This would copy the local file ami/admin/httpd.conf to the remote server into the /home/ec2-user directory. Note the trailing ':' and how the port is specified with a capital P (ssh uses a lowercase p).

Getting files back from the server is as follows:

```
scp -i credentials/admin.pem -P 38142 ec2-
user@$ip_address:httpd.conf .
```

This would copy the file /home/ec2-user/httpd.conf from the remote server to the current directory, specified by the '.' character. Obviously, port 38142 needs to be open in the AWS Security Group involved.

Including a Script in a Script

We make extensive use of the bash 'source' command, which can be abbreviated to the '.' character. Without modification, the bash shell won't let you execute a script just by typing its name - you need to issue commands like this:

```
./test.sh
```

A slight variant is:

```
. ./test.sh
```

and again:

```
source ./test.sh
```

lastly:

```
source test.sh
```

There is much confusion on the Internet concerning this topic. We have 4 examples above and different people have different opinions about what they mean. So let me explain: the 'source' command includes and runs a script *inline* in the current shell or script. That means all variables currently defined are available to the called script and if the script sets any variables, these persist in the calling environment. It's as though you copied and pasted the commands in. The '.' notation is a shorthand for 'source' and behaves in exactly the same way. so 'source test.sh' and '. test.sh' are exactly the same. The first example above is NOT a 'source' command - the dot represents the '.' meaning 'this directory'. And calling a script like that starts a new process so variables are separate. The last three examples above are synonymous. Have a look at this script which runs some tests:

[aws/snippets/snippet_sourcetests.sh]

```
#!/bin/bash

# write a test script
echo '#!/bin/bash' > test.sh
echo 'echo input=$input' >> test.sh
echo 'output=output' >> test.sh
chmod +x test.sh

# set a variable in the top context
input=input
echo input=$input

# show that output is empty
echo output=$output

# run just the filename (we get an error)
echo running: test.sh
```

```
test.sh

# run ./ version
echo running: ./test.sh
./test.sh
echo output=$output
# reset output
unset output

# run . ./ version
echo running: . ./test.sh
. ./test.sh
echo output=$output
# reset output
unset output

# run source ./ version
echo running: source ./test.sh
source ./test.sh
echo output=$output
# reset output
unset output

# run source version
echo running: source test.sh
source test.sh
echo output=$output
# reset output
unset output
```

which when run produces:

[aws/snippets/snippet_sourcetestsresult.txt]

```
input=input
output=
running: test.sh
./snippet_sourcetests.sh: line 18: test.sh: command not found
running: ./test.sh
input=
output=
running: . ./test.sh
input=input
output=output
running: source ./test.sh
input=input
output=output
running: source test.sh
input=input
output=output
```

As you can see, the first call ('./test.sh') has input and output blank - ie $input is not available to test.sh and test.sh does not set $output in the parent script. But the last three ways of calling the script ('. ./test.sh', 'source ./test.sh' and 'source test.sh') all print input and output correctly - ie $input is available to test.sh and test.sh sets $output in the calling script.

AWS CLI Query Methods

Almost all AWS CLI commands return some form of data. The standard return format is JSON. To demonstrate this, let's create a dummy IAM User:

```
aws iam create-user --user-name dummy
```

This returns:

[aws/snippets/snippet_createuseroutput.txt]

```
    "User": {
        "UserName": dummy",
        "Path": "/",
        "CreateDate": "2019-10-19T03:37:48.351Z",
        "UserId": "somestring",
        "Arn": "arn:aws:iam::000000000000:user/dummy"
    }
}
```

Delete the user and redo the creation with output set to text:

```
aws iam delete-user --user-name dummy
aws iam create-user --user-name dummy --output text
```

The output is now not in JSON:

```
USER    arn:aws:iam::000000000000:user/dummy    2019-10-
19T06:49:44.225Z          somestring        dummy
```

Let's say we wanted to retrieve a single variable form the output, we can do this with the --query option:

```
aws iam delete-user --user-name dummy
aws iam create-user --user-name dummy --query 'User.UserName'
```

This returns a JSON string:

```
"dummy"
```

Normally, we don't want JSON data back because it is more difficult to parse. So we can execute the same commands with the text output option to get a cleaner return:

```
aws iam delete-user --user-name dummy
aws iam create-user --user-name dummy --output text  --query
'User.UserName'
```

And this returns clean data:

```
dummy
```

which we can put in a bash variable with the $(...) construct.

Setting the query string can be a bit confusing. Run the command without query or output options and you'll get a lump of JSON. Then you need to specify what you want by drilling down into the returned JSON. In the example above we jumped into the 'User' aggregation and then extracted the value for 'UserName'. It's always case sensitive.

Also, if the returned JSON has arrays, you need to specify the array position or * for all items, for example, if you have no instances:

```
aws ec2 describe-instances
```

returns:

[aws/snippets/snippet_describeinstancesoutput.txt]

```
{
    "Reservations": []
}
```

The square brackets are a giveaway that the Reservations aggregation is an array, so any query string would start with 'Reservations[*].' (for all Reservations) or 'Reservations[0].' for the first Reservation only. However, you need to test, because the aws command doesn't like some combinations.

So the command:

```
aws ec2 describe-instances --output text --query
'Reservations[*].Instances[*].State.Name'
```

would return a space separated list of the State.Name property for each instance in all Reservations. However, I recommend using options in the command to return only one piece of data and avoid space separated lists if at all possible.

Note that if you want to use a variable in a query string, you need to close and open the single quotes (because bash treats text inside single quotes as real text and does not evaluate it). An example can be seen when we check if an SES email address has been verified:

```
aws ses get-identity-verification-attributes --identities
"$emailsendfrom" --region $deployregion --output text --query
'VerificationAttributes."'$emailsendfrom'".VerificationStatus'
```

Very rarely, we execute an AWS command which returns more than one piece of data that we need and which can only be run once. An example is the SES User Key generation. In this case we need to use a more cumbersome but equally effective JSON bash parser function:

[aws/snippets/snippet_jsonval.sh]

```
# extract from aws/ami/email/make.sh
# this function allows us to extract data from a json string
function jsonval {
        temp=`echo $json | sed 's/\\\\\//\//g' | sed 's/[{}]//g' |
awk -v k="text" '{n=split($0,a,","); for (i=1; i<=n; i++) print
a[i]}' | sed 's/\"\:\"/\|/g' | sed 's/[\,]/ /g' | sed 's/\"//g' |
grep -w $prop | cut -d":" -f2| sed -e 's/^ *//g' -e 's/ *$//g'`
        echo ${temp##*|}
        }

# make ses user
aws iam create-user --user-name sesuser

# we need to get 2 values from this returned data but can only call
the function once
# hence the laborious jsonval method
json=$(aws iam create-access-key --user-name sesuser)

# get key id
prop='AccessKeyId'
AccessKeyId=`jsonval`

# get secret key
prop='SecretAccessKey'
```

```
SecretAccessKey=`jsonval`
```

Fun with Quotes

It took me a long time to realise there was a difference in bash between the quote types " and '... Most of the time they work interchangeably. But they are subtly different. " evaluates it's contents (so things like variables are replaced) but ' treats it's contents as a literal string. Hence:

```
str=someval
echo "str=$str"
```

prints

```
str=someval
```

but

```
str=someval
echo 'str=$str'
```

prints

```
str=$str
```

And when I realised that's what explains similar PHP behaviour it hit me like a rock and I shall now be on the lookout for other bashisms in my PHP. You sort of always knew PHP was built on top of bash, or something bash-like, but this really exemplifies it.

One thing to be really careful about is those annoying curly quotes word processors love to convert your nice straight quotes to. They don't work on the command line and you get all sorts of weird errors. So just be careful copying and pasting from any editor or file which is not pure ASCII text.

About the Author

Many years of development have taught me 2 things:

DIVIDE AND CONQUER

or: any problem, however big, can be solved by splitting it up into smaller problems.

and

AUTOMATE, AUTOMATE, AUTOMATE

or: never give in to laziness - build that function, write that script, really tie down that issue! If at the end of a day you can sit back and say, "I made my life easier in the future", that is the most worthwhile day you could have had.

When things look bad, sit back, take a deep breath and do the Mantra:

Divide, Automate, Conquer! Divide, Automate, Conquer! Divide, Automate, Conquer...

It has always helped me.

I hope this book has inspired you to greater things.

If you automate something really cool, let everyone know at **http://www.quickstepapps.com**!

Copyright Notice

Please help others to find this book by leaving a review. Your feedback is always appreciated.

Download

All source code and scripts in this book can be downloaded at **http://www.quickstepapps.com** free of charge. You will also find related Articles and an interactive Support Forum. All code examples are tested on OSX and Amazon Linux platforms and in working order as of publishing.

Contact

Should you have questions, suggestions, difficulties or corrections, please contact the author at:

http://www.quickstepapps.com

Made in the USA
Middletown, DE
19 July 2018